Vincent van Gogh

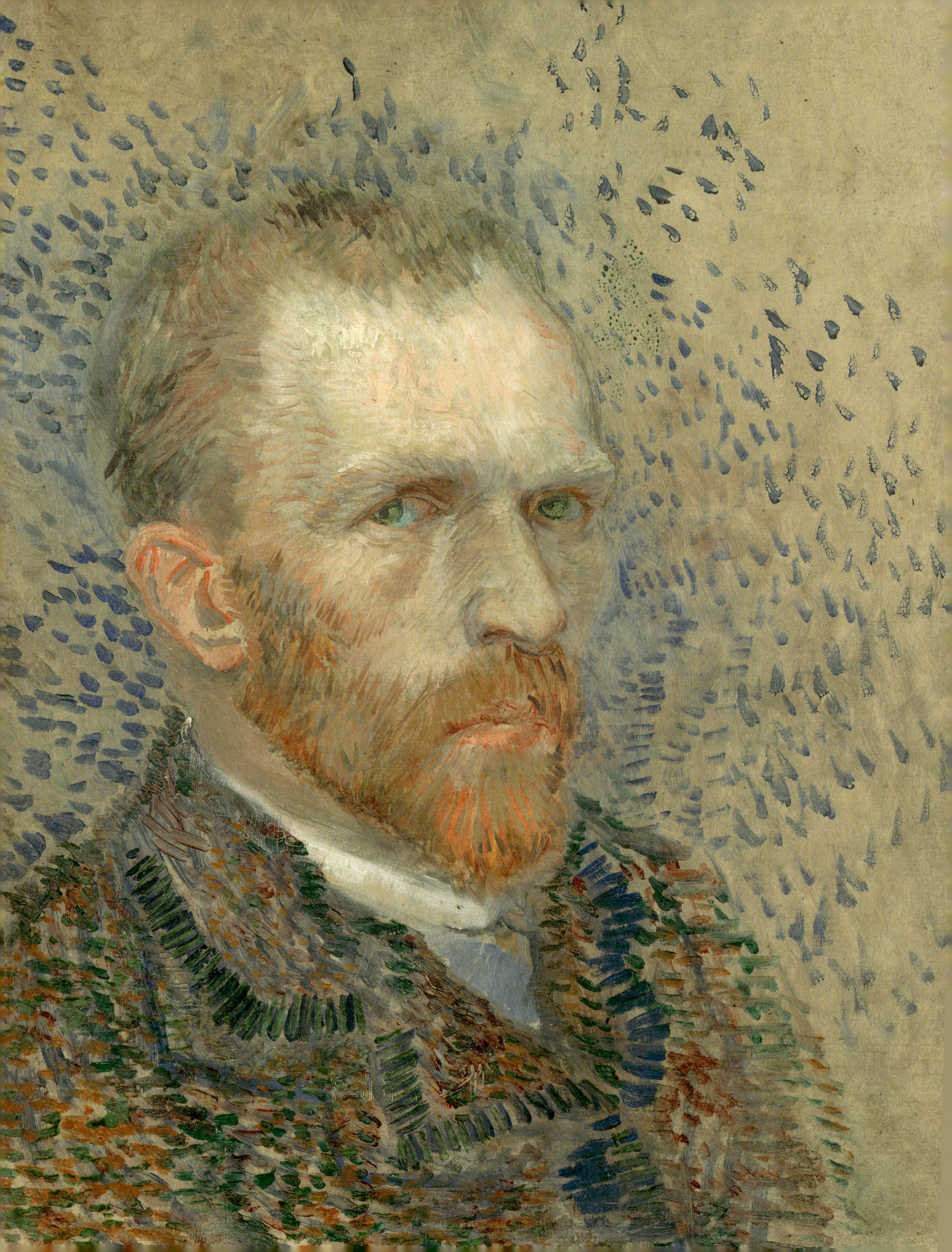

Vincent van Gogh
His Life in Art

Edited by
David Bomford

With essays by
Nienke Bakker
Renske Suijver
Renske Cohen Tervaert

Contributions by
Helga K. Aurisch
Laura Minton
Dena M. Woodall

The Museum of Fine Arts,
Houston

Distributed by
Yale University Press,
New Haven and London

Note to Reader

Numerical references to letters written by or addressed to Vincent van Gogh correspond to those in Leo Jansen, Hans Luijten, and Nienke Bakker, eds., *Vincent van Gogh – The Letters*, 6 vols., 1st ed. (Amsterdam: Van Gogh Museum, 2009); available online at vangoghletters.org.

The reference numbers beginning with "F" for works by Vincent van Gogh correlate to those listed in the catalogue raisonné by Jacob Baart de la Faille, *The Works of Vincent van Gogh: His Paintings and Drawings*, rev. ed. (New York: Reynal, 1970).

This book was published to accompany the exhibition *Vincent van Gogh: His Life in Art*, presented at the Museum of Fine Arts, Houston, March 10 through June 27, 2019.

Vincent van Gogh: His Life in Art has been organized in collaboration with the Van Gogh Museum, Amsterdam; the Kröller-Müller Museum, Otterlo; and the Museum of Fine Arts, Houston.

Produced by the Publications Department of the Museum of Fine Arts, Houston

Edited by Heather Brand and Melina Kervandjian
Translations by Ted Alkins and Diane Webb
Indexed by Kay Banning
Designed by Studio Blue, Chicago
Typeset in Rekja
Separations by Professional Graphics, Rockford
Printed by Die Keure in Belgium

Distributed by Yale University Press, New Haven and London
yalebooks.com/art

Cover illustration: Vincent van Gogh, *Irises* (detail), cat. 48.

Frontispiece: Vincent van Gogh, *Self-Portrait* (detail), cat. 24.

Pages 9–10: Vincent van Gogh, *Still Life with a Plate of Onions* (detail), cat. 37. Pages 25–26: Vincent van Gogh, *Impasse des Deux Frères* (detail), cat. 23. Pages 39–40: Vincent van Gogh, *Windmills near Dordrecht (Weeskinderendijk)* (detail), cat. 5. Pages 49–50: Vincent van Gogh, *Les Rochers (The Rocks)* (detail), cat. 32. Pages 157–58: Vincent van Gogh, *Farmhouse* (detail), cat. 51.

Library of Congress Cataloging-in-Publication Data

Names: Bomford, David, editor. | Bakker, Nienke. | Suijver, Renske. | Cohen Tervaert, Renske. | Kessler-Aurisch, Helga. | Minton, Laura. | Woodall, Dena Marie, 1969– | Museum of Fine Arts, Houston, organizer, host institution. | Van Gogh Museum, Amsterdam, organizer. | Kröller-Müller Museum, organizer.

Title: Vincent van Gogh : his life in art / edited by David Bomford ; with essays by Nienke Bakker, Renske Suijver, and Renske Cohen Tervaert, and contributions by Helga K. Aurisch, Laura Minton, and Dena M. Woodall.

Other titles: Vincent van Gogh (Museum of Fine Arts, Houston)

Description: [Houston, Texas] : Museum of Fine Arts, Houston, [2019] | "This book was published to accompany the exhibition Vincent van Gogh: His Life in Art, presented at the Museum of Fine Arts, Houston, March 10 through June 27, 2019. The exhibition was organized in collaboration with the Van Gogh Museum, Amsterdam; the Kröller-Müller Museum, Otterlo; and the Museum of Fine Arts, Houston." | Includes bibliographical references and index.

Identifiers: LCCN 2018046202 | ISBN 9780300243260 (pbk.)

Subjects: LCSH: Gogh, Vincent van, 1853–1890 — Exhibitions. | Gogh, Vincent van, 1853–1890 — Criticism and interpretation. | Painters — Netherlands — Biography.

Classification: LCC ND653.G7 A4 2019 | DDC 759.9492 — dc23

LC record available at https://lccn.loc.gov/2018046202.

Contents

Foreword

The life and work of Vincent van Gogh have come to epitomize the notion of the struggling artist, unappreciated in life and celebrated worldwide after death. His battle with depression and psychosis, his meteoric rise in French avant-garde circles, and his calamitous collapse and tragic death at age thirty-seven have fueled countless studies, novels, and films, while his images have served as inspiration for generations of subsequent artists, and his paintings and drawings continue to be sold for enormous sums. One oft-repeated component of the Van Gogh myth is that he had never sold a painting during his short-lived career. In fact, he enjoyed the patronage of his devoted brother Theo, an up-and-coming art dealer in Paris who was in touch with many of the Impressionists and Post-Impressionists, most notably Edgar Degas, Camille Pissarro, and Paul Gauguin. Once Vincent had committed himself to painting, after stints as a Protestant pastor and an art dealer, Theo paid him a monthly stipend in return for his output, which Vincent dutifully sent to Theo from the South of France at regular intervals. One could accurately say that Vincent's work that is most valued today, the production of his final two years, was sold in its entirety to his dealer.

The Museum of Fine Arts, Houston, is fortunate to have among its collections one such work by Vincent. Painted in 1888, *Les Rochers (The Rocks)* depicts the rocky terrain of Montmajour, not far from where he lived at Arles. The painting is a bravura statement of his recent advances to capture the strong light contrast of the South of France, as well as his novel brushwork that gives texture and energy to the scene. Upon receipt, Theo immediately recognized the special value of this work and framed it for display in his own apartment.

The Rocks is the point of departure for this survey of Van Gogh's life and art that we have conceived exclusively for the Museum of Fine Arts, Houston. We are very grateful to the administrations of the Van Gogh Museum and Vincent van Gogh Foundation in Amsterdam and the Kröller-Müller Museum in Otterlo for their partnership in this enterprise. No Van Gogh project can succeed without these two essential repositories of Van Gogh's oeuvre: the former representing the residual estate of Theo van Gogh, lovingly managed by his widow, Jo van Gogh-Bonger; and the latter by Anton and Helene Kröller, who began collecting Vincent's works in 1908. These two museums have generously lent most of the more than fifty works included in this exhibition. Additional select loans from the Art Institute of Chicago; Dallas Museum of Art; McNay Art Museum, San Antonio; Musée d'Orsay, Paris; Virginia

Museum of Fine Arts, Richmond; Wallraf-Richartz-Museum & Fondation Corboud, Cologne; and private collectors complete the exhibition. We are immensely grateful to our colleagues for these important contributions.

Together these works trace the artist's life and artistic development, from his early copy drawings from such masters as Jean-François Millet, through his brief embrace of Impressionism, to his vibrant late paintings executed in his own signature style. They depict the people, places, and landscapes he encountered, as well as the modest furnishings of his life. They also demonstrate the extraordinary evolution in his technique and palette as he moved from one location to another, finding different sources of inspiration as he struggled to maintain emotional equilibrium.

As a member of the supervisory board for the Van Gogh Museum, I thank my colleagues Axel Rüger, director, and Adriaan Dönszelmann, managing director, at the Van Gogh Museum, as well as Lisette Pelsers, director, and Rinus Vonhof, business director, at the Kröller-Müller Museum. I am particularly gratified that two curators from Amsterdam have contributed essays to this publication. Nienke Bakker, senior curator, has provided an overview of the artist's evolution through the various stages of his life, and Renske Suijver, curator, sheds light on how the Van Gogh Museum came to be established. Renske Cohen Tervaert has provided a complementary essay on the founding of the Kröller-Müller Museum, where she serves as curator. Texts by David Bomford, the Audrey Jones Beck Curator of European Art; Helga K. Aurisch, curator of European art; and Dena M. Woodall, associate curator of prints and drawings; all at the Museum of Fine Arts, Houston, offer insightful commentaries on the individual works.

As the sole venue for *Vincent van Gogh: His Life in Art*, we at the Museum of Fine Arts, Houston, are delighted to provide our audiences the opportunity to view beautiful and poignant works rarely seen outside of Europe. Not since 1951, when John and Dominique de Menil orchestrated an exhibition of Van Gogh works at the Contemporary Arts Museum Houston, has Houston seen so many works by Van Gogh under one roof. More than fifty years later, his works remain just as fresh, novel, inspiring, and revelatory of the life of a truly extraordinary individual. This exhibition and its accompanying catalogue are possible thanks to the generous support of the current generation of Houstonians who have followed the example of the de Menils. We are deeply grateful to these collectors and civic-minded philanthropists, and especially to the

Chairman of the Board of Trustees of the Museum of Fine Arts, Houston, Rich Kinder and his wife Nancy Kinder for their early and generous support. On behalf of the lucky visitors to this exhibition, I am honored to thank the farsighted contributors.

Gary Tinterow
Director
The Museum of Fine Arts, Houston

Acknowledgments

This exhibition and its accompanying catalogue would not have been possible without the generous support of the following individuals and organizations, to whom we wish to express our sincere gratitude.

—David Bomford
The Audrey Jones Beck Curator of European Art
The Museum of Fine Arts, Houston

Van Gogh Museum, Amsterdam
Axel Rüger, Director
Adriaan Dönszelmann, Managing Director
Nienke Bakker, Senior Curator
Renske Suijver, Curator
Geeta Bruin, Senior Project Manager Exhibitions
Stefan Wladimiroff, Safety and Security Advisor

Vincent van Gogh Foundation

Kröller-Müller Museum, Otterlo
Lisette Pelsers, Director
Rinus Vonhof, Business Director
Renske Cohen Tervaert, Curator
Ton Hoofwijk, Manager Security & Art Protection Services

Other lenders
The Art Institute of Chicago: James Rondeau, President and Eloise W. Martin Director; Kevin Salatino, the Anne Vogt Fuller and Marion Titus Searle Chair and Curator of Prints and Drawings; Emily J. Ziemba, Director of Curatorial Administration for Prints and Drawings; Natasha Derrickson, Associate Registrar, Loans and Exhibitions

Dallas Museum of Art: Agustín Arteaga, Director

McNay Art Museum, San Antonio: Richard Aste, Director; Heather Lammers, Collections Manager and Curator; Lyle W. Williams, Curator of Prints and Drawings

Musée d'Orsay, Paris: Laurence des Cars, President

Virginia Museum of Fine Arts, Richmond: Alex Nyerges, Director; Mitchell Merling, the Paul Mellon Curator and Head of the Department of European Art; Colleen Yarger, Curatorial Assistant for European Art and the Mellon Collections; and Karen Daly, Registrar for Exhibitions and Coordinator of Provenance Research

Wallraf-Richartz-Museum & Fondation Corboud, Cologne: Marcus Dekiert, Director; Barbara Schaefer, Curator

Private collectors

The Museum of Fine Arts, Houston
Amy Purvis, Chief Development Officer
Deborah L. Roldán, Assistant Director, Exhibitions
Marcelina Guerrero, Exhibitions Coordinator
Briana Gonzalez, Administrative Assistant, Exhibitions
Madison Rendall, Administrative Assistant, Curatorial
Clifford Edwards, Administrative Assistant, Curatorial
Kathleen Crain, Exhibitions Registrar
Jack Eby, Chief Exhibition Designer
William Cochrane, Exhibition Designer
Heather Brand, Head of Publications
Phenon Finley-Smiley, Manager of Graphics
Melina Kervandjian, Editor
Jon Evans, Chief Librarian and Archivist, Hirsch Library
Lynn Wexler, Reference Librarian, Hirsch Library

Thanks also to William Acquavella; Sandy Heller; and Lowell Libson and Jonny Yarker.

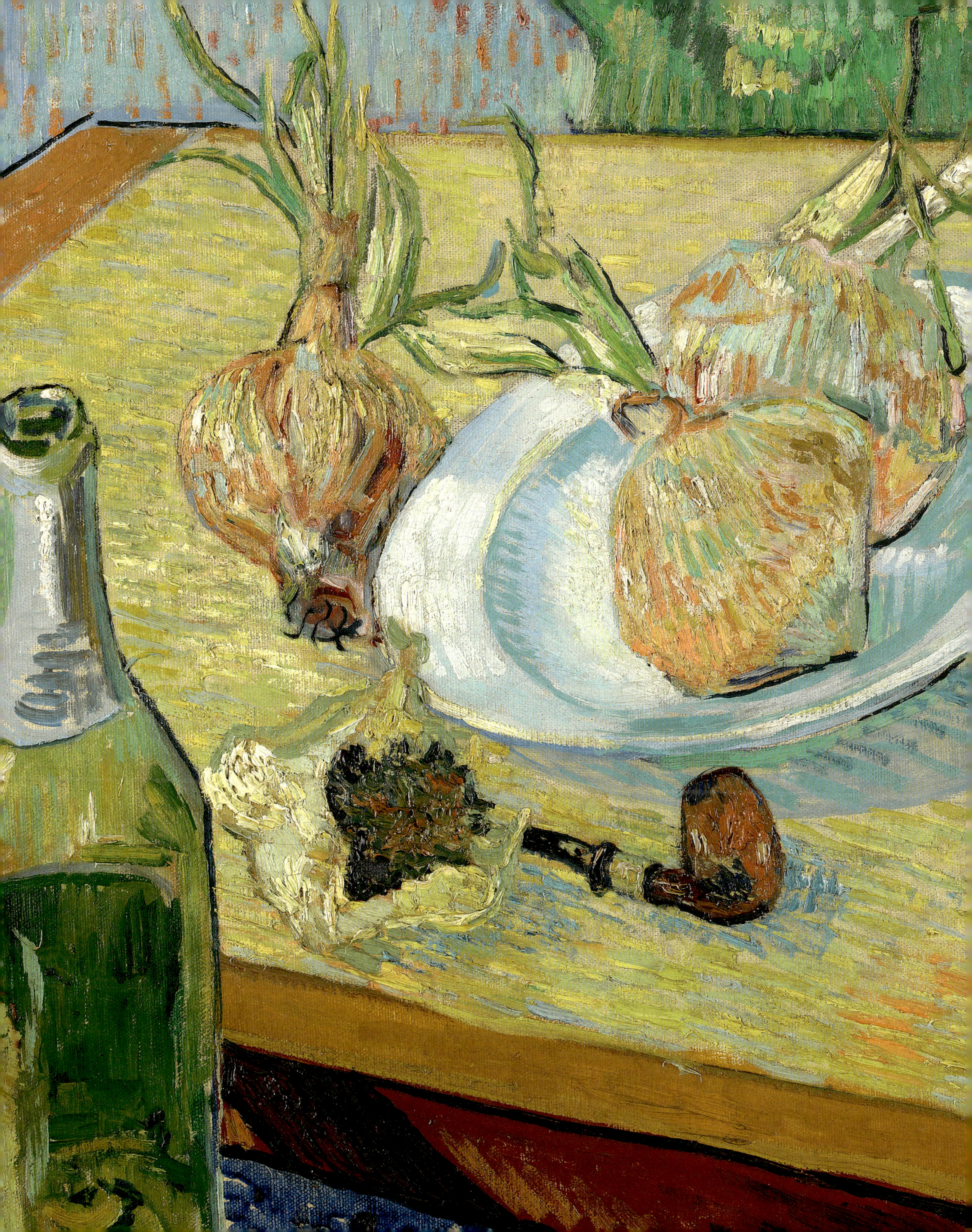

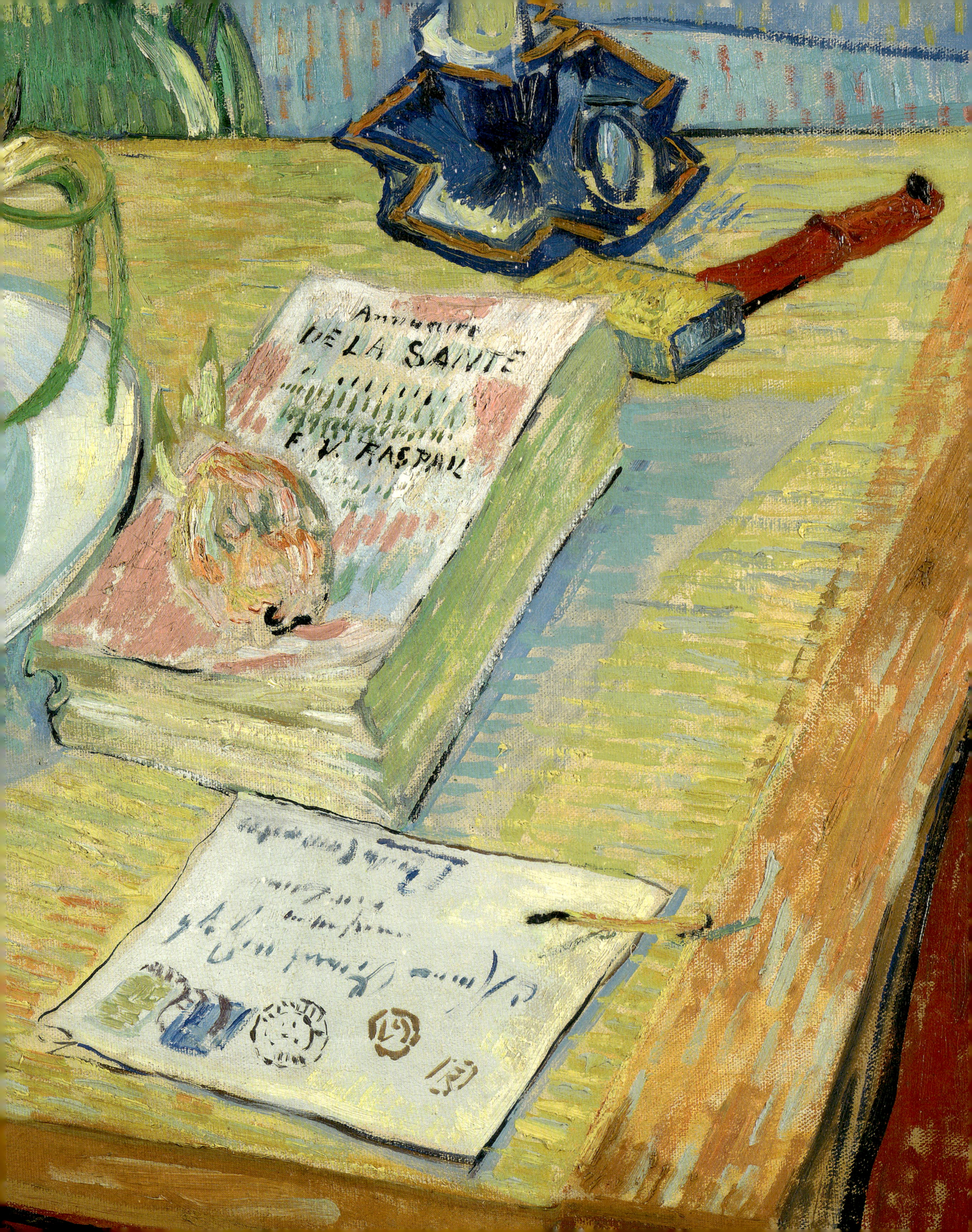

Annuaire
DE LA SANTÉ
F. V. RASPAIL

Vincent van Gogh — His Life in Art

Nienke Bakker

Becoming an artist was not Vincent van Gogh's first choice of profession. When he left home at sixteen, it was to work for an art dealer. Only after years of searching for direction did Van Gogh decide at the age of twenty-seven to pursue an artist's career. With this latest in a series of fundamental changes of course, he finally found his true destination. He would devote himself to it with great passion and to the exclusion of all else until — disillusioned and beaten after eighteen months of recurring breakdowns — the thirty-seven-year-old painter resolved to end his life. He was an artist for just ten years, which is hard to believe considering the volume of work he left behind: more than 850 paintings and some 1,300 drawings. The often difficult road he traveled prior to and during his artistic career is outlined here, along with the astonishingly rapid development that his art underwent in those ten years.

Seeking His Goal in Life

Vincent was the oldest of six children in the family of the Reverend Theodorus van Gogh and his wife, Anna. Born on March 30, 1853, he was followed by his siblings Anna (1855), Theo (1857), Elisabeth (Lies, 1859), Willemien (Wil, 1862), and Cor (1867). Theodorus served as a Protestant minister in the villages of Zundert, Helvoirt, Etten, and Nuenen in the Dutch province of Brabant. Zundert, where Vincent spent his childhood, persisted in his memory as a kind of paradise, on which he looked back wistfully. He wandered the woods and fields, either alone or with Theo, where he developed his enduring love of nature. The yearning for a rural environment in which he could draw comfort and strength from nature never left him.

Van Gogh was the proverbial jack-of-all-trades and master of none before deciding to become an artist at twenty-seven — an age by which men in the nineteenth century were expected to have long since settled down and started raising a family. Every time Vincent found a new employer or goal in life, or when he quit a job or a course of study, he would move on, leaving everything behind. The first step on many occasions was to return to his parents' house, where a plan for the next step would be thought up in the bosom of his family.

He found his first job at the international art dealers Goupil & Cie through an uncle on his father's side, who was a partner at the company. This was also the moment he embarked on the correspondence with his younger brother Theo that would continue until his death and would prove an invaluable source of information on his life and work. Vincent's work at Goupil took him from The Hague to London and Paris — major cities that were centers of the art world at the time. He took full advantage of what each of them had to offer, visiting museums, exhibitions, and galleries, and reporting on his experiences in his letters to Theo. Aside from original art, Goupil sold reproductions of artworks, which Vincent began to collect. It was during this period that the foundations were laid of his profound love of art and his impressive knowledge of artists and their work. His preferences at the time were entirely conventional: Salon painting, the Barbizon artists (Corot, Millet, and Rousseau) and the Dutch landscape painters known as the Hague School (Jozef Israëls, Jacob and Matthijs Maris, among others). His interest in literature also grew, from the Bible and other edifying texts to novels and poetry, which he read in several languages (English, French, and German, as well as his native Dutch). Art and literature shaped his view of the world and were inextricably linked: "Books and reality and art are the same kind of thing for me."[1]

Following his dismissal from Goupil, where he had neglected his work to devote himself more and more to scripture study and attending church, he sought his vocation in preaching. He tried to build a life for himself in England as a teacher and assistant minister before returning to the Netherlands to work briefly in a bookshop in Dordrecht. Van Gogh longed, however, to become a minister of the church, like his father. By this stage, his religious zeal was bordering on the fanatical, and it was decided that Vincent would move to Amsterdam to prepare for the theology entrance exam, despite his family's serious reservations as to whether this was the right career for him. His studies proved too difficult, however, and he abandoned them too. This latest failure put an end to his dream of becoming a pastor, and, looking back, Van Gogh considered this period to have been one of the most difficult in his life.[2]

Having persuaded himself that his task lay in ministering to the poor, he now hoped to be accepted for missionary training in Brussels. When this also failed, he set off for the Borinage mining region in Belgium, where he found temporary employment as a lay preacher. Van Gogh nursed the sick, taught children, and gave Bible readings. He loved the desolate landscape and even saw a certain romanticism in the harsh living conditions: "The country and the people here appeal to me more each day, one has here a familiar feeling as though on the heath or in the dunes, there's something simple and kind-hearted about the people."[3]

He came to identify so closely with the poverty-stricken population that he gave away his possessions and moved into a small cabin, where he slept on the ground.[4] His employers were not impressed by such excessive behavior and were equally dissatisfied with his performance. They duly terminated his position, making this yet another dead end and plunging Vincent into a deep personal crisis. He still had no idea what to do with his life; he had neither a job nor a family, and he was estranged from his parents, who expressed concerns in this period regarding his mental health and considered having him institutionalized. His relationship with Theo had likewise deteriorated.

It was in the Borinage late in the summer of 1880 that Vincent finally decided, on Theo's advice, to become an artist. He had drawn for his own pleasure for years, occasionally including little sketches in his letters, and had taken up drawing once more during his time in Belgium. He now decided to take Theo's suggestion seriously and try to earn his living as an artist.[5] Theo's career at Goupil had proven more successful than his brother's: he had a solid position at the firm's Paris branch and had begun to contribute to Vincent's living expenses. Henceforward, Theo would be his brother's confidant and support, accompanying him on the far-from-easy course on which he now embarked: that of becoming an artist.

Early Years: Tying in with Tradition

Having made his decision, Van Gogh threw himself into his new project. He spent the first few months working diligently through a self-compiled program of textbooks and sample drawings and copying prints of works by famous artists (cats. 1 and 2). He quickly realized, however, that he would have to go to the city if he wanted to work seriously on his artistic ambitions. Vincent duly moved to Brussels, where Theo put him in contact with several Dutch artists, including the celebrated Hague School painter Willem Roelofs, who advised him to take lessons, and Anthon van Rappard, who was also starting out as an artist and became Vincent's friend. Following Roelofs's advice, Van Gogh enrolled at the academy of art in the Belgian capital to learn how to draw after antique models. After just a month, however, he abandoned the course and decided to return to his parents,[6] now living in the village of Etten in Brabant, to continue his artistic development by drawing landscapes and peasants at work (cat. 4). He viewed figure studies as the foundation of everything: "figure drawing in particular is good … it also works indirectly to the good of landscape drawing. If one draws a pollard willow as though it were a living being, which it actually is, then the surroundings follow more or less naturally, if only one has focused all one's attention on that one tree and hasn't rested until there was some life in it."[7]

Living at home had the major advantage that Van Gogh did not have to spend any money on rent or food, but it did nothing to improve his relationship with his parents. They considered his behavior inappropriate and difficult, while he was irritated by their primness and the importance they attached to appearances and good manners. Things became even worse in his parents' eyes when Vincent proposed to his recently widowed cousin, Kee Vos, who had a young son. He had fallen passionately in love with her and was convinced that they belonged together, despite her consistent rebuffs. He stubbornly persisted, oblivious to Kee's feelings and those of his other relatives, who found his behavior highly unseemly.[8] Theo accused Vincent of making their parents' life unnecessarily difficult, but he continued to support his brother.

A vehement argument with his father on the subject of religion caused Vincent to move to The Hague in late 1881, where he hoped his cousin by marriage, the successful Hague School painter Anton Mauve, would introduce him to other artists. Mauve not only helped him in this regard, he also gave Vincent his first painting lessons (cat. 6). Van Gogh made a number of contacts in The Hague: his former boss Hermanus Tersteeg offered him support and advice, and he made the acquaintance of young artists like George Hendrik Breitner and Théophile de Bock. But he swiftly became isolated when he started a relationship with a pregnant prostitute who already had one child — a move that was wholly unacceptable to his circle. It nevertheless fulfilled his long-held desire for a family of his own and would be the only time in his life that he was able to experience domestic life in this way. He thought of marrying his girlfriend, Sien Hoornik, but faced intense resistance from his parents and from Theo, who by this stage was paying for Vincent's upkeep.

Thanks to Sien, Van Gogh now had a regular model, while her mother and daughter also posed for him on several occasions, giving him the opportunity to hone his figure-drawing skills. The residents of the local old men's home modeled for his drawings too (cats. 7 and 8). Van Gogh hoped to find work as an illustrator. He preferred workers and poor, simple people as his subjects, inspired by the realism of the wood engravings he saw in illustrated magazines,

large quantities of which he collected. He kept up a lively correspondence with Anthon van Rappard, in which the two men discussed artistic and technical matters. They also traded magazine illustrations. Van Gogh's drawing progressed significantly in his early years in The Hague. He was consumed by technical issues such as the proportions and grouping of figures and the rendering of perspective; he experimented with all sorts of materials, from pencil and charcoal to lithographic chalk; and he tried out new techniques in his city views and figure studies of working people. He captured the landscape around his studio in watercolor drawings, and produced oil studies in the woods and on the beach, using a muted palette like that of the Hague School and the Barbizon painters — the established art he saw displayed at dealers and in exhibitions.

The breakdown of Van Gogh's relationship with Sien and his need for a rural environment far from the city drove him in September 1883 to the remote northern Dutch province of Drenthe, having heard from Mauve and Van Rappard that the landscape there was beautiful and the cost of living modest. He responded lyrically to the sweeping landscape, including long descriptions of the local nature in his letters to Theo and drawing studies of workers in peat bogs and turf cottages. However, after three months and with winter approaching, he was forced to return to his parental home, afflicted by loneliness and a lack of money and painting materials.

Painter of Peasant Life

At the age of thirty-three, Van Gogh found himself moving in yet again with his parents, who were now living in Nuenen, where Theodorus was the Protestant minister. Relations with his parents — especially his father — remained difficult, with frequent disappointments on both sides. Nevertheless, the rural environment was just what he needed, and Vincent ended up staying for two years. Having focused on drawing in the early years of his artistic practice, he began to concentrate increasingly from the summer of 1883 onward on painting landscapes, with the aim of capturing the atmosphere and "feeling" of nature, as the Barbizon and Hague School painters had done so brilliantly. Van Gogh decided in Nuenen that his focus ought to be on the figure at work: the figure of the rural laborer in action was, he declared, "the heart of modern art itself."[9] The French painters Jules Breton and Léon-Augustin Lhermitte, but above all "the eternal master" Jean-François Millet, had elevated the representation of peasants and workers to the level of high art and, following in their footsteps, Van Gogh proclaimed himself a "painter of peasant life."[10]

Van Gogh had been an admirer of Millet's work long before becoming an artist himself, but after reading a biography of the artist, who died in 1875, he declared that Millet was his "counselor and guide in everything."[11] He detected in the French master's work the visualization of a religious sense of nature, "the existence of a God and an eternity,"[12] as expressed in the recurring cycle of the seasons and the associated rural labors. Like Millet, Van Gogh wanted to depict the beauty of humble peasant life and the deep connection that persisted in the countryside between human beings and nature. He produced large numbers of paintings and drawings in Nuenen of landscapes, peasants at work (cats. 14 and 15), weavers at their looms, cottages (fig. 1 and cat. 13), and head studies (cats. 9–11). The high point was *The Potato Eaters* (fig. 2), the painting he saw as marking the beginning of his career. It was the first work he did not describe as a study but as a full-fledged painting: the masterpiece, he hoped, that would establish his name both artistically and commercially. He did not consider his earlier works to be suitable for exhibition: he had yet to learn his trade at that point and regarded his entire Dutch period as one of training.

In April 1885, Van Gogh hoped to announce himself on the artistic scene with *The Potato Eaters* through Theo, who managed the Paris branch of Boussod, Valadon & Cie (formerly Goupil & Cie) on Boulevard Montmartre. But following criticism by Theo and others of the dark colors and clumsy anatomy of the figures in his painting, he was forced to conclude that he had been on the wrong track. During his time in Nuenen, he had lacked any contact with art and other artists and, with no sales in prospect, had relied on Theo for years to pay his keep. A visit to the Rijksmuseum in Amsterdam, where he studied Rembrandt's and Frans Hals's techniques and use of color, made Van Gogh even more acutely aware of how much he needed to see and learn from others' work. Spurred on by Theo, who had written to him about Impressionist art, he began to introduce a little more color into his work, to make it easier to sell. He immersed himself in color theory in Nuenen, where he became fascinated by what he read about Eugène Delacroix's use of color. Van Gogh was especially struck by "how in his paintings the mood *of colors and tone* was at one with the meaning"[13]: color, as well as the subject, could be used to convey a message. Delacroix based his unconventional color technique on the physicist Michel-Eugène Chevreul's theories on the optical function of complementary colors and the effects that could be obtained by combining them. Having read about Delacroix's use of color in Charles Blanc's textbooks, Van Gogh began to apply his new knowledge in his still lifes. However, in the absence of examples and with his continuing use of a muted palette, he was not yet able to achieve a greater intensity of color.[14]

Forced by now to acknowledge the limitations of his autodidactic approach, Van Gogh set off for Antwerp at the end of November 1885 to try his luck once more at the academy and to see if he could sell his work. For the time being, he put landscape painting to one side to focus on portraits, for which he expected there to be a better market. While in Antwerp, Van Gogh also studied Rubens's use of color, borrowing the Flemish master's technique for flesh tones in faces, which featured more color and looser brushwork (cat. 16). He took drawing and painting lessons at the academy — something he had always avoided in the past in the belief that it would hinder the development of his own style — and joined two drawing clubs. But he soon fell out with his teachers, and the hoped-for sales likewise failed to materialize. After three months, he decided enough was enough and moved on again to Paris — the world's art capital and, moreover, home to Theo, with whom he could live. Theo had actually suggested that he come to Paris years ago, but Vincent had not felt ready at that point. In the meantime, he had reached a stage in his development where he was experiencing an intense need for artistic exchange and was eager to see firsthand what Impressionism, the modern art of the time, was all about. He also wanted to take lessons once again — not at the academy, but in the studio of the Salon artist Cormon (Fernard Piestre), known for his undogmatic approach, where up-and-coming artists could work from nude and clothed models.

In Search of Renewal

His stay in the French capital brought Van Gogh everything he had hoped for: contact with other artists, plenty of inspiration and examples, and fresh impulses for his own work. Museums, art dealers, and exhibitions gave him the opportunity to study and learn from the work of predecessors and contemporaries whom he admired. He discovered the wealth of color in Delacroix, the Impressionists, and Japanese prints. Although his brief time at Cormon's studio proved less fruitful than he had hoped, as he later recalled,[15] he did meet several artists there with whom he became friends: the Australian John Russell and the

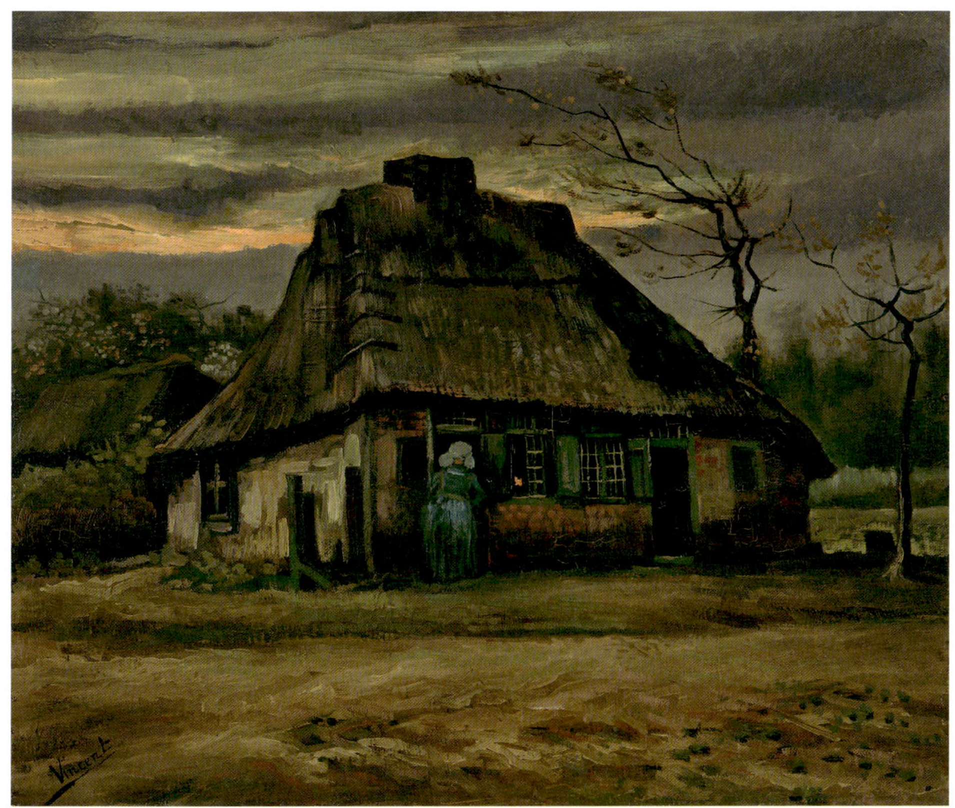

Figure 1. Vincent van Gogh, *The Cottage*, Nuenen, May 1885, oil on canvas, 25 ⅞ × 31 ¼ inches (65.7 × 79.3 cm), Van Gogh Museum, Amsterdam (Vincent van Gogh Foundation).

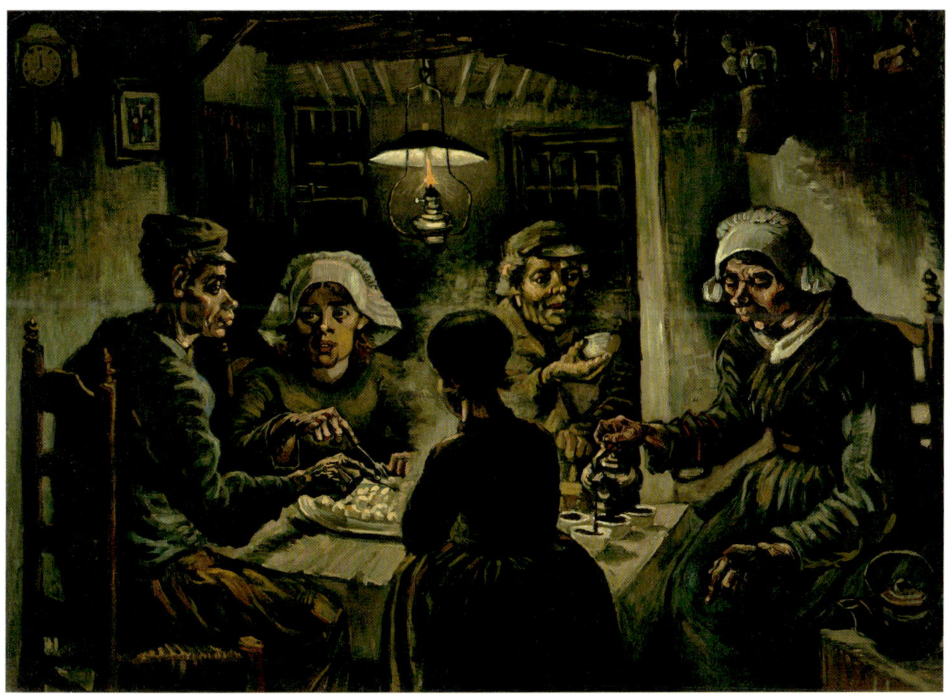

Figure 2. Vincent van Gogh, *The Potato Eaters*, Nuenen, April–May 1885, oil on canvas, 32 ¼ × 44 ⅞ inches (82 × 114 cm), Van Gogh Museum, Amsterdam (Vincent van Gogh Foundation).

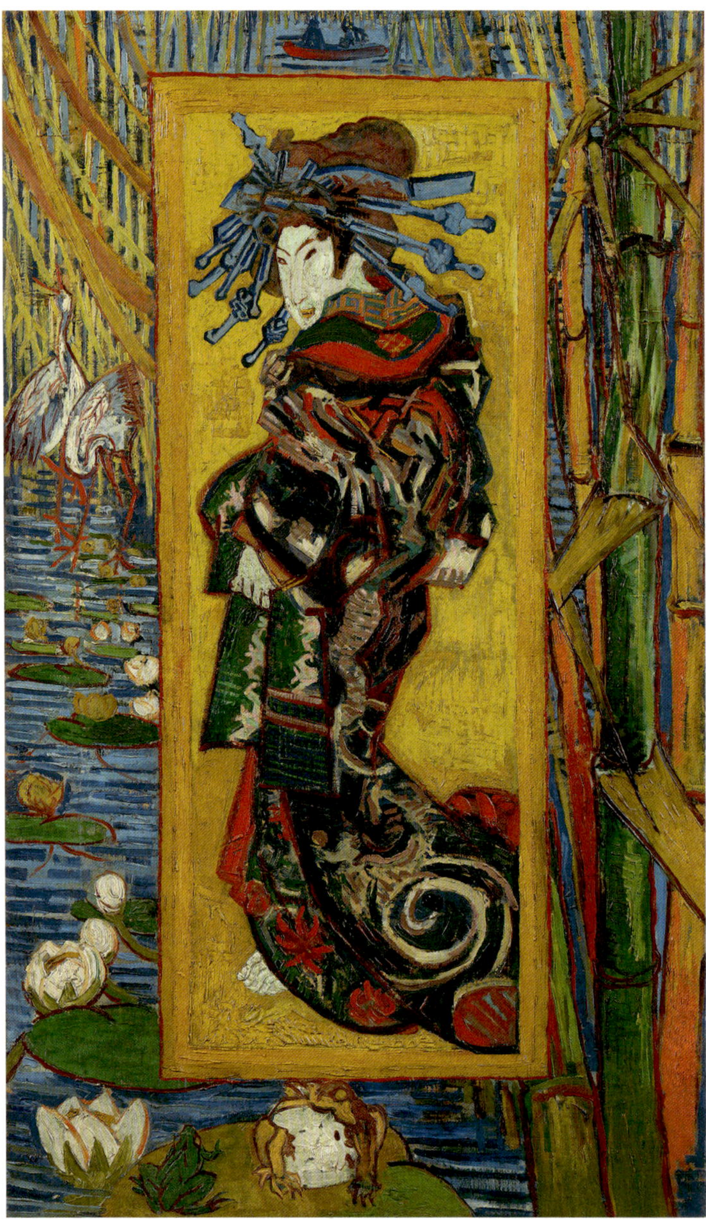

French artists Émile Bernard and Henri de Toulouse-Lautrec. He made the acquaintance of several members of the Impressionist group, including Armand Guillaumin and Camille Pissarro, but also Paul Gauguin, who was viewed in artists' circles as a promising painter, and the Neo-Impressionists Georges Seurat and Paul Signac, who, with their technique of dots and dashes based on scientific color theory, had embarked on an entirely different course. In this manner, Van Gogh gradually found his way into the avant-garde.

In the meantime, his art was developing in spectacular fashion in response to all these fresh impulses. Van Gogh no longer painted dark landscapes and figural works, but used brighter colors and above all lighter shades, and he experimented with different techniques and brush-strokes.[16] In a series of flower studies made in the summer of 1886 (cats. 19 and 20), he worked with a more colorful palette of complementary contrasts and with thick brush-strokes, inspired by the expressive impasto of Adolphe Monticelli, which was well suited to his own pursuit of an unpolished look. He also aimed for more color in the landscapes he painted at Montmartre, in which he continued to work at first in a traditional style reminiscent of the Barbizon and Hague Schools, with lighter but not yet pronounced colors (cat. 17). A marked change occurred in his work in the winter of 1886–87, when he began to apply the innovations of the Impressionists in earnest: his palette now became even brighter, and his brushwork considerably looser (cat. 23). Like Toulouse-Lautrec, he experimented with *peinture à l'essence* — a technique using highly diluted oil paint to obtain a refined, flowing brushstroke that was the complete opposite of the thick, heavily loaded strokes he had been using up to then and to which he would later return.[17] Van Gogh also explored the Neo-Impressionist stippling technique, although he was less than stringent in the theory's application (cat. 25). He tried out the new techniques — from *pointillé* to *à l'essence* (cat. 24) — in both landscapes and self-portraits, a practical and inexpensive way to practice portrait-painting.

In addition to his Impressionist and Pointillist experiments, Japanese prints played an extremely significant role in Van Gogh's development as a modern artist. He purchased hundreds of prints with a view to selling them, and later studied them intensively as artistic examples. Following the loose brushstrokes of Impressionism and the dots and dashes of Pointillism, the clear lines and expanses of color that he found in Japanese printmaking offered an ideal point of departure for his own powerful style (fig. 3).[18]

In this way, the character of Van Gogh's work changed fundamentally in the space of a year through his contact with modern art and artists: he had found the artistic progress he yearned for. What's more, he had generated some attention for his work within Parisian artistic circles by trading paintings with artist friends and exhibiting at several art dealers' shops. He also showed a large number of paintings — mostly floral still lifes — at the café Le Tambourin, run by the Italian Agostina Segatori, with whom he had a brief relationship (cat. 21), and organized an exhibition of his own paintings and those of his friends at a Montmartre bistro. Although none of these efforts resulted in sales, he nevertheless managed to carve out a modest place for himself within the avant-garde.[19] Theo also had an unshakable faith now in Vincent's abilities as an artist. The brothers' relationship had indeed improved considerably, even though sharing a home proved challenging at times. Theo would continue to support Vincent financially after his time in Paris, but they now found themselves on a more equal footing.

Nevertheless, metropolitan life was having an adverse effect on Vincent's well-being, and after two exhausting years he decided to move again. The unhealthy bohemian life he had been leading in the cafés of Montmartre began to take its toll: he was smoking and drinking far too much and eating poorly, and by the winter of 1887–88 he was all but drained. Living too long in the city was not good for him: "we painters work better in the country, everything there speaks more clearly, everything holds firm, everything explains itself, now in a city when one is tired one no longer understands anything and feels as if one is lost."[20] His journey south was thus motivated by the desire for a warmer climate and a quiet, rural environment. But there was a more important reason, too, as he later wrote: "To want to see another light, to believe that looking at nature under a brighter sky can give us a more accurate idea of the Japanese way of feeling and drawing. Wanting, finally, to see this stronger sun, because one feels that without knowing it one couldn't understand the paintings of Delacroix from the point of view of execution, technique, and because one feels that the colors of the prism are veiled in mist in the north."[21]

Light and Color in the South

When Van Gogh arrived in Arles at the end of February 1888, he was deeply impressed by the sunny and colorful southern French landscape. It was here that he would develop a style identifiably his own, with elongated, rhythmic brushstrokes, which he applied thickly and in increasingly bright colors, unmistakably influenced by the Japanese example. He also remained faithful to Delacroix's lessons, as he consistently pursued contrasts between complementary colors to maximize the chromatic impact. The hues of Provence lent themselves wonderfully to "the simplification of color in the Japanese manner,"[22] as Van Gogh wrote to Émile Bernard, with whom he had begun a lively correspondence after leaving Paris.

For the first time in years, Van Gogh was able in Arles to create a domestic base for himself in the shape of the "Yellow House" on Place Lamartine, where he set up his studio in May before moving in fully in September (fig. 4). Following his hectic and unhealthy time in Paris, the Provençal countryside came as a breath of fresh air, and he set about capturing it in paintings and drawings almost systematically. Although his ultimate ambitions lay primarily in the field of portraiture, Van Gogh achieved an unprecedented degree of accomplishment as a landscape painter in Provence (cats. 31 and 34). To properly understand the character of a region, he once wrote to Theo,[23] you had to experience it in all seasons, and, interestingly enough, the period of just over a year he spent in Arles both began and ended with a series of paintings of orchards in blossom. He devoted an intensive "campaign," as he called it, to them in the spring of 1888: "I'm in a fury of work as the trees are in blossom and I wanted to do a Provence orchard of tremendous gaiety," he informed Theo.[24] After the blossoming orchards, the next campaign — harvest — began in June. He had to work hard then too, as the wheat was brought in within a short period. The fruits of a week's hard work out in the fields in the sweltering heat and direct sun, which he enjoyed "like a cicada,"[25] consisted of a series of paintings of wheat fields and one of a sower. They were studies in yellow, just as the orchards had been studies in white and pink, and the sea views he painted during his trip to the coast were studies in blue. He already knew what the next step would be: the vineyards in autumn. "Perhaps now I'll have a try at doing greens. Now autumn — that gives you the whole range of tones."[26] In early October, he painted *The Green Vineyard* (cat. 35) near Arles, which featured prominently among the "poetic subjects" with which he decorated the Yellow House, where he was now living.[27]

As soon as he rented the house, Van Gogh came up with the idea of turning it into an artists' colony, where like-minded painters could come together to create a new art. With the agreement of Theo, whose money was needed to fund the

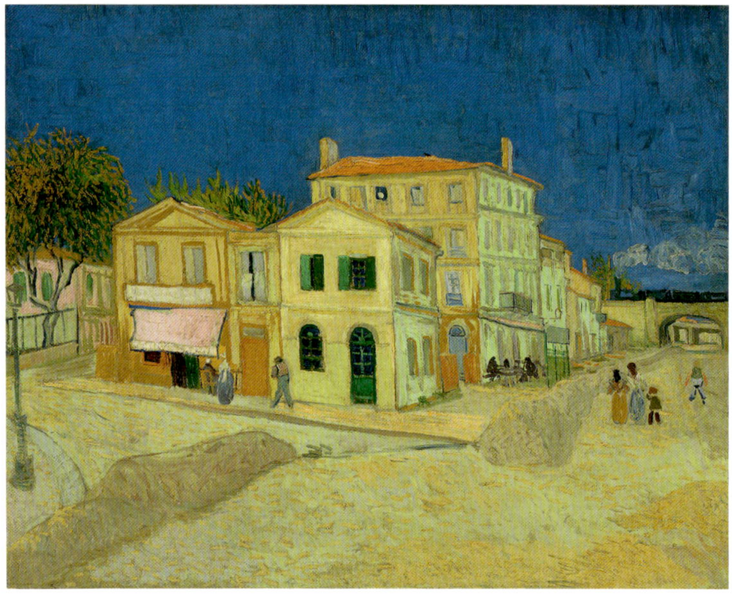

Figure 4. Vincent van Gogh, *The Yellow House (The Street)*, Arles, September 1888, oil on canvas, 28⅜ × 36 inches (72 × 91.5 cm), Van Gogh Museum, Amsterdam (Vincent van Gogh Foundation).

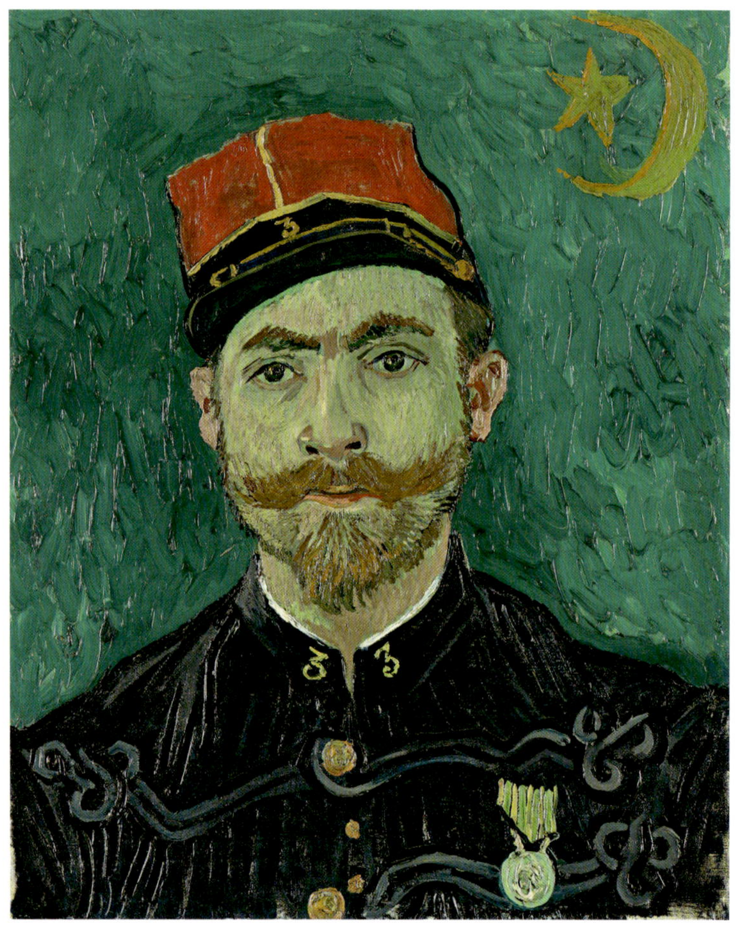

Figure 5. Vincent van Gogh, *The Lover (Portrait of Lieutenant Milliet)*, Arles, late September–early October 1888, oil on canvas, 23¾ × 19½ inches (60.3 × 49.5 cm), Kröller-Müller Museum, Otterlo.

venture, Vincent invited Paul Gauguin — who had been complaining from Brittany about his ill health and lack of money — to come to Arles to lead this "studio in the south."[28] Gauguin agreed after some initial hesitation, but took his time before actually setting off for Provence. While he waited for his fellow artist to arrive, Van Gogh painted a series of canvases to decorate the house, including large sunflowers, park views, landscapes, and portraits (fig. 5). His friends in Arles sat for portraits of "everyday people" — the soldier, the café owner (cat. 36), the postman, the Arlésienne — in which, using heightened colors, he attempted to say something about "the model's thoughts, his soul,"[29] and simultaneously about human existence in a more universal sense. Color had the capacity to convey emotion and did not have to be naturalistic: in *The Night Café* (Yale University Art Gallery, New Haven, Connecticut), for instance, red and green were used to communicate "the terrible human passions," while the color contrasts in *The Bedroom* (Van Gogh Museum, Amsterdam) were meant, conversely, as an expression of "utter repose."[30]

To maintain this immense productivity, Van Gogh needed large amounts of paint and canvas, which Theo sent to him from Paris. When his supplies ran low or he was forced to economize, he drew with reed pens, which he cut from the plants growing by the riverside. He used pen and ink to create a series of landscapes in which he achieved the same supple and seemingly effortless drawing style he so admired in the work of Japanese artists (fig. 6). Van Gogh's painting and drawing achieved unparalleled heights in this period, but the unceasing work made huge demands of him, and his physical and mental health came under increasing strain. His collaboration with Gauguin, who had finally turned up in late October, brought the creative exchange he so fervently desired, but growing tension too, due to their incompatible personalities and differing ideas about art.[31]

On December 23, 1888, the situation escalated to such an extent that Van Gogh suffered a breakdown and cut off his own ear during a psychotic episode, following which he was hospitalized. Gauguin left immediately for Paris, leaving the dream of a shared studio in tatters. Van Gogh now entered a period of uncertainty, with recurring breakdowns and hospital admissions interspersed with periods in which he continued to work intensively, convinced it would help him overcome his illness.[32] Despite the support he received from friends such as the postman Joseph Roulin, Dr. Félix Rey, and the minister Frédéric Salles,

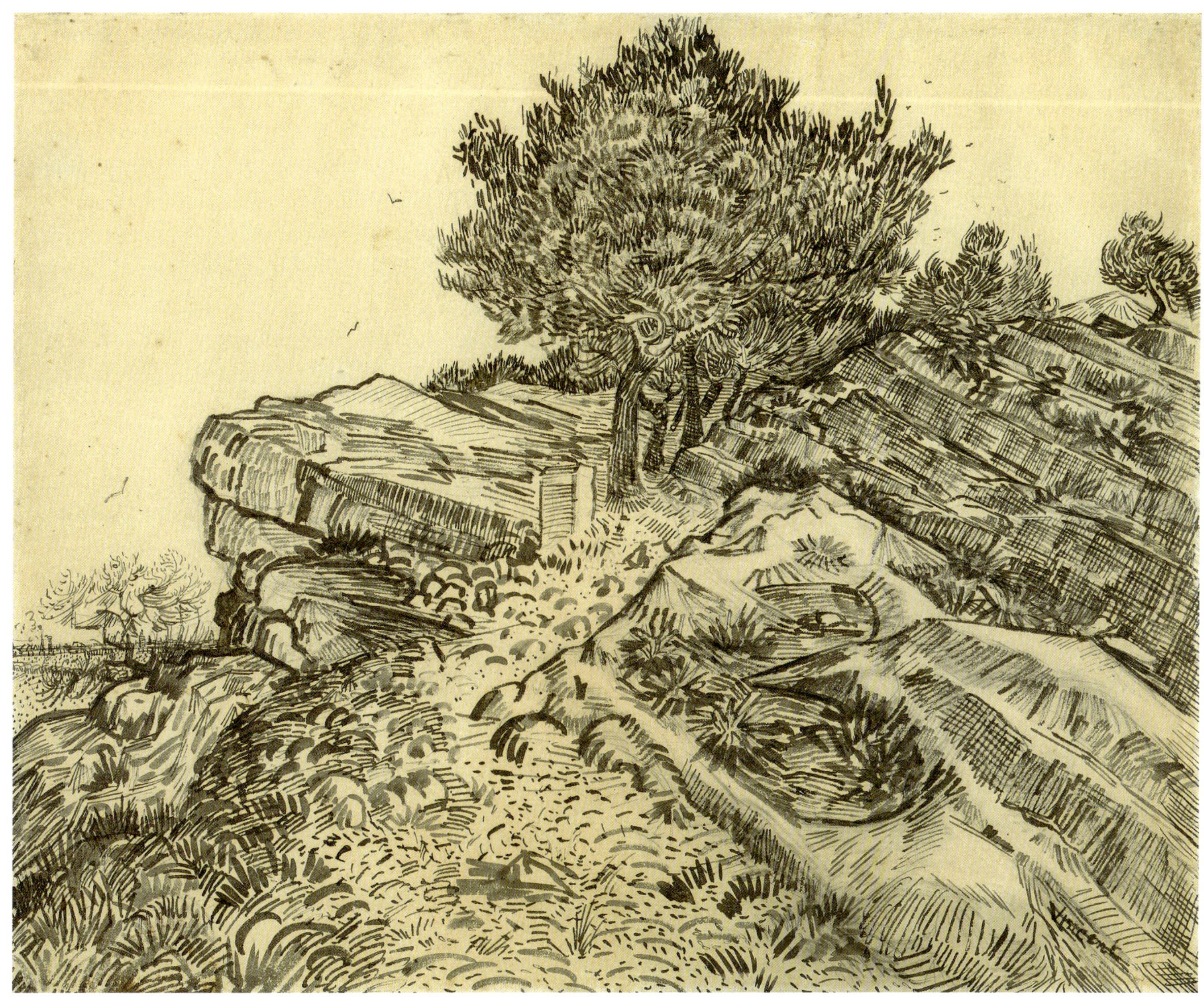

Figure 6. Vincent van Gogh, *The Rock of Montmajour with Pine Trees,* Arles, July 1888, pencil, pen, and reed pen and brush and ink, on paper, 19⅜ × 24 inches (49.1 × 61 cm), Van Gogh Museum, Amsterdam (Vincent van Gogh Foundation).

he felt lonely. The fact that Theo was engaged and planning his wedding in April made Vincent's own situation even more painful, although he did his best to downplay it: "I wouldn't exactly have chosen madness if there had been a choice, but once one has something like that one can't catch it anymore."[33] But the ambition he had brought with him to Arles of contributing to a new art had been seriously undermined by his illness, and he fretted about the future.

Van Gogh did not want to give up the Yellow House, his studio and refuge. However, the local people no longer wanted him around and, following several episodes of his illness, he was scared of living alone. Ultimately, he decided to leave Arles.

Nature as a Source of Enduring Inspiration

Van Gogh spent his second year in southern France at an institution for the mentally ill in Saint-Rémy-de-Provence, twenty-five kilometers northeast of Arles, to which he had himself admitted voluntarily at the beginning of May 1889. He was able to paint and draw in peace at the institution, where his condition was extremely variable: there were periods in which he felt good and could be highly productive, and others when he was ill and incapable of working. During these crises, which could last for days or sometimes weeks at a time, Van Gogh was, according to his doctors, "highly agitated," "delirious," "uttering only incoherent words and confused sentences," or "subject to terrifying fears." However, they wrote, "in the intervals between the attacks the patient is perfectly calm and lucid, and passionately devotes himself to painting."[34]

Although his illness reduced his confidence in his own ability, Van Gogh continued to work just as hard as before. During his first weeks at the clinic, he painted frequently in the walled garden with its tall pines and ivy-covered trees (cats. 39 and 41). After a couple of weeks, he was also allowed to venture beyond the walls of the institution, and he set off every day to draw and paint the wheat fields, olive groves, and cypress trees in the immediate surroundings (fig. 7). After his intense coloristic experiments in Arles, he now sought tranquility and harmony in his color combinations. He set the extremes of color to one side to concentrate instead on how the style of a painting could intensify the image — a quest for stylization that went furthest in *The Starry Night* (fig. 8).

Things initially went well for Van Gogh in Saint-Rémy; he cautiously began to hope that the worst was over, and he grew somewhat more optimistic about the future. But he then suffered another, severe attack in the middle of July while painting (cat. 40). The unwelcome recurrence of his illness left him frightened and uncertain, and when he tentatively resumed work in September, he did so in his studio at first, as he was afraid to venture outside immediately. He began a series of copies of lithographs and etchings after paintings by artists whom he admired, such as Delacroix (cat. 47) and Millet (cats. 42 and 43), which meant he could devote himself to figure studies even without models. He compared the "translation into color" of these black-and-white prints with a musician interpreting a piece of music: "And then I improvise color on it … but seeking memories of *their* paintings — but the memory, the vague consonance of colors that are in the same sentiment, if not right — that's my own interpretation."[35]

He began to work further afield again from October onward, culminating in, among other things, a new series of olive-grove paintings (cat. 45). Having experimented with working from the imagination, as Gauguin had encouraged him to do during their collaboration, Van Gogh firmly anchored himself in nature once more, which meant the modern biblical scenes that Bernard and Gauguin were painting at the time irritated him. Reality had to be the point of departure at all times — abstraction to him was "enchanted ground" that he was eager to avoid, due in part to his illness.[36]

When Van Gogh headed back to northern France in May 1890 following a difficult and lonely year at the institution, his destination was Auvers-sur-Oise. Living among mentally ill people had become oppressive, and he was eager to move closer to Theo, who responded by seeking out a peaceful location where Vincent would be able to work under a doctor's supervision. Through Camille Pissarro, Theo had heard about Paul Gachet, a doctor based in Auvers who was a friend of the Impressionists and an amateur artist himself. When Gachet expressed his willingness to take Vincent under his wing, arrangements were swiftly made.

It pained Van Gogh to leave Provence, but he looked forward to working on studies of rural people and landscapes in the north. His illness had substantially reduced his faith in the future and in the value of his work — something that an article in the magazine *Mercure de France* praising his paintings in an exhibition by Les Vingt in Brussels could do little to alter.[37] "Ah, if I'd been able to work

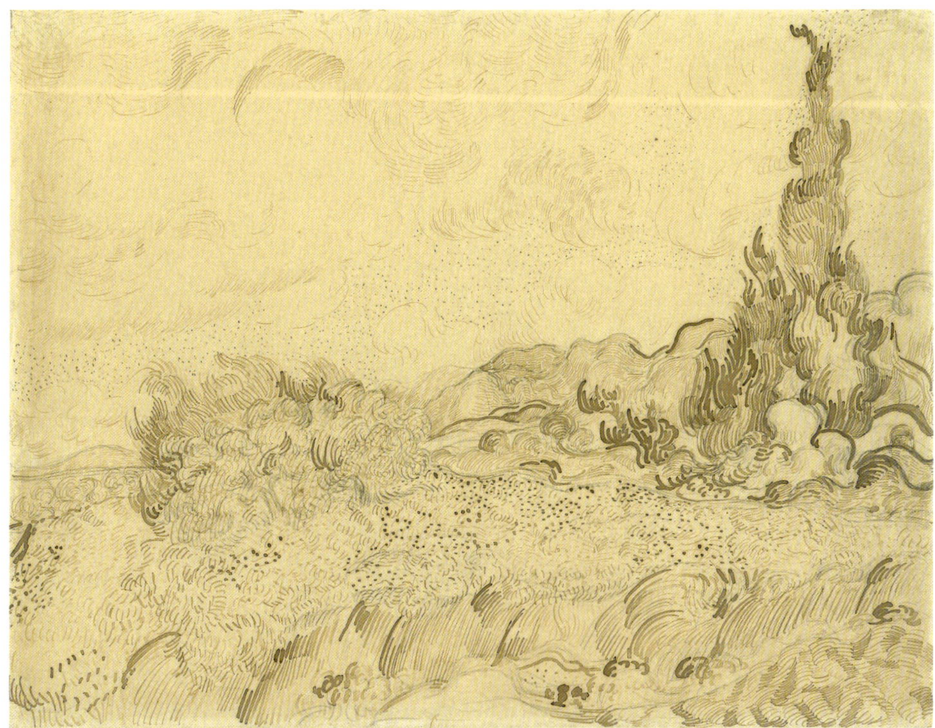

Figure 7. Vincent van Gogh, *Wheatfield and Cypresses*, Saint-Rémy-de-Provence, June–July 1889, pencil, reed pen, and pen and ink on paper, 18 ½ × 24 ½ inches (47.1 × 62.3 cm), Van Gogh Museum, Amsterdam (Vincent van Gogh Foundation).

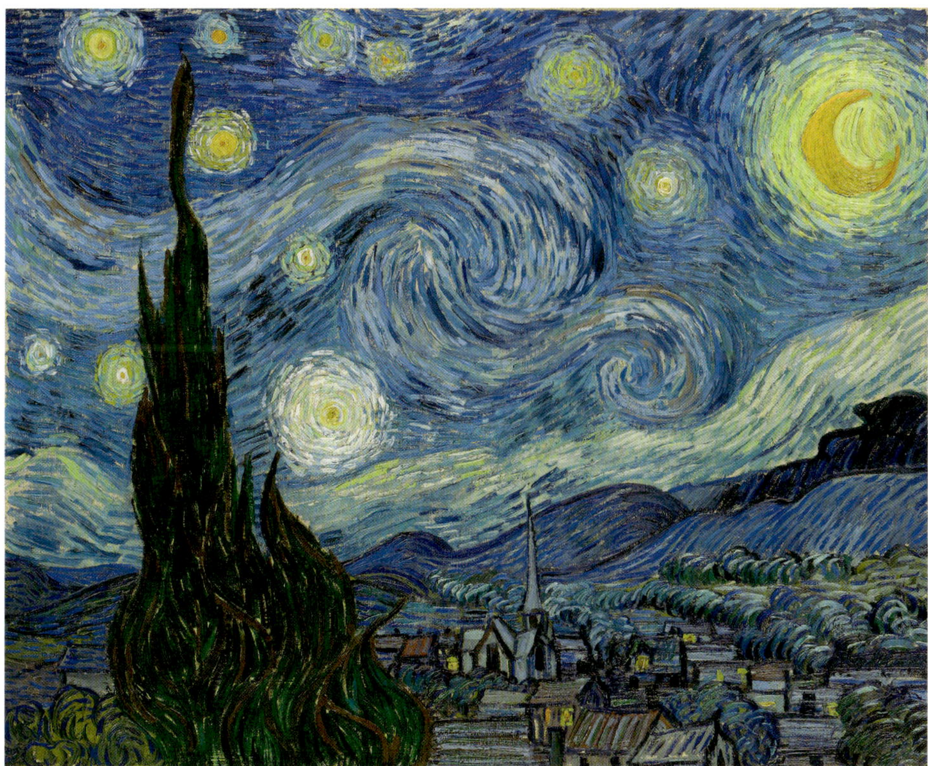

Figure 8. Vincent van Gogh, *The Starry Night*, Saint-Rémy-de-Provence, June 1889, oil on canvas, 29 × 36 ¼ inches (73.7 × 92.1 cm), acquired through the Lillie P. Bliss Bequest, The Museum of Modern Art, New York.

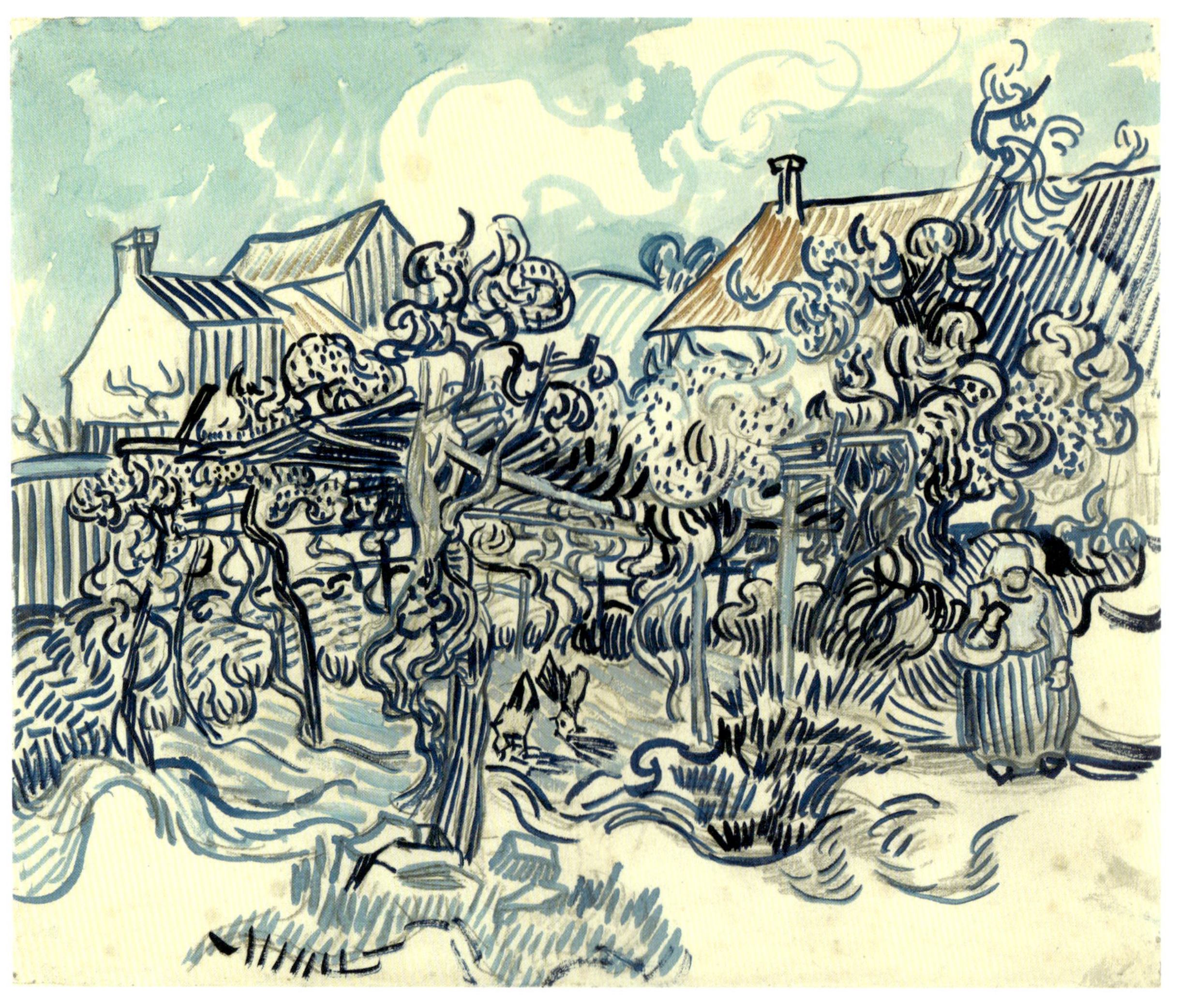

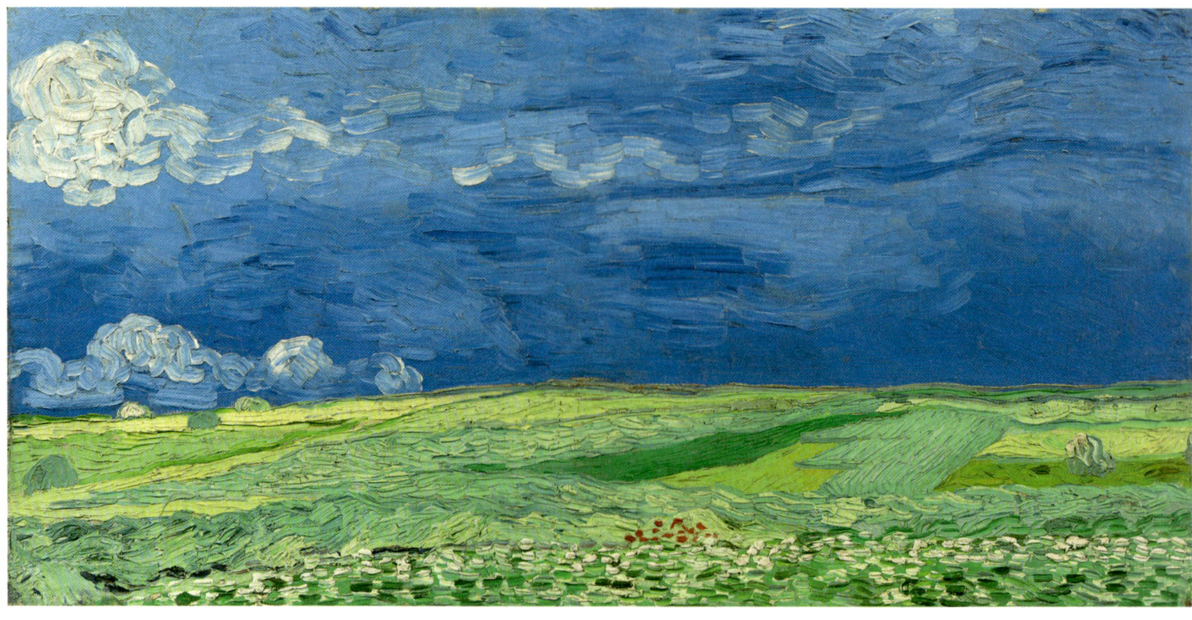

without this bloody illness! How many things I could have done," he lamented, shortly before leaving the clinic.[38] He rounded off his time at Saint-Rémy at the beginning of May 1890 with four impressive still lifes with irises (cat. 48) and roses.

During a short visit to Paris on his way to Auvers, Van Gogh was glad to see Theo again and to meet his brother's wife, Jo, and their three-month-old son (and his namesake), Vincent. Following his arrival in Auvers, a quiet, picturesque village on the river Oise, he wrote to Theo: "I perceive already that it did me good to go into the south the better to see the north."[39] This was the beginning of an unprecedented period of productivity: in the seventy days he spent in Auvers, Van Gogh completed about seventy-five paintings and more than a hundred sketches and drawings, including views of the village (fig. 9 and cat. 49), cottages with thatched roofs (cat. 51), floral still lifes, and portraits, but above all a great many landscapes. In "immense stretches of wheat fields under turbulent skies" (fig. 10), he sought to convey "sadness, extreme loneliness," but also "what I consider healthy and fortifying about the countryside."[40]

Nature offered him consolation in Auvers; his art continued to develop; and he was gradually beginning to receive greater recognition. All the same, he wrote at the end of May, "I feel — a failure — that's it as regards me — I feel that that's the fate I'm accepting. And which won't change any more."[41] It was most likely a combination of deep disquiet that Theo might no longer be able to look out for him, a growing sense of loneliness, and fear that his nervous attacks would return that drove Van Gogh to shoot himself in the chest on July 27, 1890, with the intention of ending his life.[42] He died of his injuries two days later, with Theo at his bedside.

Notes

I am grateful to Renske Suijver and Marije Vellekoop for their comments for this text, and I wish to thank Ted Alkins for translating this essay.

1 Letter 312, Vincent van Gogh to Theo van Gogh, The Hague, Sunday, February 11, 1883. The numbers used for Van Gogh's letters refer to Leo Jansen, Hans Luijten, and Nienke Bakker, *Vincent van Gogh — The Letters: The Complete Illustrated and Annotated Edition*, 6 vols. (London and Amsterdam: Thames & Hudson / Van Gogh Museum, 2009), available online at www.vangoghletters.org.

2 Letter 154, Vincent van Gogh to Theo van Gogh, Cuesmes, between about August 11 and 14, 1879.

3 Letter 150, Vincent van Gogh to Theo van Gogh, Wasmes, between March 4 and 31, 1879.

4 Letter from Anna van Gogh-Carbentus to Theo van Gogh, February 27, 1879 (Van Gogh Museum, inv. b2463).

5 See letters 156 (Vincent van Gogh to Theo van Gogh, Cuesmes, August 20, 1880) and 214 (Vincent van Gogh to Theo van Gogh, The Hague, on or about April 2, 1882).

6 Teio Meedendorp, "Van Gogh in Training: The Idiosyncratic Path to Artistry," in Marije Vellekoop et al., eds., *Van Gogh's Studio Practice* (Amsterdam and Brussels: Van Gogh Museum / Mercatorfonds, 2013), 45–48.

7 Letter 175, Vincent van Gogh to Theo van Gogh, Etten, between October 12 and 15, 1881.

8 Hans Luijten, *Van Gogh and Love* (Amsterdam: Van Gogh Museum, 2007), 16–18.

9 Letter 515, Vincent van Gogh to Theo van Gogh, Nuenen, on or about July 14, 1885.

10 Letter 489, Vincent van Gogh to Theo van Gogh, Nuenen, on or about April 4, 1885.

11 Letter 493, Vincent van Gogh to Theo van Gogh, Nuenen, April 13, 1885.

12 Letter 288, Vincent van Gogh to Theo van Gogh, The Hague, November 26 and 27, 1882.

13 Letter 526, Vincent van Gogh to Anthon van Rappard, Nuenen, between about August 8 and 15, 1885.

14 Louis van Tilborgh and Marije Vellekoop, *Vincent van Gogh Paintings*, vol. 1, *Dutch Period 1881–1885, Van Gogh Museum* (Amsterdam and Blaricum: Van Gogh Museum / V+K Publishing, 1999), 164–78.

15 Letter 569, Vincent van Gogh to Horace Mann Livens, Paris, September or October 1886.

16 For a detailed analysis of Van Gogh's development from realist to modernist, see Louis van Tilborgh and Ella Hendriks, *Vincent van Gogh Paintings*, vol. 2, *Antwerp and Paris 1885–1888, Van Gogh Museum* (Amsterdam and Zwolle: Van Gogh Museum / Waanders, 2011), 51–89.

17 See ibid., 74–77, and Fleur Roos Rosa de Carvalho, "Degas, Toulouse-Lautrec and Van Gogh: The Use of Diluted Paint," in Vellekoop et al., eds., *Van Gogh's Studio Practice*, 330–49.

18 See Louis van Tilborgh et al., *Van Gogh and Japan* (Amsterdam and Brussels: Van Gogh Museum / Mercatorfonds, 2018).

19 For a survey of Van Gogh's attempts to sell and exchange work in Paris, see Van Tilborgh and Hendriks, *Vincent van Gogh Paintings,* vol. 2, 17–25.

20 Letter 841, Vincent van Gogh to Willemien van Gogh, Saint-Rémy-de-Provence, January 20, 1890.

21 Letter 801, Vincent van Gogh to Theo van Gogh, Saint-Rémy-de-Provence, September 10, 1889.

22 Letter 622, Vincent van Gogh to Émile Bernard, Arles, June 7, 1888.

23 Letter 384, Vincent van Gogh to Theo van Gogh, The Hague, September 10, 1883.

24 Letter 592, Vincent van Gogh to Theo van Gogh, Arles, on or about April 3, 1888.

25 Letter 628, Vincent van Gogh to Émile Bernard, Arles, on or about June 19, 1888.

26 Letter 631, Vincent van Gogh to Theo van Gogh, Arles, on or about June 25, 1888.

27 Letter 697, Vincent van Gogh to Theo van Gogh, Arles, October 4 or 5, 1888.

28 Letter 674, Vincent van Gogh to Theo van Gogh, Arles, September 4, 1888.

29 Letter 673, Vincent van Gogh to Theo van Gogh, Arles, September 3, 1888.

30 Letter 676, Vincent van Gogh to Theo van Gogh, Arles, September 8, 1888; letter 706, Vincent van Gogh to Paul Gauguin, Arles, October 17, 1888.

31 See Douglas W. Druick and Peter Kort Zegers, *Van Gogh and Gauguin: The Studio of the South* (Chicago: The Art Institute of Chicago; Amsterdam: Van Gogh Museum, 2001).

32 On Van Gogh's illness, see Nienke Bakker, Louis van Tilborgh, and Laura Prins, *On the Verge of Insanity: Van Gogh and His Illness* (Amsterdam and Brussels: Van Gogh Museum / Mercatorfonds, 2016).

33 Letter 760, Vincent van Gogh to Theo van Gogh, Arles, April 21, 1889.

34 Bakker, Tilborgh, and Prins, *On the Verge of Insanity*.

35 Letter 805, Vincent van Gogh to Theo van Gogh, Saint-Rémy-de-Provence, September 20, 1889.

36 Letter 822, Vincent van Gogh to Émile Bernard, Saint-Rémy-de-Provence, November 26, 1889.

37 Gabriel-Albert Aurier, "Les Isolés: Vincent van Gogh," *Mercure de France*, January 1890.

38 Letter 865, Vincent van Gogh to Theo van Gogh, Saint-Rémy-de-Provence, on or about May 1, 1890.

39 Letter 874, Vincent van Gogh to Theo van Gogh and Jo van Gogh-Bonger, Auvers-sur-Oise, on or about May 21, 1890.

40 Letter 898, Vincent van Gogh to Theo van Gogh and Jo van Gogh-Bonger, Auvers-sur-Oise, on or about July 10, 1890.

41 Related manuscript 20, Vincent van Gogh to Theo van Gogh and Jo van Gogh-Bonger, Auvers-sur-Oise, May 24, 1890.

42 Bakker, Tilborgh, and Prins, *On the Verge of Insanity*, 80–81.

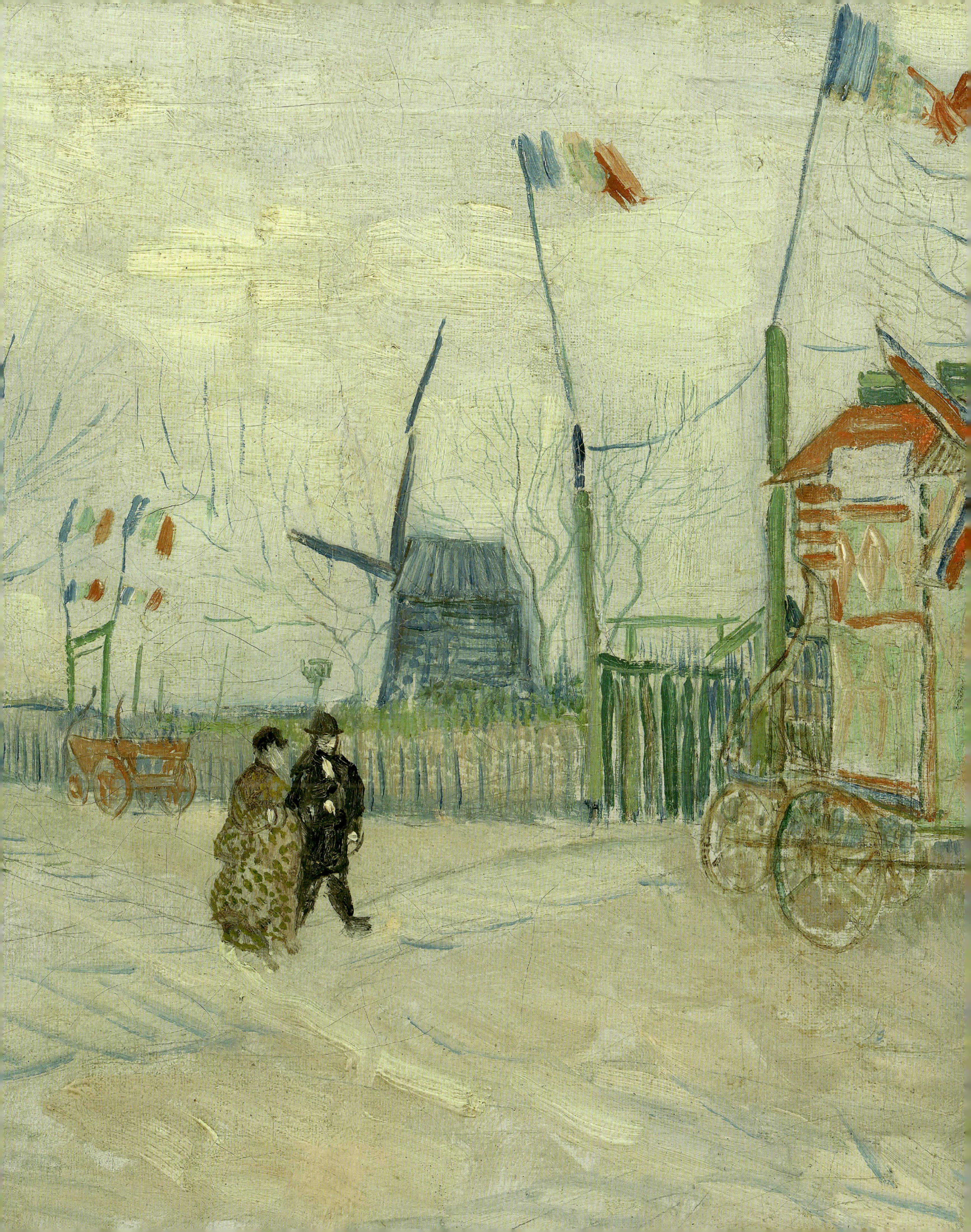

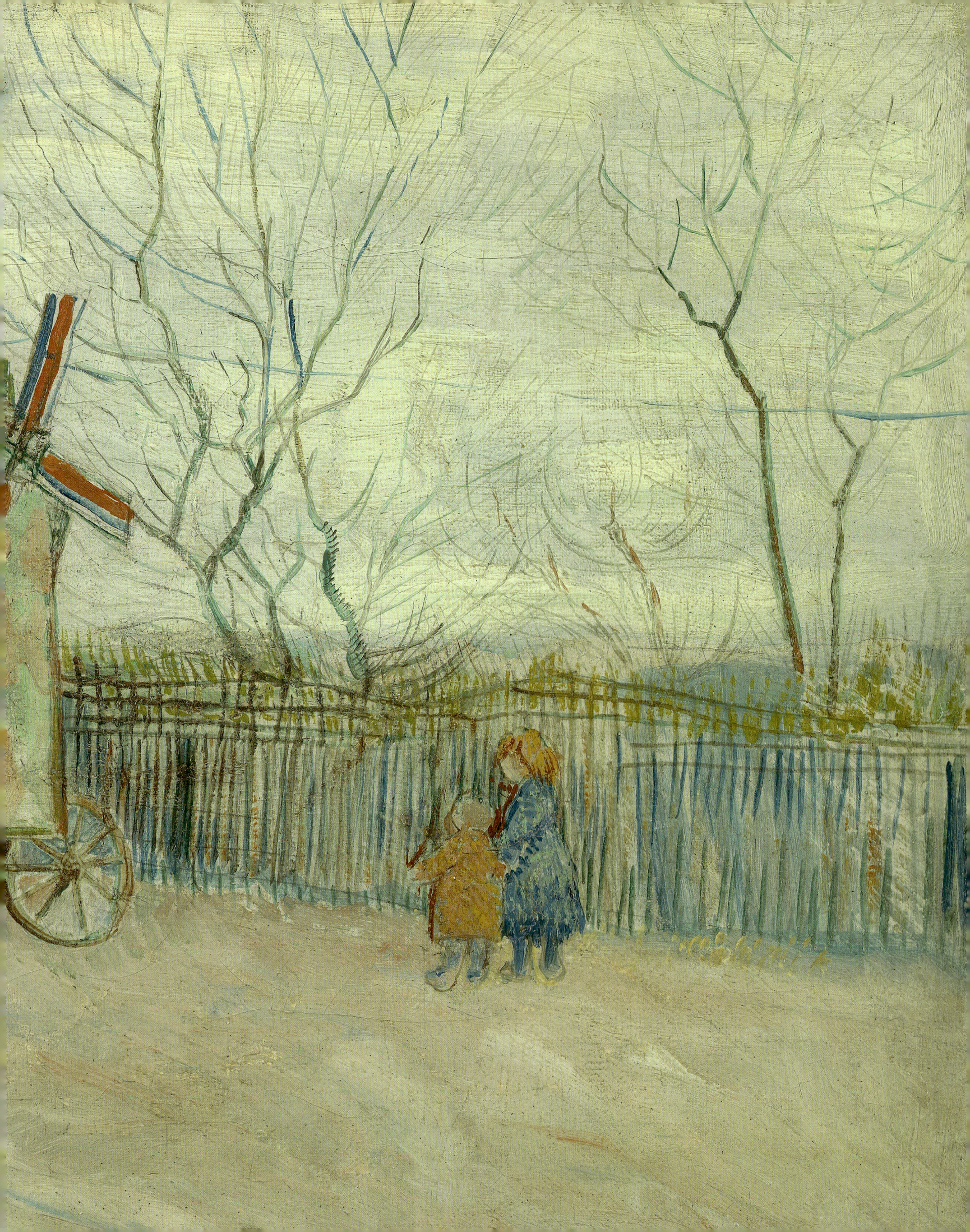

Family Matters
The History of the Van Gogh Museum and Its Collection

Renske Suijver

Vincent van Gogh died on July 29, 1890, two days after shooting himself in the chest. Even though he sold a few works and earned the esteem of his fellow artists during his lifetime, he did not live long enough to enjoy his eventual fame. In 1888, however, he had written to Theo with surprising foresight: "I can do nothing about it if my paintings don't sell. The day will come, though, when people will see that they're worth more than the cost of the paint and my subsistence, very meagre in fact, that we put into them."[1] Today, people from all over the world are inspired by Van Gogh's art and views on life, and many of them also visit the museum in Amsterdam that has been dedicated to him since 1973. The very existence of the Van Gogh Museum is due to the boundless devotion of Vincent's brother Theo (1857–1891) and his wife, Jo van Gogh-Bonger (1862–1925), and of their son, Vincent (1890–1978), who was named after the artist.

Brotherly Love: Theo

Theo van Gogh was grief-stricken by the death of his elder brother and kindred spirit (fig. 1). Theo, an art dealer, had the majority of his brother's paintings and drawings in his possession. It stands to reason, therefore, that he immediately wished to generate interest in Vincent's work by organizing an exhibition, so that everyone would know "that he was a great artist.... Time will bring the honor due him, and many a one will grieve to think he died so young.... I have decided to organize an exhibition of his works in Paris within the next few months. I wish you could see a collection of his pictures. One has to see them together to understand them truly," he wrote to his sister Lies.[2]

The hoped-for exhibition at the famous Paris gallery of Durand-Ruel did not take place.[3] In the meantime, Theo— in an effort to give people an opportunity to become acquainted with Vincent's work—had exhibited as many of his brother's paintings as possible in the apartment in Paris that he had rented for his young family. Theo could not pursue his mission, however, because of his rapidly deteriorating health. He had a nervous breakdown and was admitted to a clinic in the Netherlands shortly afterward. Less than six months after Vincent's death, Theo died too.

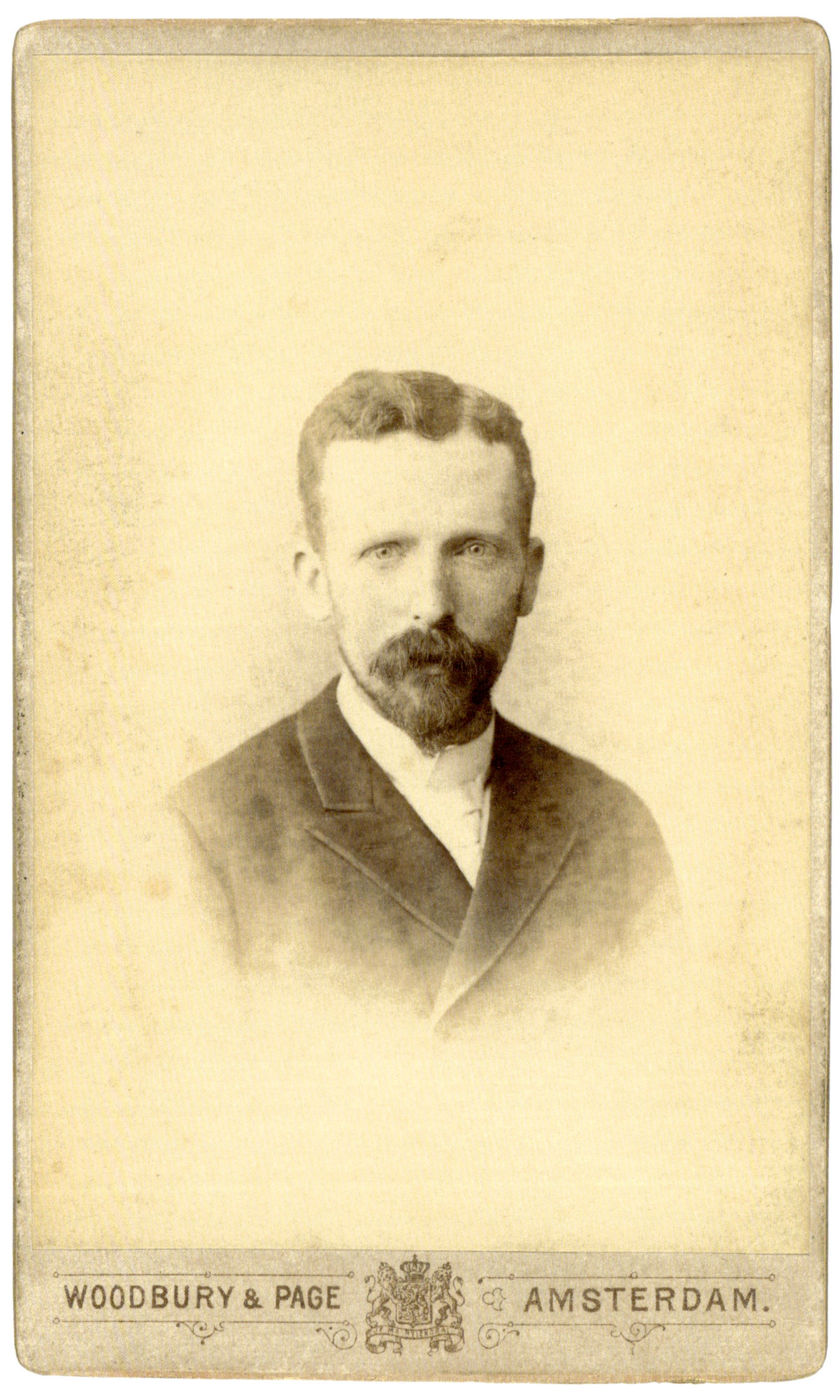

Figure 1. Theo van Gogh, 1889, Van Gogh Museum, Amsterdam (Vincent van Gogh Foundation).

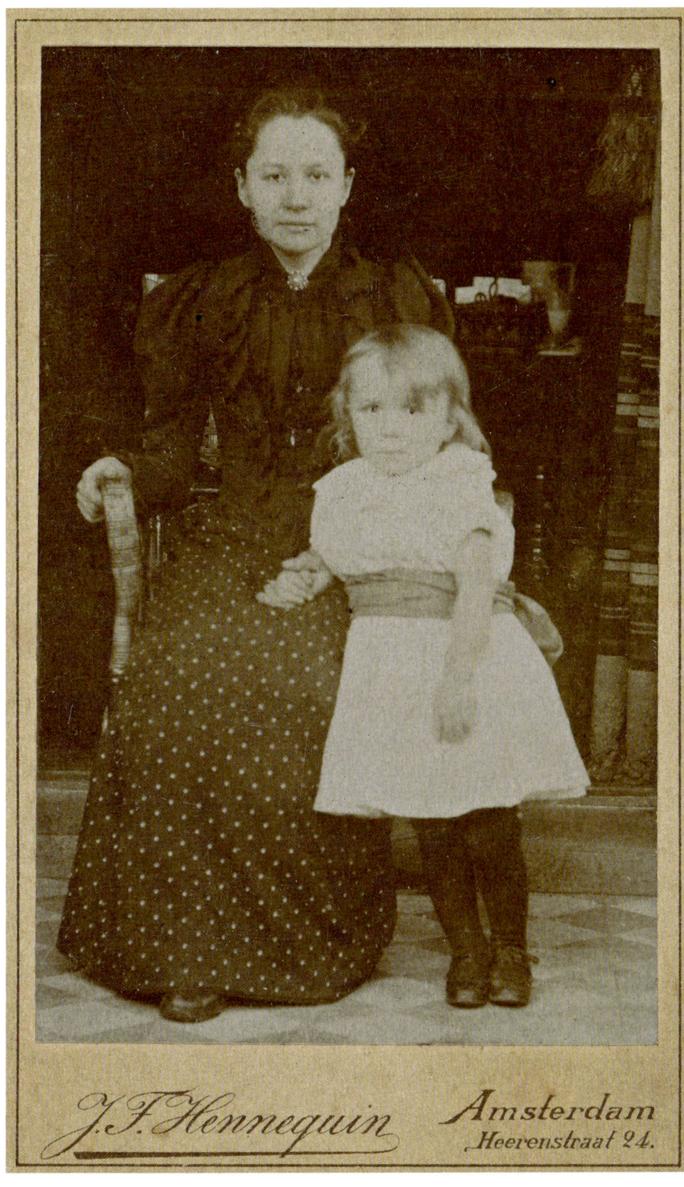

Figure 2. Jo van Gogh-Bonger with her son, Vincent van Gogh, 1892, Van Gogh Museum, Amsterdam (Vincent van Gogh Foundation).

A Devoted Sister-in-Law: Jo

At the age of twenty-eight, Jo van Gogh-Bonger became a widow with a son who was less than a year old (fig. 2). Together, they inherited Theo's possessions, including all the works by Vincent, the brothers' correspondence, and the art collection they had formed together. As long as little Vincent was still underage, Jo was responsible for administering the entire collection. "As well as the child, he has left me another task — *Vincent*'s work — getting it seen and appreciated as much as possible — keeping all the treasures that Theo and Vincent had collected intact for the child — that, too, is my work," she wrote in her diary in 1891.[4]

To support herself and her child, Jo established a guest-house in the Netherlands. Over the years, she also sold quite a few works from the collection to boost Van Gogh's reputation. She sent works to various art dealers for sale exhibitions, by far the most to the German dealer and publisher Paul Cassirer.[5] Jo sold some 240 works by Van Gogh and a dozen paintings and drawings by other artists from the brothers' collection.[6] In retrospect, it is of course a pity that so many works were dispersed from the family collection, but without these often strategic sales, Van Gogh's popularity would have been longer in coming and less widespread.

In the spirit of Theo, Jo too organized exhibitions of Vincent's paintings and drawings, and she collaborated on initiatives of artists in her circle of acquaintances. It gave Jo a great deal of satisfaction to see that the public and the critics were increasingly positive about Van Gogh's work: "The art appreciation session on Vincent's drawings is in Arti tomorrow evening. — I have high hopes — I have a feeling of indescribable triumph when I think that it's finally arrived — the appreciation — the liking — I must go to hear what people are saying — what their attitude is. The ones who used to ridicule Vincent and call him a fool."[7] The first large retrospective followed in 1905 at the Stedelijk Museum in Amsterdam, with 474 works by Van Gogh, largely from the family collection.[8]

Jo read the extraordinary correspondence between the brothers, most of which survives, thanks to Theo. After years of preparation, she launched the first extensive publication of Vincent's letters in 1914: the three-volume *Brieven aan zijn broeder* (Letters to His Brother). A German translation appeared that same year, and Jo, who had been trained as an English teacher, also translated the bulk of the letters into English. All of these publications served to acquaint a broad public with the human side of the artist.

The Nephew Who Founded the Museum: Vincent

On January 31, 1890, nine months after Theo and Jo were married, their son, Vincent, was born.[9] That same day, Theo wrote to his brother: "As we told you, we'll name [our little one] after you, and I'm making the wish that he may be as determined and as courageous as you."[10] The boy amply fulfilled his father's wish, for he ensured the founding of the Van Gogh Museum.

After the death of Jo in 1925, her son had full responsibility for the collection. Following his mother's example, Vincent published various editions of the letters in the 1930s. Even so, until 1950 he spent most of his time simply working as an engineer. According to Bram Hammacher, former director of the Kröller-Müller Museum, Vincent's dilemma was "that he was fatally bound up with that fame and, being the nephew, had to show respect while at the same time wanting to prove to himself and the world that he was someone in his own right, irrespective of artistic values."[11] After the Second World War, "the engineer" — as Vincent was often called, to prevent confusion with his famous uncle — set to work on the four-volume edition of the collected letters, the *Verzamelde brieven van Vincent van Gogh* (1952–54), which soon appeared in various other languages.

The paintings to which Vincent was most attached hung on the walls of his house in Laren; the others stood rows deep in a room reserved for Van Gogh's paintings (fig. 3). He stopped selling off paintings from the collection and gave away only a few works as personal presents. He did, however, collaborate on exhibitions. In 1930 there was another large Van Gogh exhibition at the Stedelijk Museum in Amsterdam, which also included pieces from the collection of Anton Kröller and Helene Kröller-Müller. When the director cautiously asked if the family paintings could perhaps remain on display in the museum for an extended period, Vincent gave a number of works on long-term loan, partly at the urging of his wife, Josina van Gogh-Wibaut.[12] Those works remained on display there for decades. This permanent presentation of his work in the capital city further enhanced Van Gogh's reputation.

Keeping the collection together for posterity became more and more of a priority, and Vincent's thoughts on this matter were steered by his concern that his children would

Figure 3. The artist's nephew Vincent van Gogh and his second wife, Nelly van der Goot, in their living room in Laren, 1949, The Art Institute of Chicago.

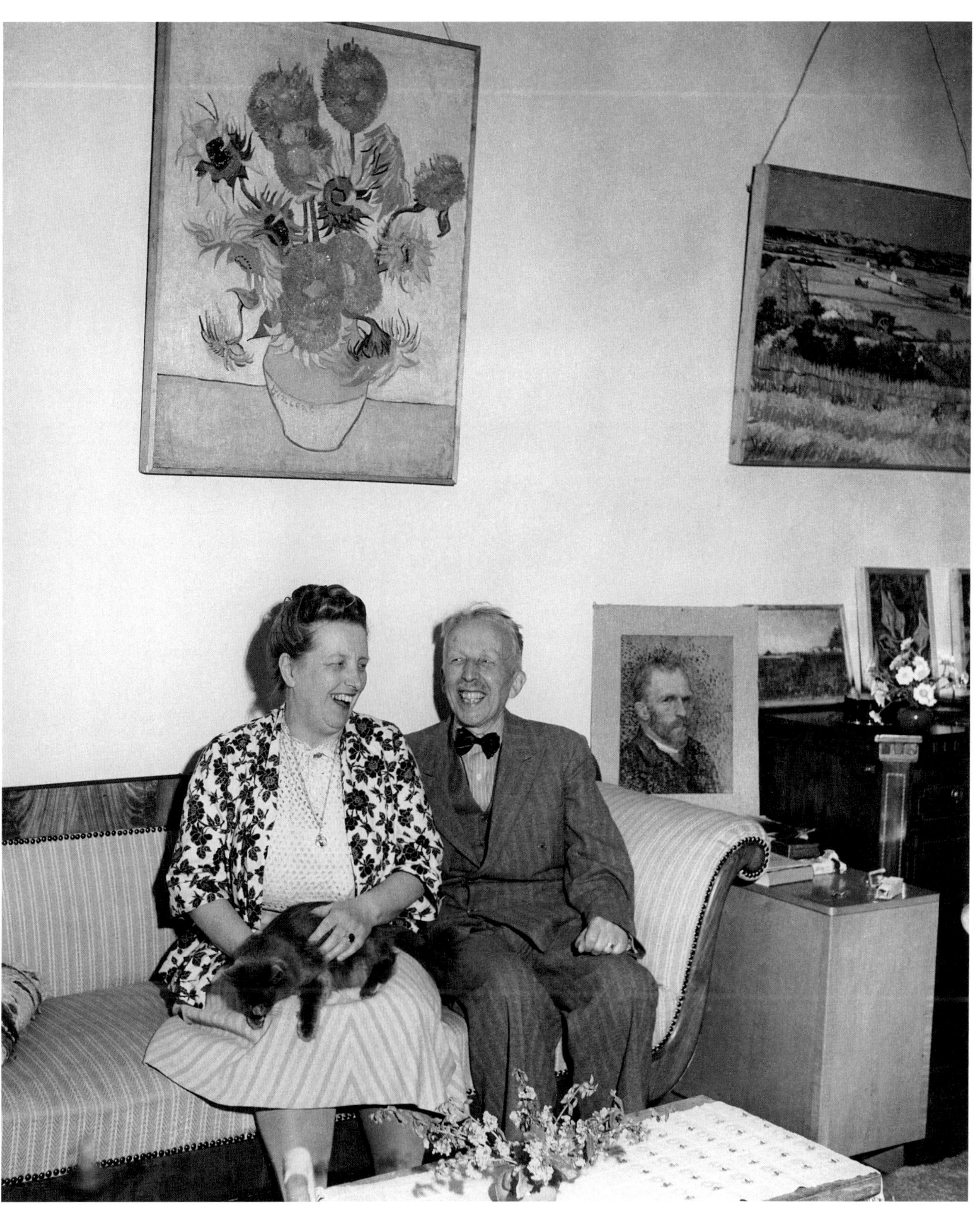

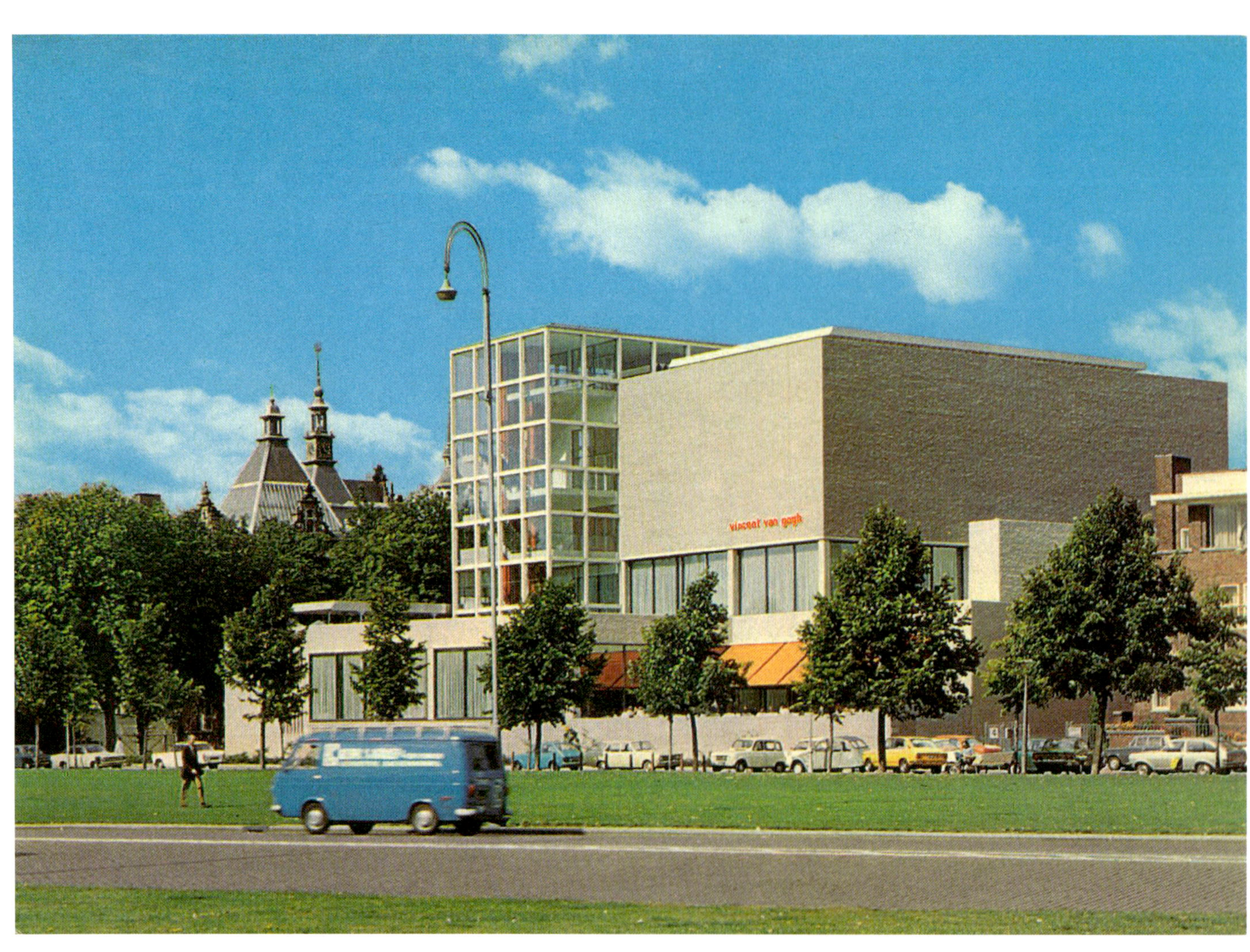

Figure 4. Postcard of the Van Gogh Museum, 1970s.

have to pay sky-high inheritance tax on the collection
after his death. The solution was found in the 1960s: Hendrik
Jan Reinink, director-general for the arts and international cultural relations, put forward a proposal, backed
by Hammacher, to build a museum for the collection.
This idea was well received. The collection was transferred
to the Vincent van Gogh Foundation, which concluded an
agreement with the Dutch government in 1962. After the
payment of 18,470,000 guilders, responsibility for the
collection and its housing in a museum in Amsterdam was
entrusted to the Dutch state.[13] The city of Amsterdam
bore the costs of building the museum. It was also agreed
that the Van Gogh family would always remain closely
involved as members of the board of the foundation.[14] The
famous architect Gerrit Rietveld was chosen to design
the museum, owing to his modernist vision and his empha-
sis on geometrical forms and light, open spaces. After
Rietveld's death, his task was taken over first by Joan van
Dillen and then by Johan van Tricht. Vincent was also
closely involved in the process. On June 2, 1973, the Van Gogh
Museum, situated between the Stedelijk Museum and the
Rijksmuseum, opened its doors (fig. 4).

Vincent had clear ideas about the role of a museum in
society. He dreamed of an active museum that would contribute to the self-development of its visitors.[15] In the
speech he gave to mark the driving of the first pile into
the ground, he stressed that the Van Gogh Museum
would focus on "collecting and exhibiting art of the past" —
in this period he was still acquiring many artworks for
the collection — and on the active practice of art by visitors
to the museum, with a view to bringing about "a better
appreciation of the works exhibited," but above all to give
them an opportunity to "express their own feelings."[16]

A Unique Museum

The Van Gogh Museum administers the largest and most
representative collection of Van Gogh's work in the
world: 205 paintings, more than 500 drawings, four sketchbooks, and impressions of all his graphic output.[17]
Many paintings of special significance for the artist have
naturally remained in the family collection, such as
his masterpiece *The Potato Eaters* (see page 15, fig. 2), the
Self-Portrait as a Painter, in which he consciously presents
himself as a modern artist, and *Almond Blossom*, which
Van Gogh painted for his newborn nephew (figs. 5–6).

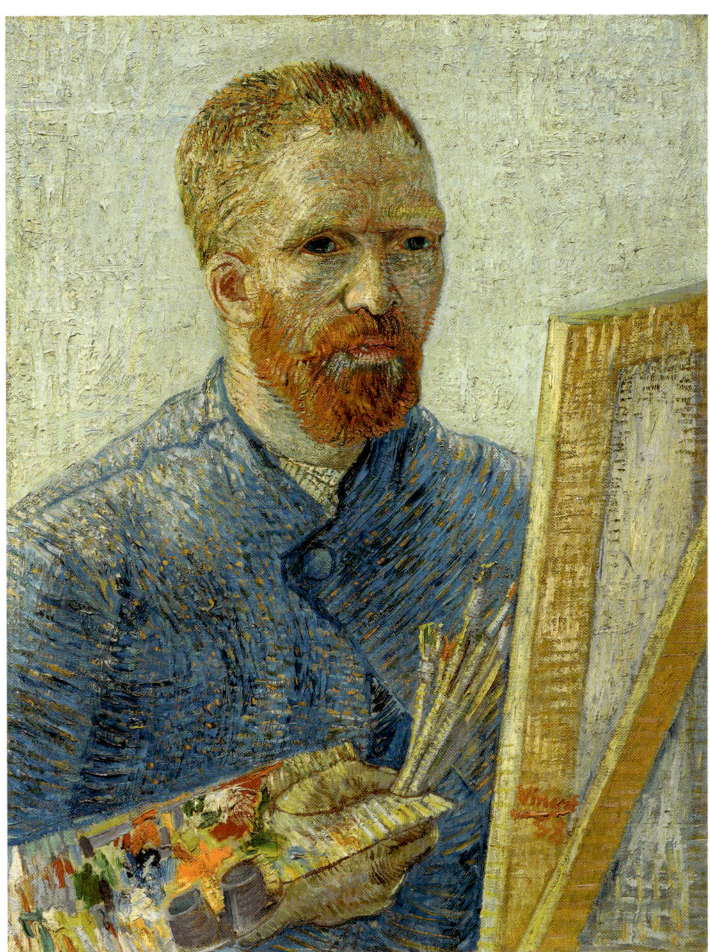

Figure 5. Vincent van Gogh, *Self-Portrait as a Painter*, Paris, December 1887–
February 1888, oil on canvas, 25 ⅝ × 19 ⅝ inches (65.1 × 50 cm), Van Gogh
Museum, Amsterdam (Vincent van Gogh Foundation).

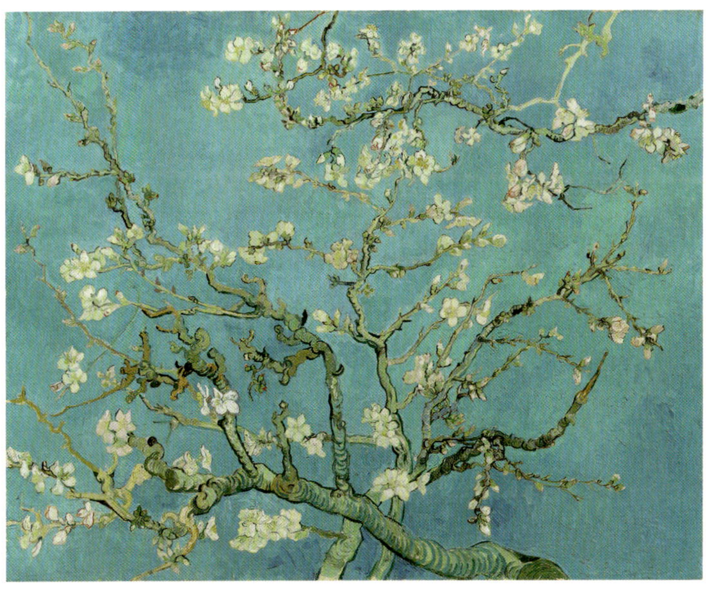

Figure 6. Vincent van Gogh, *Almond Blossom*, Saint-Rémy-de-Provence,
February 1890, oil on canvas, 28 ⅞ × 36 ⅜ inches (73.3 × 92.4 cm), Van Gogh
Museum, Amsterdam (Vincent van Gogh Foundation).

Figure 7. Vincent van Gogh, *Irises*, from the Paris and Auvers-sur-Oise sketchbook, 1890, pencil on paper, 5 ¼ × 3 ⅜ inches (13.4 × 8.5 cm), Van Gogh Museum, Amsterdam (Vincent van Gogh Foundation).

Figure 8. Vase, earthenware, 8 ⅝ × 5 ⅛ × 5 ⅛ inches (22 × 13 × 13 cm), Van Gogh Museum, Amsterdam (Vincent van Gogh Foundation).

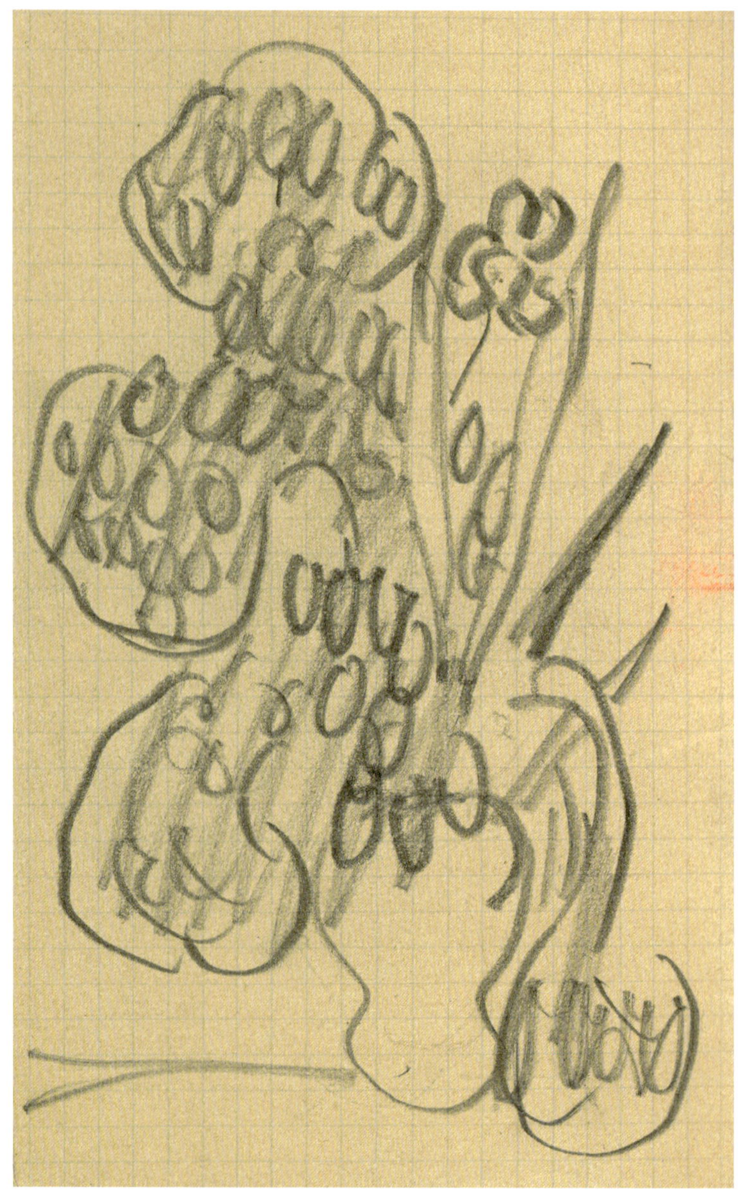

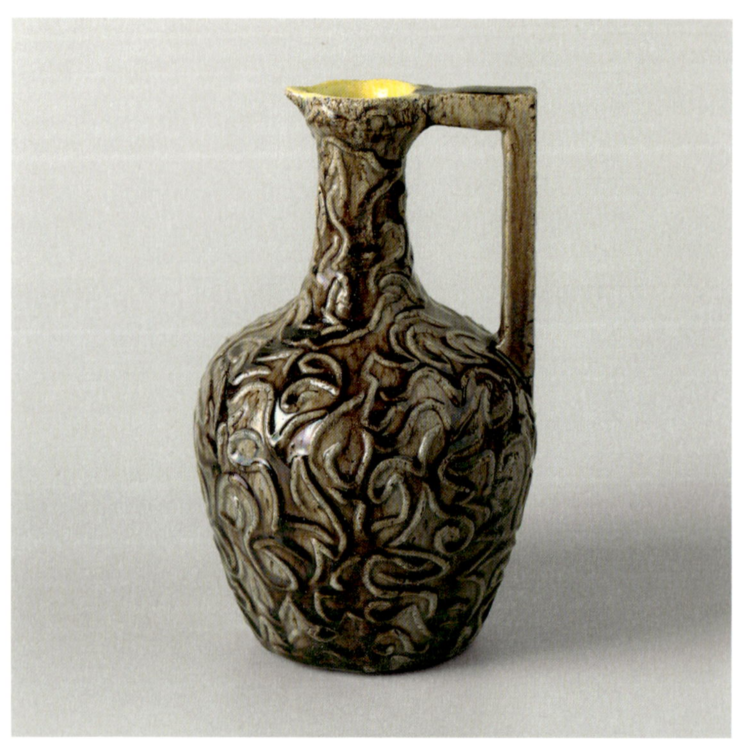

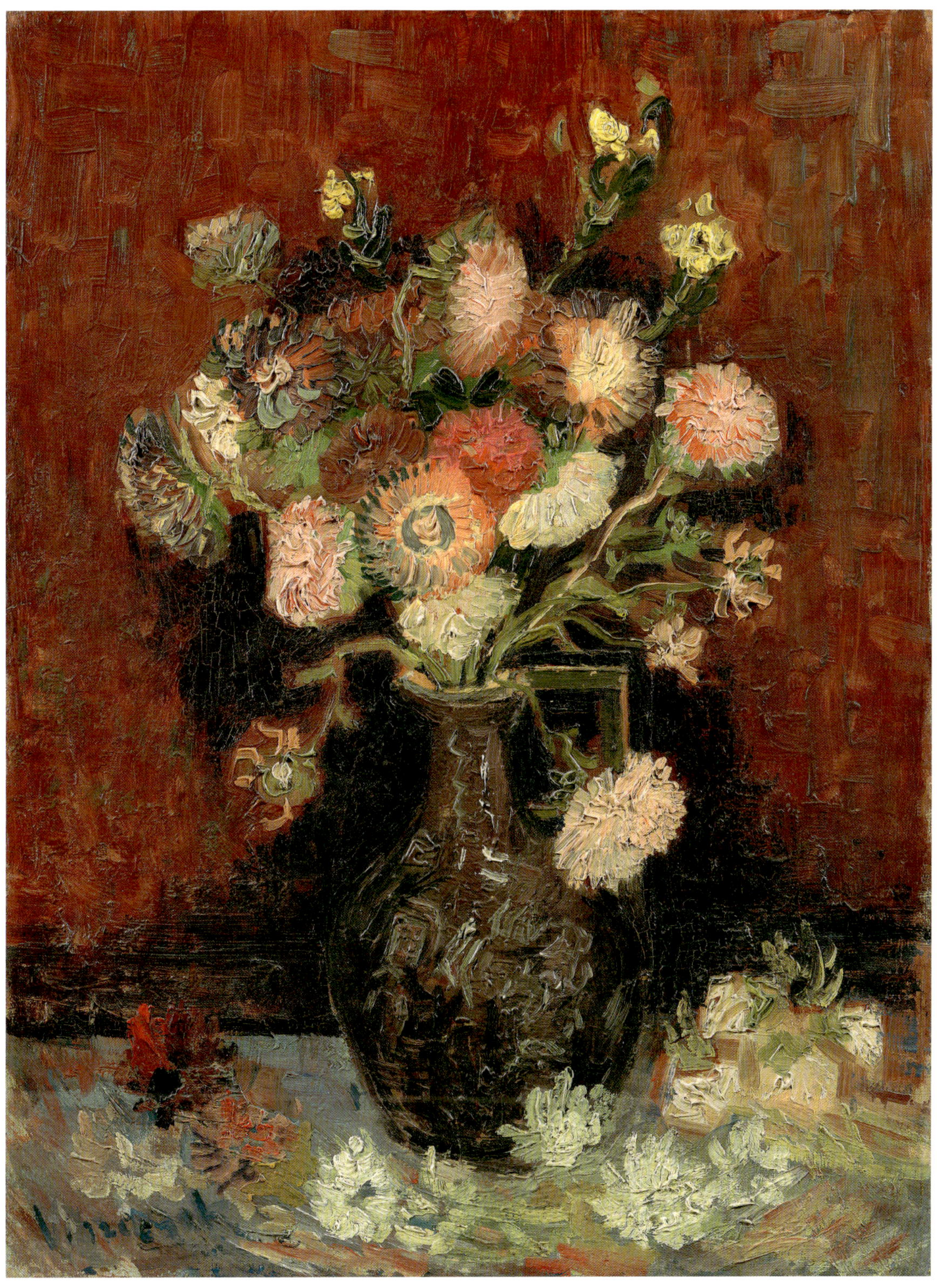

Figure 9. Vincent van Gogh, *Vase with Chinese Asters and Gladioli*, Paris, August–September 1886, oil on canvas, 24 × 18⅛ inches (61.1 × 46.1 cm), Van Gogh Museum, Amsterdam (Vincent van Gogh Foundation).

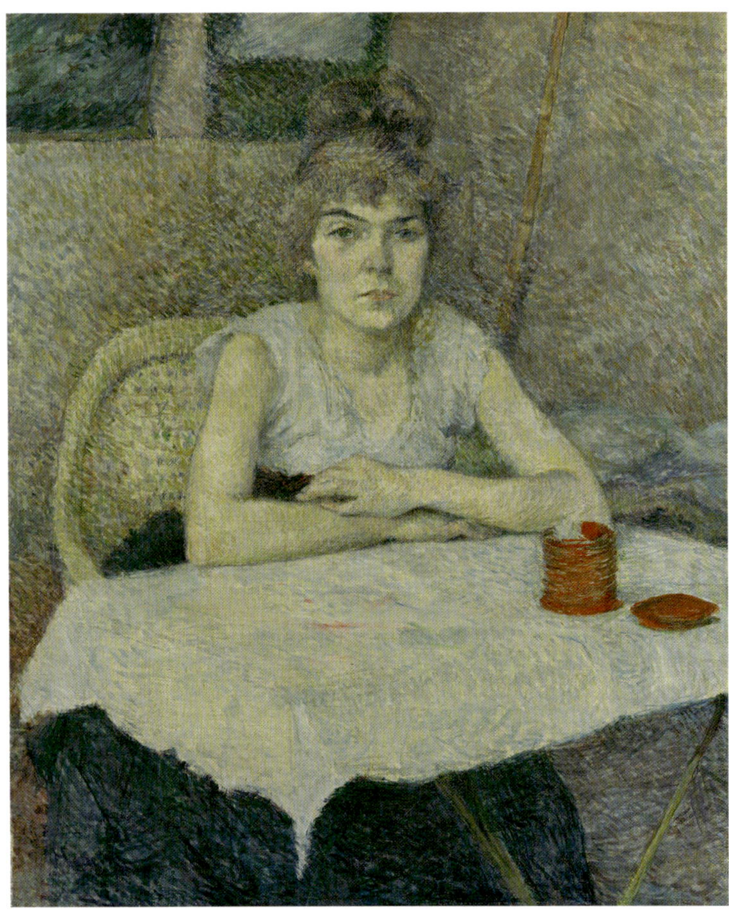

Figure 10. Henri de Toulouse-Lautrec, *Young Woman at a Table, "Poudre de riz,"*
1887, oil on canvas, 22 × 18 ⅛ inches (56 × 46 cm), Van Gogh Museum, Amsterdam
(Vincent van Gogh Foundation).

In addition to the artworks, the museum holds 850 of the
903 known letters from Van Gogh's correspondence with
family and friends, as well as other correspondence and
archival documents pertaining to the family. The variety
of objects once belonging to the artist makes it possible
to establish remarkable links between artworks in various
media, such as the painting *Irises*, of which Van Gogh
drew a recollection in his sketchbook (cat. 48 and fig. 7).
Conversely, family objects can sometimes be seen in
the paintings, such as a vase that is depicted in several
flower still lifes from Van Gogh's time in Paris (figs. 8–9).

The art collection assembled by Vincent and Theo is also
part of the museum. Theo bought or received the bulk of the
collection; Vincent expressed his preference for certain
artists and sometimes exchanged work with colleagues.
Van Gogh also amassed an extensive collection of magazine
illustrations and Japanese prints, which he drew upon as
inspiration for his own art. Supplemented with later acquisitions, the collection now contains some 270 paintings
and 680 drawings by artist friends and contemporaries, as
well as sculptures, objects, and prints. This collection
provides a context for Van Gogh's work, and shows that he
worked in an artistic tradition. A substantial part of this
collection is by artist friends of the avant-garde, such as Paul
Gauguin, Émile Bernard, and Henri de Toulouse-Lautrec.
A comparison of Toulouse-Lautrec's *Young Woman at a
Table, "Poudre de riz"* and Van Gogh's *In the Café: Agostina
Segatori in Le Tambourin* shows that the two artists briefly
shared similar aspirations (fig. 10 and cat. 21). Theo bought
this painting from Toulouse-Lautrec, probably at Vincent's
suggestion.[18]

When the Van Gogh Museum was built, it was predicted
to attract 60,000 visitors a year, but in the first six months
after the opening there were already 345,590 visitors.[19]
Meanwhile, their numbers have increased to more than
two million a year. By the 1990s, it had become clear
that an extension would be necessary, and there was also
a great desire for a separate space for exhibitions eluci-
dating Van Gogh's connections with nineteenth- and early
twentieth-century art. The exhibition wing designed
by the Japanese architect Kisho Kurokawa opened in 1999.
In 2015 the new entrance building, realized jointly by
the architectural bureau of Kurokawa, who had meanwhile
died, and Hans van Heeswijk Architecten, completed
the wing's semicircle, which now provides the perfect coun-
terpoise to Rietveld's cube (fig. 11).

Museum visitors who come to look at Van Gogh's paintings, drawings, and letters will focus mainly on the expressiveness of his oeuvre and his artistry (figs. 12–13). Yet there is a special and very personal history underlying the museum and its collection. Clearly, Van Gogh owes a great deal of his fame and appreciation to the unconditional trust and unflagging efforts of Theo, Jo, and their son, Vincent, who understood the importance of propagating his work, as do the family members now represented on the board of the Vincent van Gogh Foundation. As Theo wrote to Jo, "He is one of the most progressive of the painters & even I, who am so close to him, find him difficult to understand. He holds such sweeping ideas on questions of what is humane and how we should regard the world, that one first has to relinquish all one's conventional ideas in order to grasp what he means. But one day he will be understood. When? That is the question."[20]

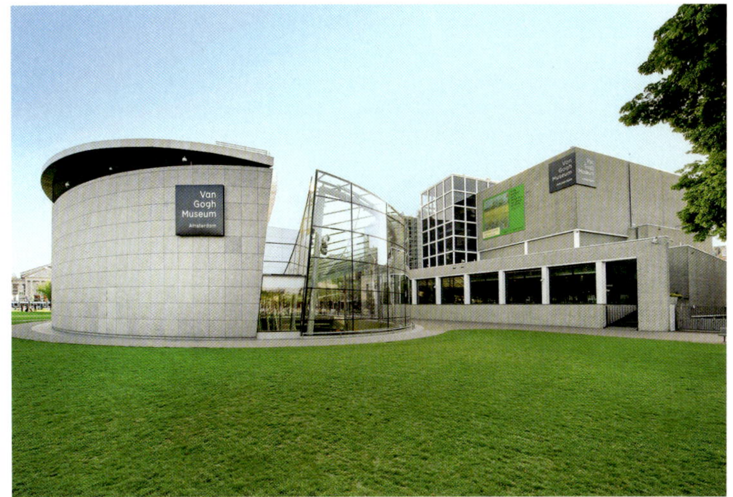

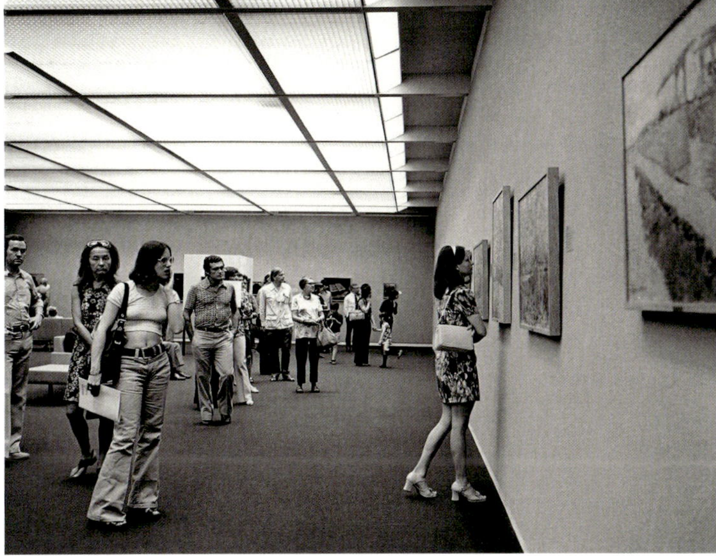

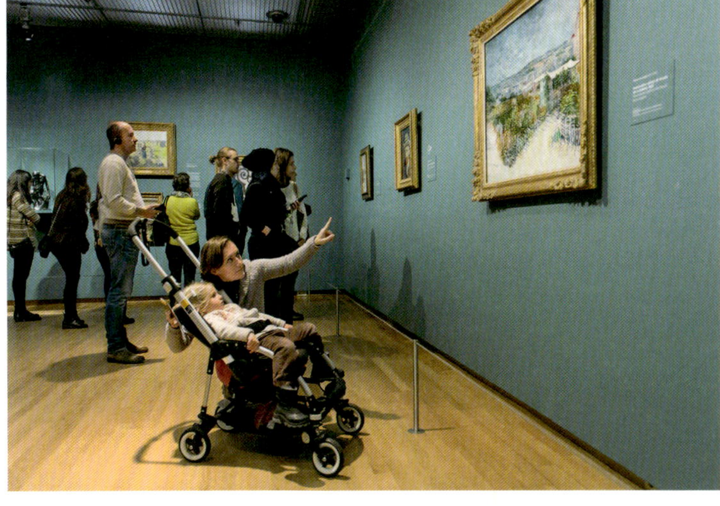

Figure 11. The Van Gogh Museum today.

Figure 12. Visitors at the Van Gogh Museum in 1973.

Figure 13. Visitors at the Van Gogh Museum today.

Notes

I am grateful to Hans Luijten and Roelie Zwikker for allowing me to make use of their research for the biographies of Jo van Gogh-Bonger and her son, Vincent van Gogh, forthcoming. I am also indebted to Nienke Bakker and Marije Velle-koop for their comments on this essay, which was translated by Diane Webb.

1 Letter 712, Vincent van Gogh to Theo van Gogh, Arles, about October 25, 1888.

2 Theo van Gogh to Lies van Gogh, August 5, 1890, letter's whereabouts un-known, quoted in Lies's memoires: *Elizabeth du Quesne Van Gogh*, with a foreword by Arthur B. Davies, *Personal Recollections of Vincent van Gogh* (Boston and New York: Houghton Mifflin, 1913), 53.

3 Theo van Gogh to Dr. Paul Gachet, September 12, 1890, b2015V/1982, Van Gogh Museum, Amsterdam (Vincent van Gogh Foundation). Theo did, in fact, take the first steps toward organizing an exhibition, which was to take place in April 1892 at Le Barc de Boutteville in Paris. After Theo's death, Vincent's artist friend Émile Bernard took over the organization of that exhibition.

4 Jo van Gogh-Bonger in diary number 3, November 15, 1891. Jo Bonger, *Diaries*, ed. Hans Luijten (Amsterdam: Van Gogh Museum, 2019. See www.vangoghmuseum.nl/publications.

5 The painting *Les Rochers (The Rocks)* (cat. 32), now in the collection of the Museum of Fine Arts, Houston, was also sold through Paul Cassirer to a German collector in 1905 and eventually ended up in the United States.

6 Chris Stolwijk and Han Veenenbos, *The Account Book of Theo van Gogh and Jo van Gogh-Bonger* (Amsterdam: Van Gogh Museum; Leiden: Primavera Pers, 2002), 27, 167.

7 Jo van Gogh-Bonger in diary number 4, February 24, 1892, in Bonger, *Diaries*. Arti et Amicitiae is an artists' society in Amsterdam.

8 *Catalogus der tentoonstelling van schilderijen en teekeningen door Vincent van Gogh*, with a foreword by Johan Cohen Gosschalk (Amsterdam: Stedelijk Museum, 1905).

9 In most publications, this Vincent van Gogh is called Vincent Willem, but he was always addressed simply as Vincent.

10 Letter 847, Theo van Gogh to Vincent van Gogh, Paris, January 31, 1890.

11 Bram Hammacher, "Vincent Willem van Gogh 1890–1978," *Museumjournaal* 23, no. 2 (1978): 50–52, 51. English translation taken from *Van Gogh Museum Journal* 1995, p. 24 (https://www.dbnl.org/tekst/_van012199501_01/_van012199501_01_0003.php).

12 Johan van Gogh, "The History of the Collection," in *The Rijksmuseum Vincent van Gogh*, ed. Evert van Uitert and Michael Hoyle (Amsterdam: Meulenhoff/Landshoff, 1987), 1–8, 5.

13 This sum is equivalent to more than 52 million euros in today's money (www.iisg.nl/hpw/calculate-nl.php).

14 Van Gogh, "The History of the Collection," 6; agreement between the State of the Netherlands and the Vincent van Gogh Foundation, July 21, 1962, explanatory memorandum 6827, p. 3.

15 Letter from Vincent van Gogh to Anne Vondeling, a member of parliament, October 8, 1962, Van Gogh Museum, Amsterdam (Vincent van Gogh Foundation), mentioned in Gerald Bronkhorst, "Vincent Willem van Gogh and the Van Gogh Museum's Pre-History," *Van Gogh Museum Journal* (1995): 24–33.

16 Vincent Willem van Gogh, "De vier functies van het museum," *Museumjournaal* 14, no. 6 (1969): 291–92. The other functions of a museum that he named, but those he did not wish to pursue, were exhibiting the art of artistic movements occurring elsewhere in the world and offering living artists an opportunity to show their work to the public.

17 The vast majority of these belong to the Vincent van Gogh Foundation; a few works were acquired later or received as gifts.

18 Sjraar van Heugten and Chris Stolwijk, "Theo van Gogh: The Collector," in Chris Stolwijk and Richard Thomson, with a contribution by Sjraar van Heugten, *Theo van Gogh 1857–1891: Art Dealer, Collector and Brother of Vincent* (Amsterdam: Van Gogh Museum; Zwolle: Waanders, 1999), 153–79.

19 Hans Ibelings, "Nuances in Grey," in Andreas Blühm, Hans Ibelings, and Jannes Linders, *Van Gogh Museum Architecture: Rietveld to Kurokawa* (Amsterdam: Van Gogh Museum; Rotterdam: NAi, 1999), 7–25, 13; *Rijksmuseum Vincent van Gogh te Amsterdam. Verslag van de Directeur over het jaar 1973. Overdruk uit de Nederlandse Rijksmusea*, vol. 95 (The Hague: Ministry of Culture, Recreation, and Social Work, 1975), 11 (p. 139).

20 Theo van Gogh to Jo Bonger, February 9 and 10, 1889, in *Brief Happiness*, ed. Leo Jansen and Jan Robert, with an introduction and explanation by Han van Crimpen (Amsterdam: Van Gogh Museum; Zwolle: Waanders, 1999), 146.

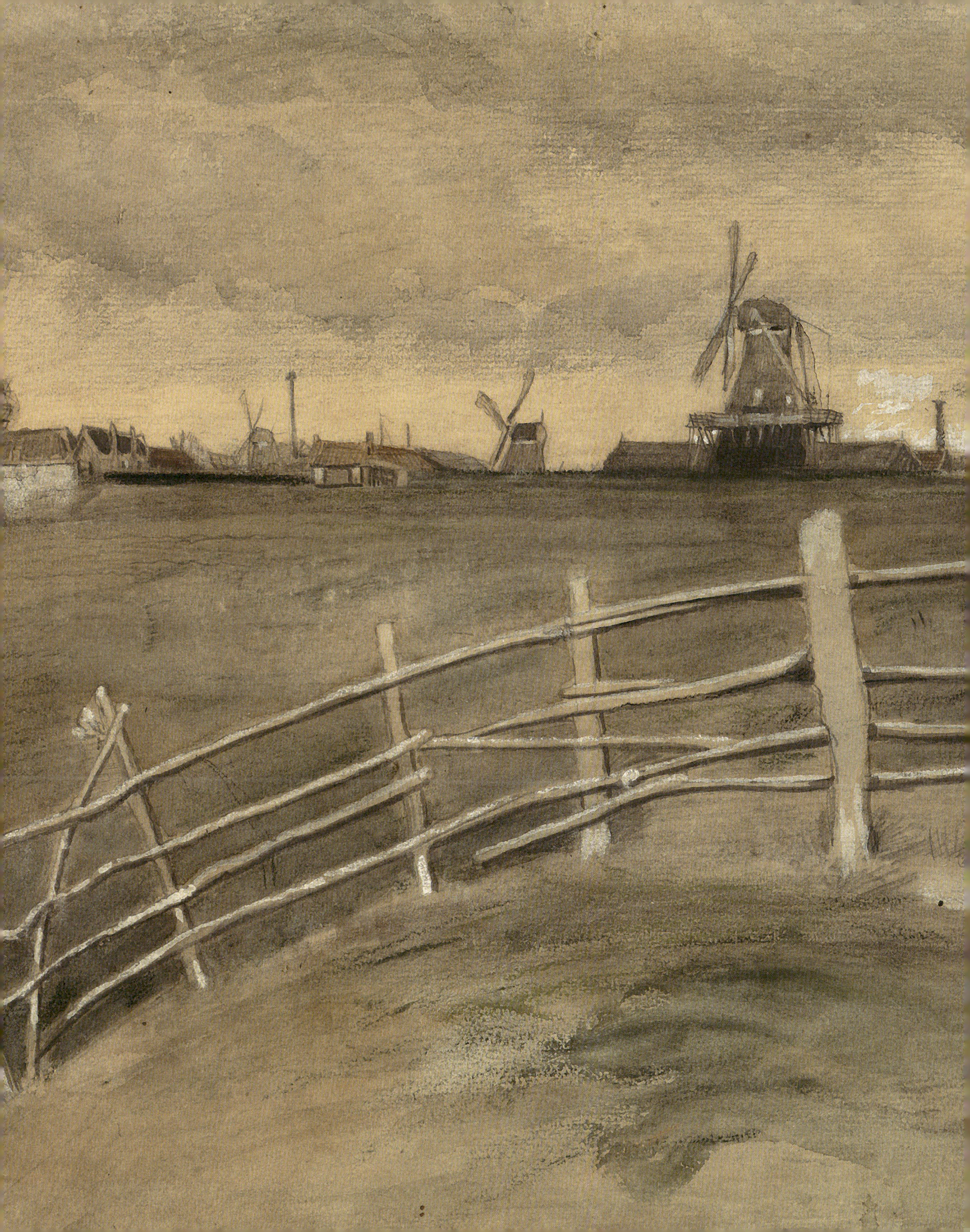

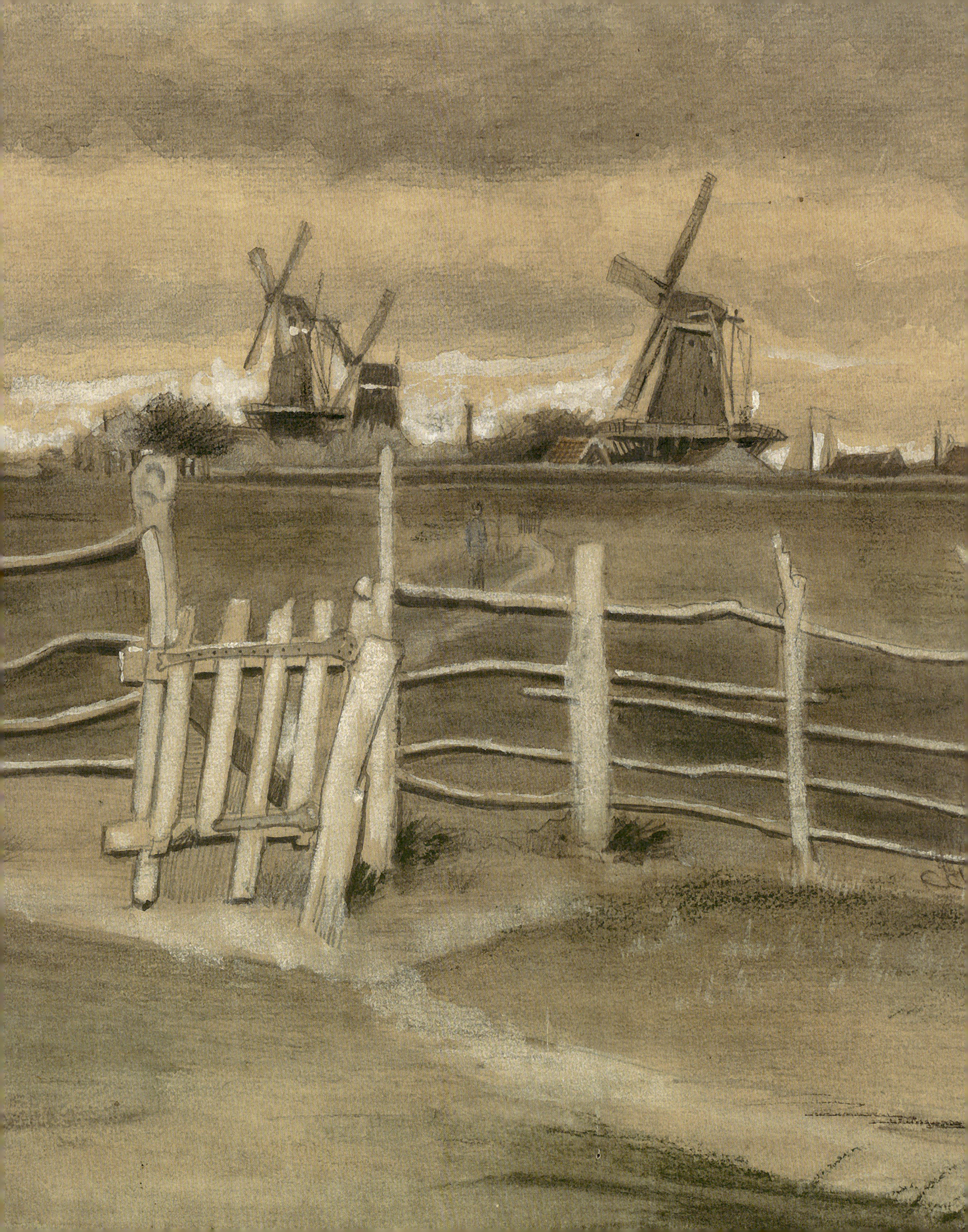

The Vincent van Gogh Collection

The Heart of the Kröller-Müller Museum

Renske Cohen Tervaert

Vincent van Gogh's work occupies a prominent place within the collection of the Kröller-Müller Museum. Thanks to the museum's founders, Anton and Helene Kröller, the Van Gogh collection — consisting of eighty-eight paintings and over a hundred and eighty works on paper — is the second-largest collection of the artist's work in the world. When the museum opened in 1938, Van Gogh's work was given pride of place at the very heart of the museum in what is now the Van Gogh Gallery. This central location emphasized not only the vital role the Kröllers felt Van Gogh's work had played in the development of modern painting, but also the special place held by his work in the hearts of these two passionate collectors.

Helene and Anton Kröller

On May 15, 1888, the German-born Helene Müller married the Dutch Anton Kröller (fig. 1).[1] In 1883 young Anton had come to work at the Düsseldorf offices of Helene's father's company, Wm. H. Müller & Co., which is where the couple met. After their wedding, the pair relocated to the Dutch port city of Rotterdam, where the company had a branch office. They went on to have four children together.

Following the sudden death of Helene's father, Anton took over the business. He was twenty-seven years old at the time.[2] Under his leadership, the company grew into a profitable international enterprise in shipping, buying and selling iron ore, and the transshipment of goods. Thanks to Anton's clever head for business, the family gradually became one of the wealthiest in the Netherlands.

Around 1900, Anton decided to shift the company's headquarters to The Hague, the city that was (and still is) the seat of the Dutch government. The family made the move as well; in keeping with their newfound prosperity, they took up residence in a specially commissioned villa that they called "Huize ten Vijver." To feather her new nest, Helene began collecting antique furniture, ceramics, and Asian art.

The fall of 1905 marked a turning point in the Kröllers' lives, and in Helene's life in particular. During this period, she and her daughter attended a course taught by H. P. Bremmer, an art educator from The Hague (fig. 2). It was Helene's first encounter with modernist painting. Bremmer's lessons left an indelible impression on her. From 1908 onward, she arranged for him to come to her home for private instruction.[3] This pursuit marked the start of a lifelong mission.

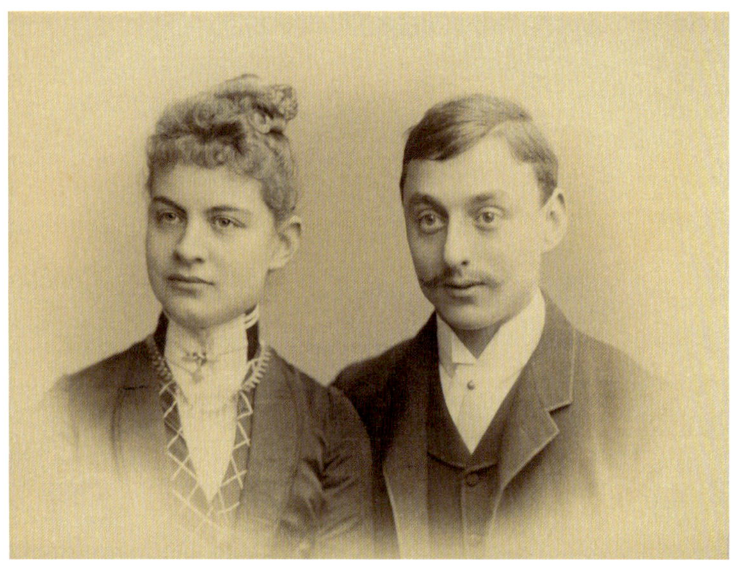

Figure 1. Helene Müller and Anton Kröller at the time of their engagement, c. 1887/88.

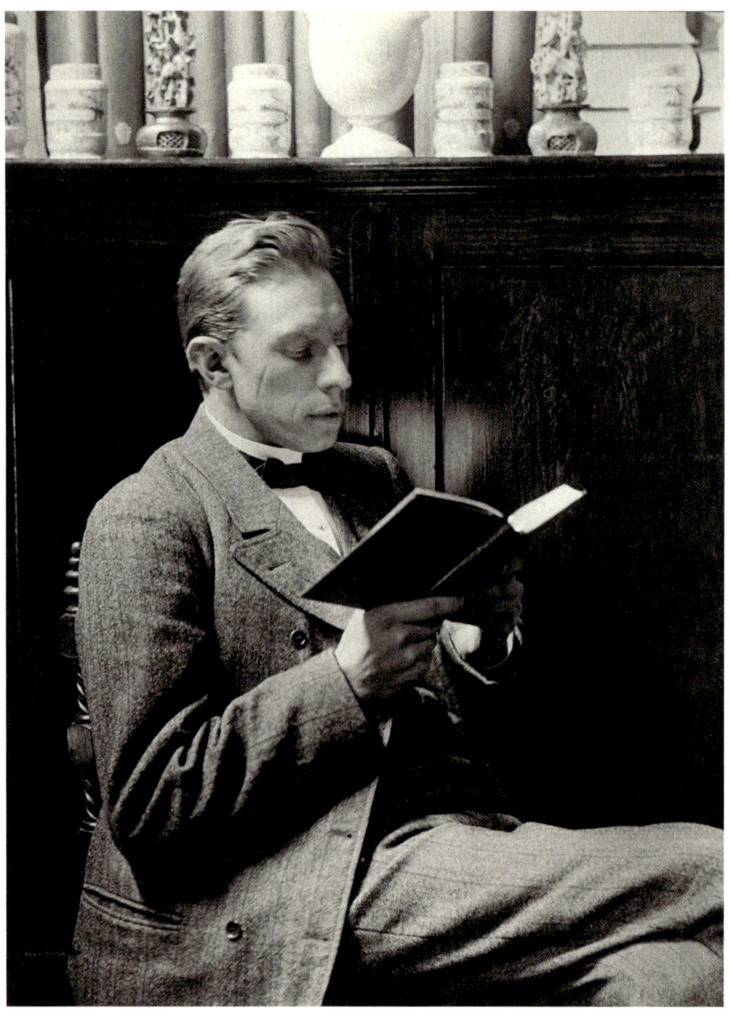

Figure 2. H. P. Bremmer, c. 1909.

A Burgeoning Love for Van Gogh

Bremmer was passionate in his teaching.[4] In his *Practical Aesthetics*,[5] he railed against the dominant art-historical paradigm, which approached a given artwork based on knowledge of facts, styles, and historical context. His lessons focused instead on the artwork itself. To that end, he examined the painting and drawing techniques applied and the relationship between form and color. He also emphasized the artist's emotional motives: "Art is that which instills an emotion and has been created with the intention of provoking an emotional response."[6] By *emotion*, Bremmer was referring to the spiritual charge communicated by an artist through his or her work. For that reason, he identified strongly with the as-yet relatively unknown artist Vincent van Gogh. Bremmer, himself one of the first in the Netherlands to collect Van Gogh's work, considered Van Gogh to be the ultimate example of an artist imbued with a sacred reverence for everyday reality. Regarding the piece *Kettle and Two Bowls*, Bremmer wrote in 1904, "No *belle peinture* or aristocratic attitude here; [the painting] suggests human beings, work, the struggle of life.... Does it not seem as if the kettle has turned into a thing that has taken life's knocks, as if the misshapen features and bruises are like peasant bodies grown crooked under life's struggle?"[7] Like Van Gogh, Bremmer adopted art as a new form of religion.

Thanks to this approach, which emphasized the spiritual aspect that could be captured by true art, Helene learned to appreciate and understand Van Gogh's work. Bremmer taught her that the earthly and the divine — like the mind and the body — are not distinct phenomena but rather the component parts of a larger whole. Following a lesson by Bremmer on *Basket of Lemons and Bottle* (1888, cat. 28), she wrote: "I was so struck by Bremmer's words 'This is what heaven looks like' and the longer I look at the painting the more I see an explanation, which has nothing to do with the material.... [Human beings have] developed to such a high degree that they can look at things in an abstract manner.... If I want to understand Van Gogh's lemons, I just place a few lemons beside them in my imagination — as I see them, and then I feel the enormous difference."[8]

Though Helene was reluctant to compare her own life to that of Van Gogh, she nevertheless saw quite a few similarities between their stories.[9] Van Gogh's struggle with organized religion and his ability, despite that conflict,

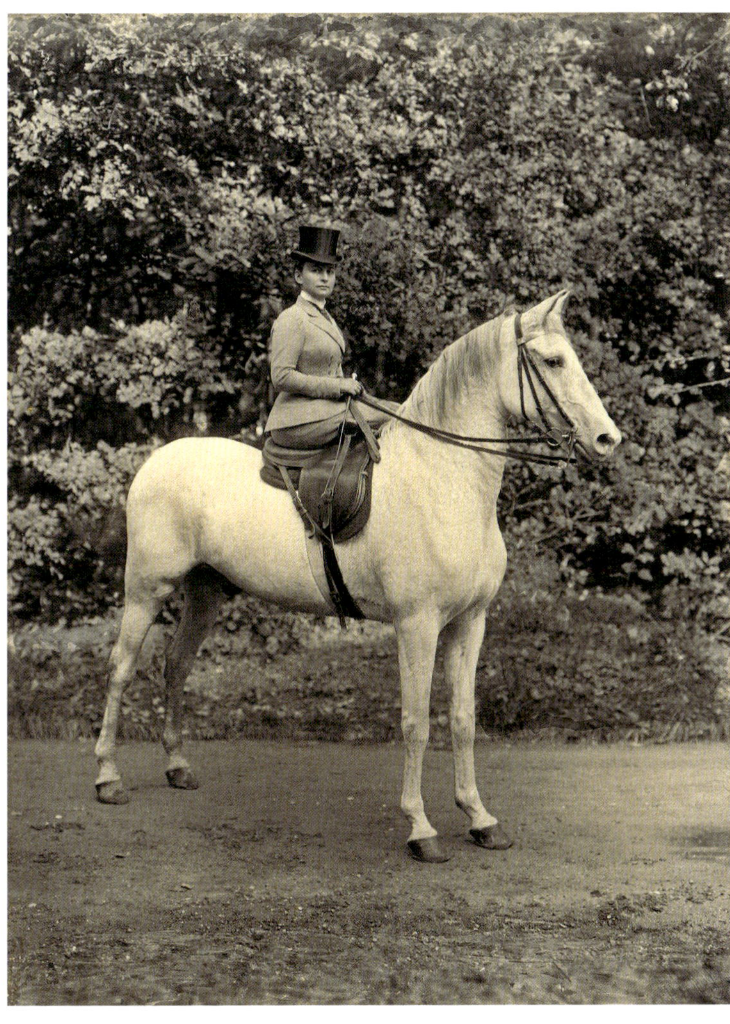

Figure 3. Helene Kröller-Müller, c. 1900.

to maintain his belief in God appealed to Helene (fig. 3). She, too, felt a strong need for spirituality in her life, yet — like the artist — had been unable to satisfy this need through church tradition. Helene related to the way in which Van Gogh sought that spiritual aspect in everyday life, in people, and in nature. She firmly believed that Van Gogh was one of the great minds of modern art.

Initially, Anton Kröller was less than enthusiastic about Helene's interest in modern art. He referred to Vincent van Gogh's work as art from a "madhouse."[10] Quickly, however, he realized that works of art, like land, can appreciate in value; he began to see opportunities with regard to his own passion: speculation. Van Gogh's work was still relatively inexpensive, making it an attractive investment.[11]

A Growing Collection

In 1907 Helene appointed Bremmer as her personal adviser to "assist [her] in establishing an art collection."[12] Together with Bremmer, Helene and Anton would collect some 11,500 works of art between 1907 and 1939. Their acquisitions included not only paintings by famous artists such as Paul Gauguin, Piet Mondrian, Pablo Picasso, August Renoir, and Georges Seurat, but also drawings, sculptures, Delftware, antique pottery, Chinese art, and graphic art. Up until 1922, their budget was virtually unlimited.[13] This mania for collecting resulted in the pair spending thousands of guilders a day at times.[14] The Van Gogh collection was compiled between 1908 and 1929; during this period, the couple purchased a total of ninety-one paintings and a hundred and eighty works on paper (including those drawings on the reverse of eighteen sheets).[15]

The first works by Van Gogh that Helene acquired (via Bremmer) in 1908 were *Edge of a Wood* (1883) and *Four Sunflowers Gone to Seed* (1887), followed a year later by the purchase of *The Sower (after Millet)* (1890) and *Basket of Lemons and Bottle* (1888). Sam van Deventer, a close friend of the family and former director of the museum, described the purchase of those first two Van Gogh works as a moment of euphoria: "I have a vivid picture in my mind of Bremmer, flushed with excitement, stepping into Mrs. Kröller's boudoir with two paintings by Vincent, and I can still hear the joyous rapture that issued from herself and her daughter. . . . It struck me how everyone experienced the acquisition as something quite extraordinary."[16]

As the years passed, Helene more and more frequently accompanied Bremmer to galleries and auctions both in the Netherlands and abroad. When Anton traveled to Paris for business in April 1912, Helene and Bremmer followed a few days later so that the three of them could go in search of works by Van Gogh. On the very first evening, they found the painting *La Berceuse* (1888–89). Helene felt that the tranquility in this work, with which the artist "confronted the complexity of it all," demonstrated "what was actually the greatness of Van Gogh in his French period."[17]

It was far from their only purchase on that trip, according to Helene: "This morning … we went to get the other Van Goghs. They were fantastic. … We saw more, but Bremmer felt only these were better than or equal to the ones we have, and he secured them with a bid. … He was so excited with his haul that he went out quite shaking like a leaf."[18] The total "haul" at the end of their visit to Paris was fifteen paintings by Van Gogh, dating primarily from his French period, and two works by Georges Seurat and Paul Signac. Less than a month later, Helene purchased fifteen additional paintings at an auction, four of which were by Van Gogh; these included *Bridge at Arles (Pont de Langlois)* (1888, fig. 4), for which she gave Bremmer permission to bid five times the recommended price.

In a few cases, the couple went so far as to snatch up whole groups of works accumulated by other collectors the instant they came on the market, such as the Lodewijk Cornelis Enthoven collection in 1920 (containing twenty-six Van Gogh paintings, including *The Green Vineyard* [1888, cat. 35]) and, in 1928, a lot of some hundred drawings belonging to the Dordrecht art collector Hidde Nijland. These bulk purchases piqued the curiosity of art-world denizens in both France and the Netherlands, which strongly boosted public appreciation for Van Gogh's work.[19]

Bremmer had a deciding role in virtually every art purchase. Very rarely did the Kröllers buy a Van Gogh without his say-so; on one occasion, it was a decision for which they would pay a heavy price. During a visit to Berlin, they bought *Reaper with a Scythe (after Millet)* (1889) from the German dealer and collector Paul Cassirer. Bremmer, irritated by this turn of events, immediately claimed the work was a forgery. The Kröllers subsequently brought legal proceedings against Cassirer — and lost. To this day, the work is considered to be a genuine Van Gogh.[20]

Van Gogh at the Heart of Things

It was not only the spectacular purchases (which occasionally made headlines) that brought Van Gogh's work to the attention of a wider audience; it was also the fact that, from 1913, Helene opened her collection to the public in a small museum within the main offices of Müller & Co. in The Hague (fig. 5). Helene viewed this museum as a temporary means for realizing a larger dream of hers: to erect a monument to culture. This dream — which took shape during a period in 1911 when she was seriously ill and began to feel a desire to leave some kind of enduring legacy after her death — fanned the embers of the collector's mania.

Her goal was, through her collection, to give visitors insight into the development of painting from 1860 to the present: the progression from realism to abstraction, or (as she preferred to put it) from realism to idealism. To Helene, Vincent van Gogh was instrumental to this development and superior to every other artist. The Van Gogh works were the cornerstone around which she built the rest of her collection. She acquired pieces by artists whom she considered practitioners of realism, including Henri Fantin-Latour, Jean-François Millet, Auguste Renoir, and Jan Weissenbruch. To illustrate the further progression of painting, she added works by Odilon Redon, Georges Seurat, Paul Signac, and Jan Toorop to her collection. The final step was then embodied by artists such as Juan Gris, Piet Mondrian, Pablo Picasso, and Bart Anthony van der Leck. Helene additionally purchased works by sixteenth- and seventeenth-century artists (such as Hans Baldung and Lucas Cranach) whom she considered precursors to the modernists.

The museum — the monument to culture she had in mind — was to be built in the Hoge Veluwe, a nature reserve in the central Netherlands where Anton had acquired six thousand hectares of land between 1906 and 1916. In 1921 builders broke ground on a museum designed by the Belgian architect Henry van de Velde. Helene envisioned that "a hundred years from now it would already be an interesting monument to culture, a great lesson on how much inner civilization a merchant family could achieve at the beginning of the century. It would be a museum as natural and vibrant as had never been seen before."[21] Yet just one year later, construction work and art purchases were abruptly halted when Müller & Co. found itself precariously close to bankruptcy.[22] Helene refused to give up on her plans for a museum and tasked Van de Velde with designing a more modestly sized museum to house the Van Gogh collection.

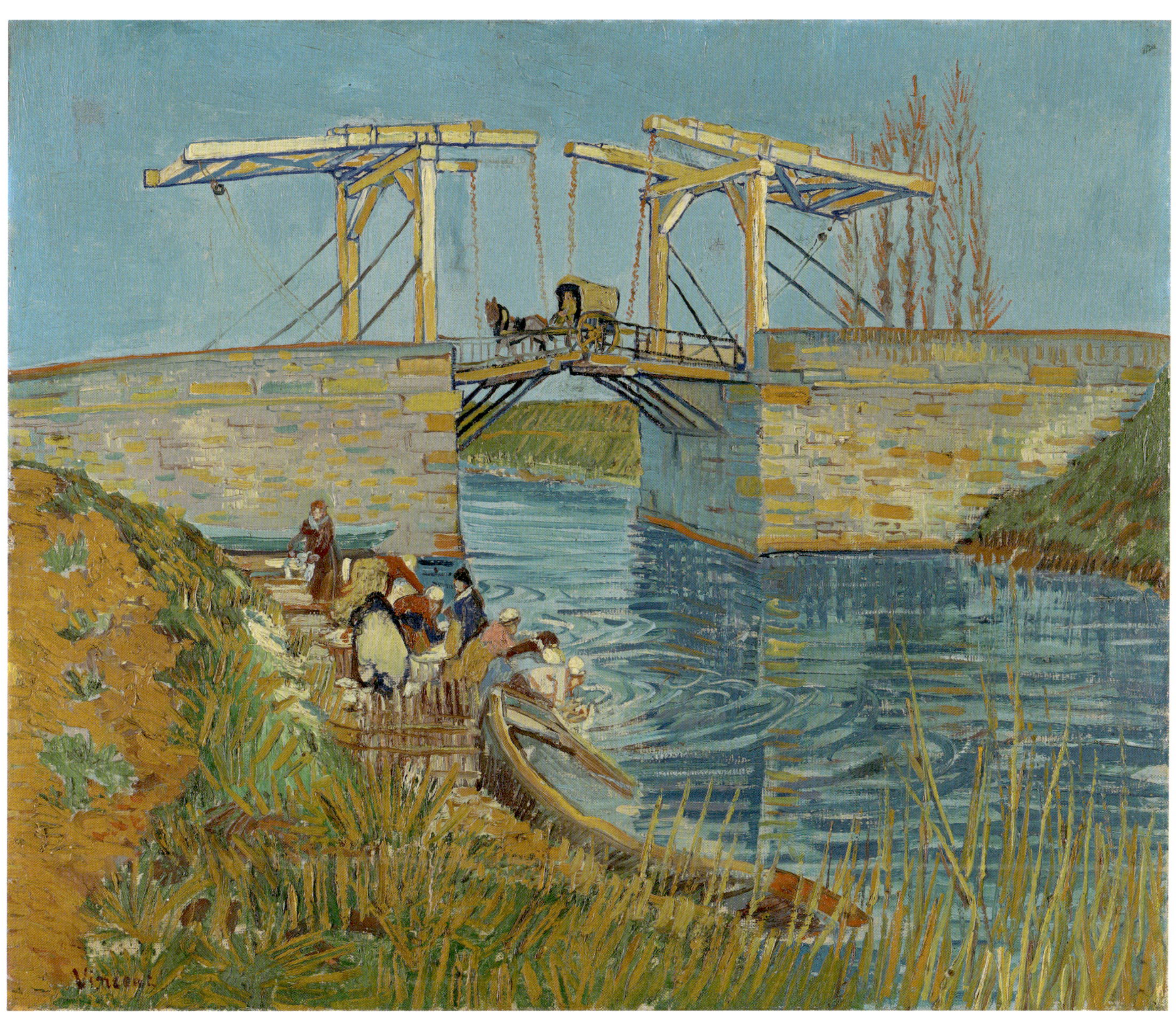

Figure 4. Vincent van Gogh, *Bridge at Arles* (*Pont de Langlois*), Arles, mid-March 1888, oil on canvas, 21 × 25 ¼ (53.4 × 64 cm), Kröller-Müller Museum, Otterlo, the Netherlands, KM 111.056, F397.

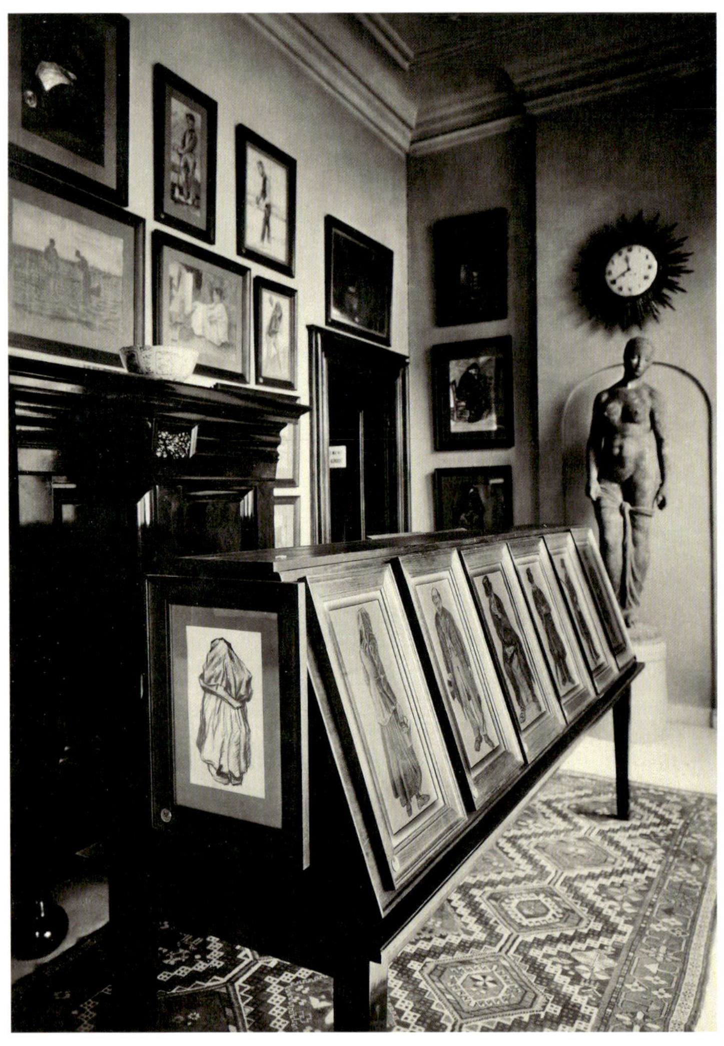

Figure 5. Interior of the Museum Kröller on the Lange Voorhout in The Hague, view of the collection of drawings by Van Gogh, November 1933.

The collection remained accessible to the public in The Hague, and from 1927 Helene began lending out her Van Gogh works as well. One hundred and forty of the drawings and paintings in her possession were included in a large traveling retrospective that was displayed in Switzerland, Belgium, and Germany. This marked the start of extensive lending from the collection, such as in 1935–36 to an exhibition titled *Vincent van Gogh*, which made its way across the United States starting at the Museum of Modern Art in New York.[23]

With support from the Dutch government and thanks to a number of private donations, construction of the "temporary" smaller museum was able to move forward starting in May 1937. The doors of the Rijksmuseum Kröller-Müller [National Museum Kröller-Müller], today the Kröller-Müller Museum, opened on July 13, 1938 (fig. 6). At the age of sixty-eight, Helene became its first director, but she passed away only eighteen months later as a result of pneumonia (fig. 7).[24]

More than eighty years later, the Van Gogh Gallery is still the cornerstone of the museum — and, more important, it is the most dynamic part of the permanent exhibition. These works by Van Gogh, which embark on journeys to far-flung corners of the globe and return to the gallery each year, are the heart of the Kröller-Müller Museum.

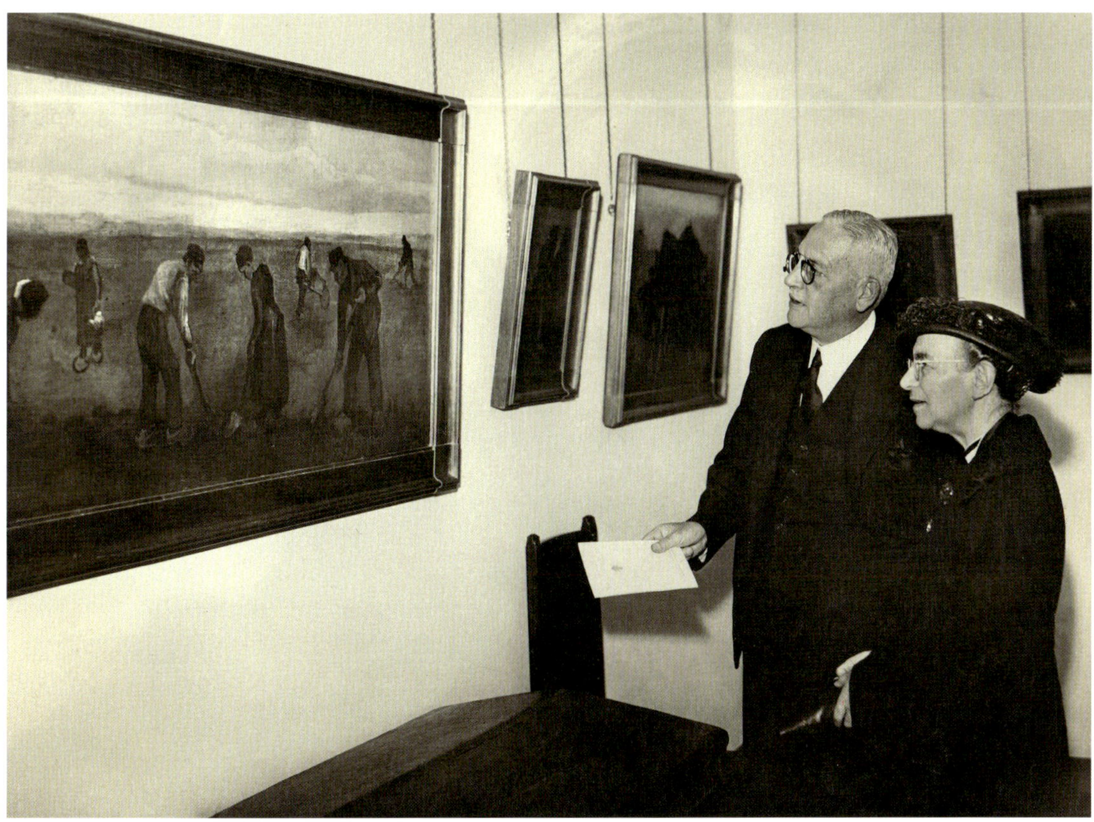

Figure 6. Opening of the Rijksmuseum Kröller-Müller on July 13, 1938, with Helene Kröller-Müller and government representative minister Charles Welter looking at Van Gogh's *Peasants Planting Potatoes*.

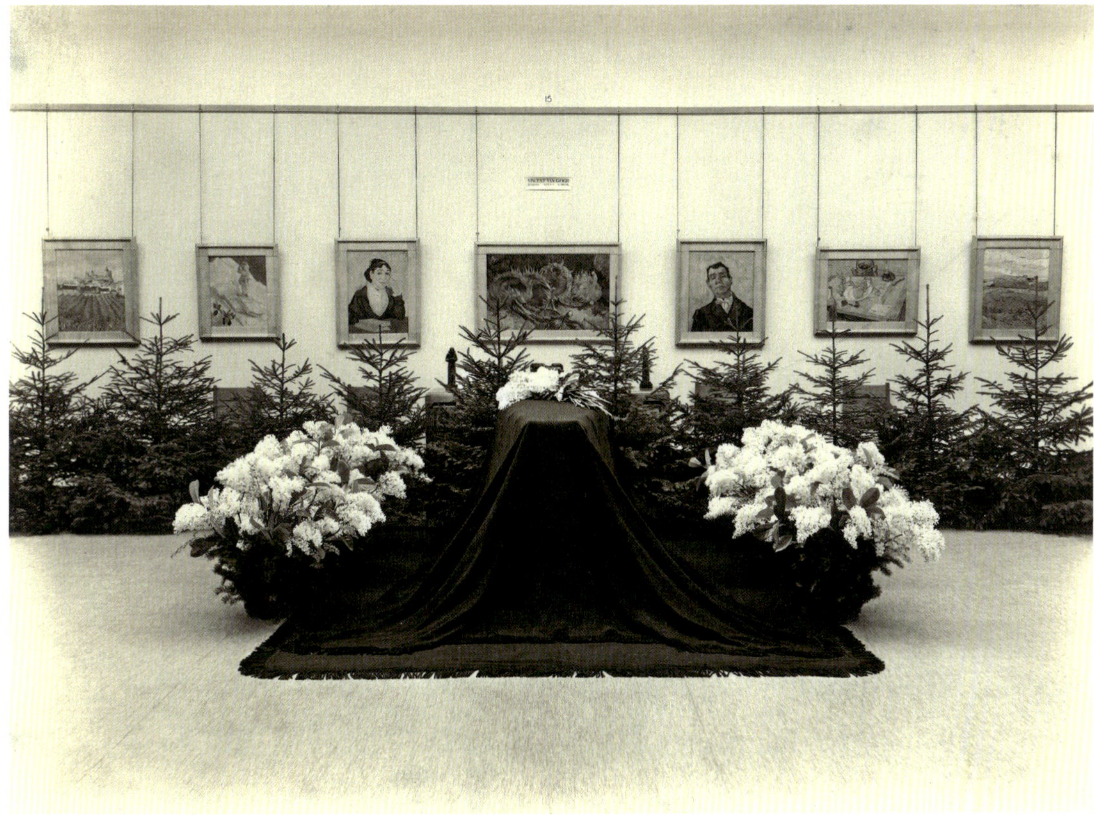

Figure 7. The casket of Helene Kröller-Müller on public view in front of *Four Sunflowers Gone to Seed* and six other works by Van Gogh, December 15, 1939.

Notes

I wish to thank Liz Gorin for translating this essay.

1 Comprehensive biographies have been published on both Helene and Anton Kröller. For Helene's biography, see Eva Rovers, *Voor de eeuwigheid verzameld: Helene Kröller-Müller 1869–1939* [Collected for All Time: Helene Kröller-Müller 1869–1939] (Amsterdam: Prometheus / Bert Bakker, 2010); for Anton's, see Ariëtte Dekker, *Leven op krediet: Anton Kröller (1862–1941)* [An Indebted Life: Anton Kröller (1862–1941)] (Amsterdam: Prometheus / Bert Bakker, 2015).

2 See Dekker, *Leven op krediet*, for more about Anton Kröller's business acumen and the history of Wm. H. Müller & Co.

3 See Hildelies Balk, *De Kunstpaus: H. P. Bremmer 1871–1956* [The "Art Pope": H. P. Bremmer 1871–1956] (Bussum: Thoth, 2006), 159.

4 See ibid. for more on the life and work of H. P. Bremmer.

5 Bremmer's art-historical approach became known as "Practical Aesthetics." Ibid., 82.

6 Rovers, *Voor de eeuwigheid verzameld*, 90.

7 See H. P. Bremmer, *Moderne Kunstwerken* 2 [Modern Works of Art 2] (1904), sheet 59. Cited in Hildelies Balk, Jos ten Berge, et al., *The Paintings of Vincent van Gogh in the Collection of the Kröller-Müller Museum* (Otterlo: Kröller-Müller Museum, 2003), 430.

8 Letter from Helene Kröller-Müller to Sam van Deventer, March 26, 1909, Kröller-Müller Museum archive. Cited in Sam van Deventer, *Kröller-Müller: De geschiedenis van een cultureel levenswerk* [The History of a Lifelong Cultural Undertaking] (Haarlem: Joh. Enschedè & Zonen, 1956; reprinted Arnhem: Roos & Roos, 1998), 34–36.

9 See Rovers, *Voor de eeuwigheid verzameld*, 106, and Eva Rovers, "Collecting for the Future: Helene Kröller-Müller's Love of Vincent van Gogh," in *Van Gogh & Co: Criss-crossing the Collection*, exh. cat. (Otterlo: Kröller-Müller Museum, 2015), 80.

10 See Dekker, *Leven op krediet*, 232.

11 See ibid., 232. For more on how Bremmer and Helene Kröller-Müller attempted to involve Anton Kröller in purchasing art, see also Balk, *De Kunstpaus,* 209–10.

12 See ibid., 210.

13 In order to buy art and private estates, Anton Kröller funneled resources from his company in a creative (and since outlawed) fashion. In 1922 Müller & Co. narrowly escaped bankruptcy due to difficulties securing financing following the end of the Great War. See Rovers, *Voor de eeuwigheid verzameld*, 332.

14 Helene and Anton paid — to the extent that records of the purchase amounts exist — about 585,000 guilders for the Van Gogh collection; see Balk et al., *The Paintings of Vincent van Gogh in the Collection of the Kröller-Müller Museum*, 443–46, and Jos ten Berge, Teio Meedendorp, et al., *Drawings and Prints by Vincent van Gogh in the Collection of the Kröller-Müller Museum* (Amersfoort: ThiemeArt, 2007), 431–34. Adjusted to today's currency, this would be about $5,385,000 (as per the International Institute of Social History, http://www.iisg.nl/hpw/calculate.php).

15 This number of paintings does not match the current number of works in the collection. Although one or two of these paintings may have been sold or given away, several works have since been attributed to other artists. For more information on paintings that were previously part of the collection, see Balk et al., *The Paintings of Vincent van Gogh in the Collection of the Kröller-Müller Museum,* 387–402. For the drawings, see Ten Berge et al., *Drawings and Prints by Vincent van Gogh in the Collection of the Kröller-Müller Museum,* 377–95.

16 See van Deventer, *Kröller-Müller,* 34. Cited in Balk et al., *The Paintings of Vincent van Gogh in the Collection of the Kröller-Müller Museum,* 435.

17 Rovers, *Voor de eeuwigheid verzameld*, 191.

18 Letter from Helene Kröller-Müller to Sam van Deventer, April 13, 1912, Kröller-Müller Museum archive. Cited in Van Deventer, *Kröller-Müller*, 62. From Eugène Druet, the trio purchased *Basket with Apples*, 1887 (KM 108.800); *Olive Grove*, 1889 (KM 104.278); *Portrait of a Man*, 1888 (KM 103.189); *The Ravine (Les Peiroulets)*, 1889 (KM 106.109); and *Loom with Weaver*, 1884 (KM 111.301).

19 Rovers, "Collecting for the Future," 84.

20 *Reaper with a Scythe (after Millet)* (F688) now belongs to a private collection in the United States.

21 Letter from Helene Kröller-Müller to Sam van Deventer, September 7, 1911, Kröller-Müller Museum archive.

22 See note 12.

23 From New York, the exhibition traveled to Philadelphia, Boston, Cleveland, San Francisco, Kansas City, Minneapolis, Chicago, Detroit, and Toronto.

24 The history of the Kröller-Müller Museum, including stories about the later directors, their most important acquisitions, and the collaboration with artists and architects, can be found on the digital *Timeline* of the museum: https://kroller-muller.nl/en/a-timeline-full-of-stories.

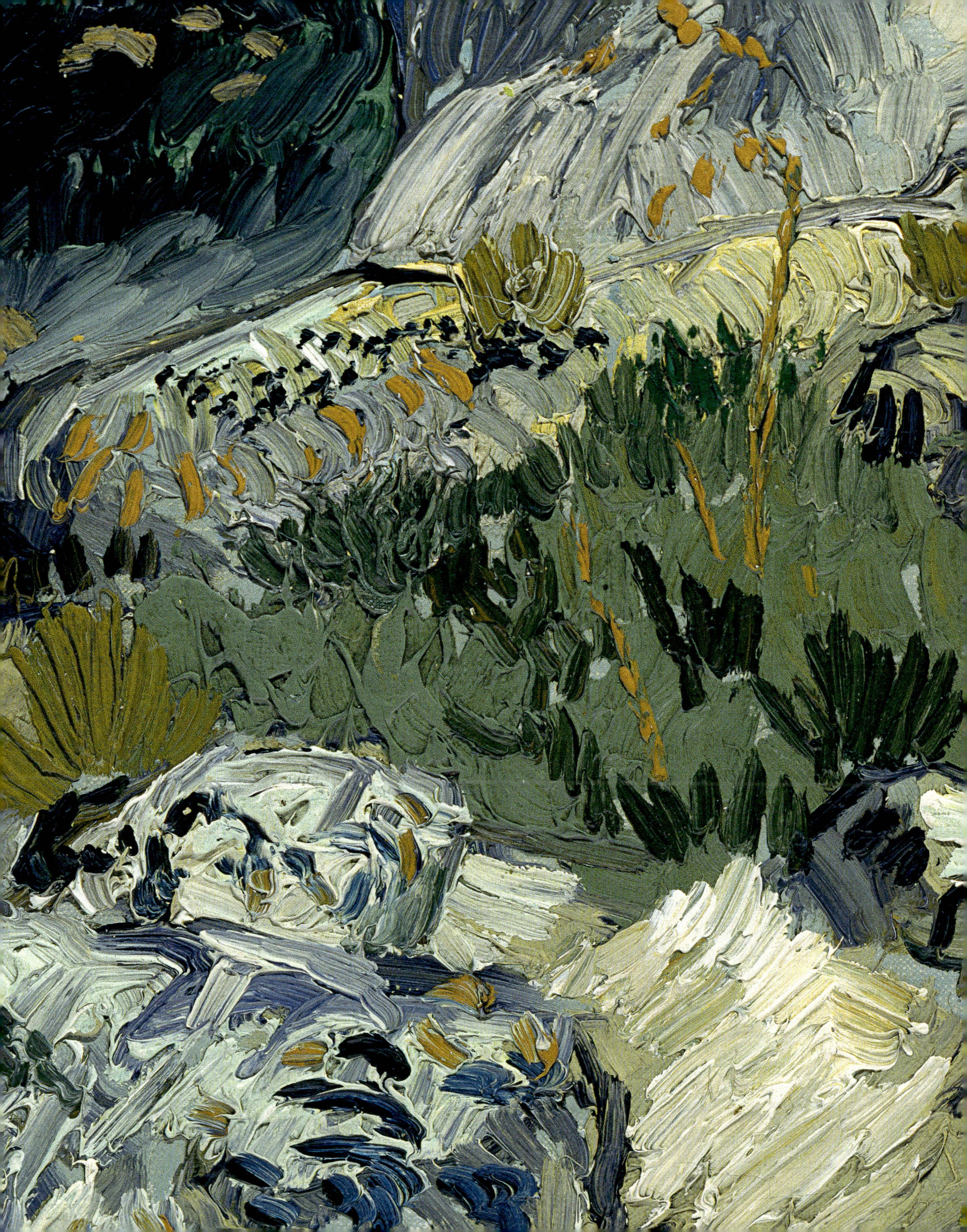

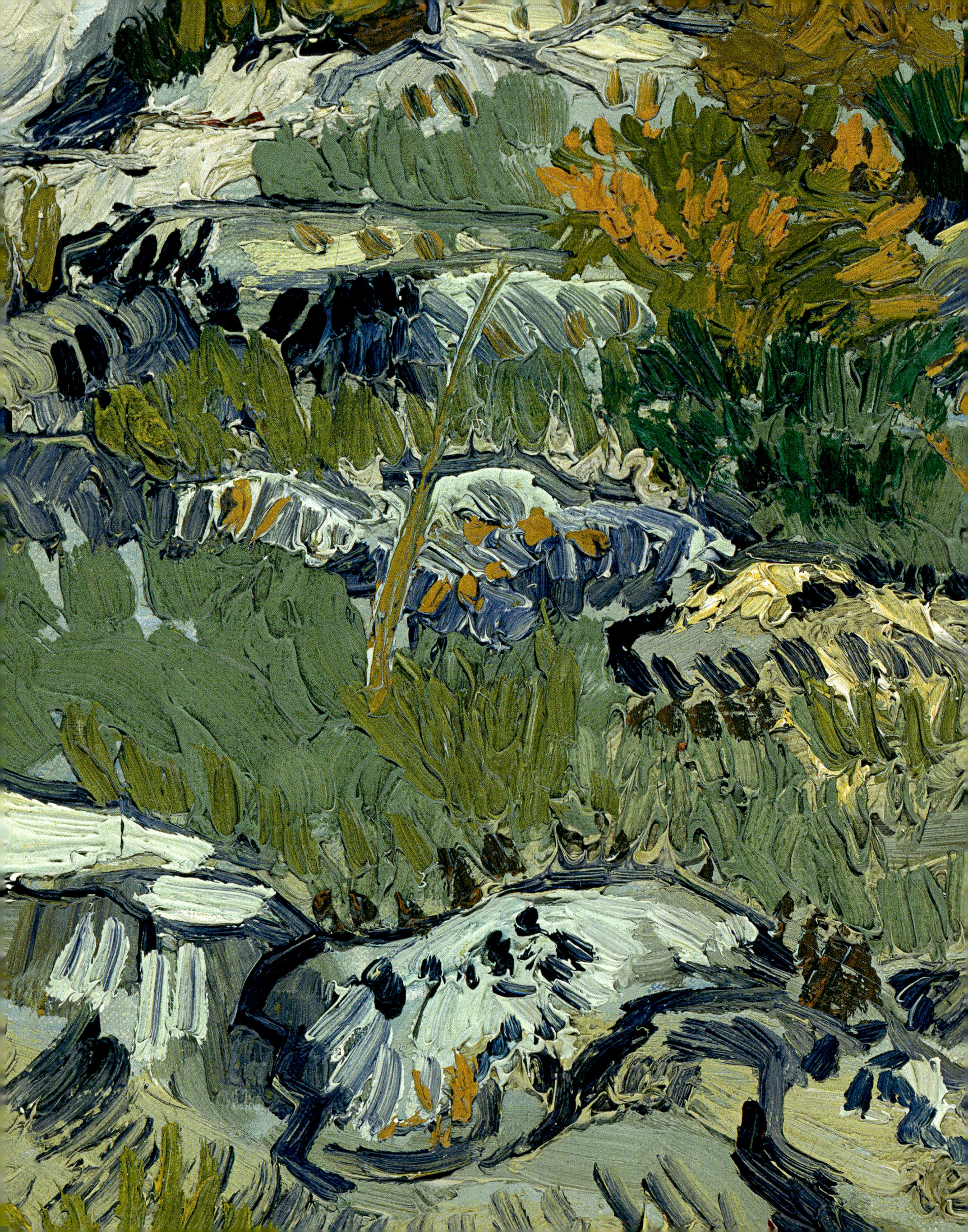

Plates

with entries
by David Bomford,
Helga K. Aurisch,
and Dena M. Woodall

Cat. 1
The Diggers (after Millet)
Graphite and black
chalk on wove paper,
14 ¾ × 24 ¼ inches
(37.5 × 61.5 cm)
Kröller-Müller Museum,
Otterlo
KM 119.703
F829

Provenance
Acquired by Hidde Nijland,
Dordrecht, before 1904; purchased
from Hidde Nijland by A. G. Kröller,
The Hague, July 1928; donated to the
Kröller-Müller Foundation by A. G.
Kröller, December 1928.

Notes
1 He studied Armand T. Cassagne, *Guide de l'alphabet du dessin* (1880);
John Marshall, *Esquisses anatomiques à l'usage des artistes*; Charles Bargue,
Exercices au fusain pour preparer à l'étude de l'académie d'après nature (Paris,
1871); and Charles Bargue, *Cours de dessin, avec le concours de J.-L. Gérôme*
(Paris, 1868–70).

2 See Sharon Gregory, *Vasari and the Renaissance Print* (Burlington, VT:
Ashgate, 2012), 161–228.

3 Letter 156, Vincent van Gogh to Theo van Gogh, Cuesmes, August 20,
1880. See also after J. F. Millet, *Labours of the Field*, 1853, ten wood engravings on wove paper, 17 ⅛ × 26 ⅝ inches (43.6 × 67.5 cm), Van Gogh Museum,
Amsterdam (Van Gogh Foundation), t0913V1962.

4 They include *The Sower, The Reaper, L'Angelus de soir*, and two versions
of *The Diggers*. The other drawing of *The Diggers* is also in the Kröller-
Müller Museum, Otterlo (F828). It lacks the inscription "d'après J. F. Millet,"
but has a signature. Van Gogh would return to this subject in September
1889 for a painting copied after Millet made in Saint-Rémy. See letter 805,
Vincent van Gogh to Theo van Gogh, Saint-Rémy-de-Provence, September
20, 1889. The painting is now located in the Stedelijk Museum, Amsterdam.

5 See letters 159 and 160, Vincent van Gogh to Theo van Gogh, Brussels,
October 15, and November 1, 1880, respectively. Jos ten Berge, Teio
Meedendorp, et al., *Drawings and Prints by Vincent van Gogh in the
Collection of the Kröller-Müller Museum* (Amsfoort: ThiemeArt, 2007), 18.

At the age of twenty-seven, Van Gogh resolved to become an
artist after abandoning other career paths — he had previously worked as a clerk at Goupil & Cie, the international fine
art and print dealers (located in The Hague, London, and
Paris), a teacher, a bookstore assistant, and a lay preacher. He
was determined to teach himself how to draw. His preparation consisted of studying manuals on anatomy and
perspective and copying figure studies from model books.[1]
Van Gogh also copied reproductive prints after famous
masters, a tradition that extends back to artistic training in
the Renaissance.[2] He had immeasurable admiration for
the French Realist artist Jean-François Millet, notable for
his scenes of peasants and physical labor in rural France;
consistently throughout his career, Van Gogh would return
to drawing after Millet's images.

In a letter to his brother Theo while living in Cuesmes in
the mining district of the Borinage, Belgium, Van Gogh
wrote that he was sketching large drawings after Millet. He
requested that Theo send by post *The Labours of the Fields*,
a set of ten small-scale reproductive prints after Millet that
Van Gogh copied several times.[3] Only a few of his drawings
after Millet survive from 1880–81.[4]

In this drawing, two men arduously till the earth with
flat-bladed spades in preparation for sowing the seed,
symbolically signifying the toil and drudgery that humans
endure in life. Instead of Millet's print as his guide, here
Van Gogh utilized a photograph from Ad. Braun & Co. after
a Millet print that Tobias Victor Schmidt, an art dealer at
Goupil, had lent to the young artist in October 1880 upon his
recent move to Brussels.[5] Van Gogh did not make an exact
copy of the photograph, which was lightly squared for transfer; rather, he elongated the scene. He drew in graphite and
added black chalk on the figure and stones to the right and
shadows in the foreground. The tone of the brown paper
has altered over time and suggests that it was perhaps once
tinted blue. DMW

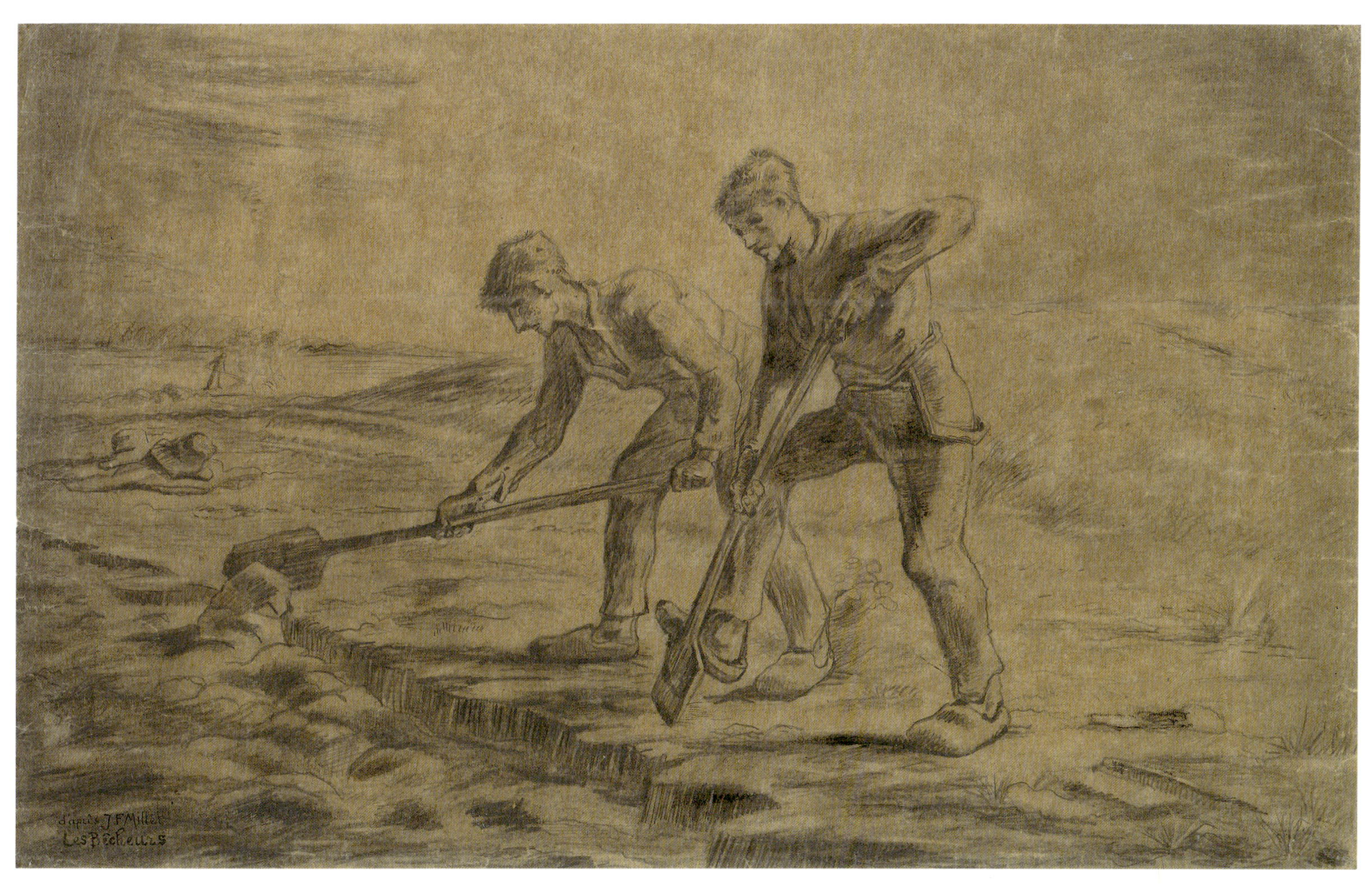

d'après J.F.Millet
Les Bêcheurs

Cat. 2
*The Daughter of Jacob Meyer
(after Bargue after Holbein)*
Graphite on wove paper,
16 ¾ × 12 inches (42.6 × 30.5 cm)
Kröller-Müller Museum,
Otterlo,
and Van Gogh Museum,
Amsterdam
(purchased with support
 from the BankGiroLoterij)
KM 131.050
VGM d112552005
F847

Provenance
H. P. Bremmer collection, The Hague,
probably acquired between 1915–22;
inherited by the heirs of H. P. Bremmer,
1956; F. Bremmer, The Hague, 1970–90;
sale, London, Christie's, *Impressionist
and Modern Art from the Collection of the
Late Mrs. A. A. Bremmer-Hollmann*,
The Hague, December 12, 1990, lot 254
(as *Jacob Meyer's Daughter — After Hans
Holbein*); purchased by the Kröller-
Müller Museum, Otterlo, and the Van
Gogh Museum, Amsterdam, with the
support of the BankGiroLoterij, 2005.

Van Gogh was not a natural at drawing, and he had to work tirelessly to master this skill. In a letter from Etten in July 1881, Van Gogh wrote to his brother Theo, "I have made another drawing in the Liesbos, and now it's become surprisingly hot, too hot to sit on the heath during the day, and I'm working at home these days, copying drawings by Holbein &c. from the Bargue."[1] He had received *Exercices au fusain pour preparer à l'étude de l'académie d'aprés nature* (1871) by Charles Bargue (1826/27–1883) from Hermanus Gijsbertus Tersteeg, the manager of the art gallery Goupil & Cie in The Hague, where Van Gogh had previously worked. He also sketched repeatedly from Bargue's full *Cours de dessin*, which was organized in three parts — drawings after casts, copies after Old Master drawings, and the aforementioned life studies of the male nude in varied poses.[2]

Anna, the teenage daughter of Jacob Meyer, sits at an angle, her head in profile and her long, loose hair falling on her back. The sixteenth-century painter and printmaker Hans Holbein the Younger, who was among Van Gogh's favorite Old Masters to draw after, had originally captured Anna with colored chalks, but here Van Gogh portrays her in metallic gray with his graphite pencil.[3] He closely followed Bargue's charcoal drawing, reproduced in lithographic form in the *Cours de dessin*, paying attention to the measurements and broad outlines.[4] He believed it was essential to draw only in black and white before attempting to work in color. The artist repeatedly drew the subjects from the manual, strictly adhering to the images with only a few alterations — enlarging her nose, lowering her eye, and disheveling her hair.[5] DMW

Notes
1 Letter 169, Vincent van Gogh to Theo van Gogh, Etten, between about July 15 and on or about July 20, 1881.

2 Van Gogh worked from the drawing manual by Bargue in 1880–81 while in Cuesmes, Brussels, and Etten. Bargue's *Cours de dessin* was made with the famed artist Jean-Léon Gérôme and contained 197 lithographs, in three parts: *Modèles d'après la bosse* (70 sheets), *Modèles d'après les maîtres de toutes les époques et de toutes les écoles* (67 sheets), and *Exercices au fusain pour preparer à l'étude de l'académie d'aprés nature* (60 sheets). It was published between 1868 and 1873.

3 See Hans Holbein (1497/1498–1543), *Portrait of Anna Meyer*, c. 1525–26, black and colored chalks with lead point and scored lines, 15 ¼ × 10 ¾ in. (39.1 × 27.5 cm), Kupferstichkabinett, Kunstmuseum, Basel, 1823.142. Jacob Meyer was the mayor of Basel, Switzerland. See Charles Chetham, *The Role of Vincent van Gogh's Copies in the Development of His Art* (New York: Garland, 1976), 72–74.

4 See letter 172, Vincent van Gogh to Theo van Gogh, Etten, mid-September 1881.

5 Van Gogh's image of Anna is extant in two forms; this one in graphite and another in pen and ink with a graphite underdrawing from July 1881.

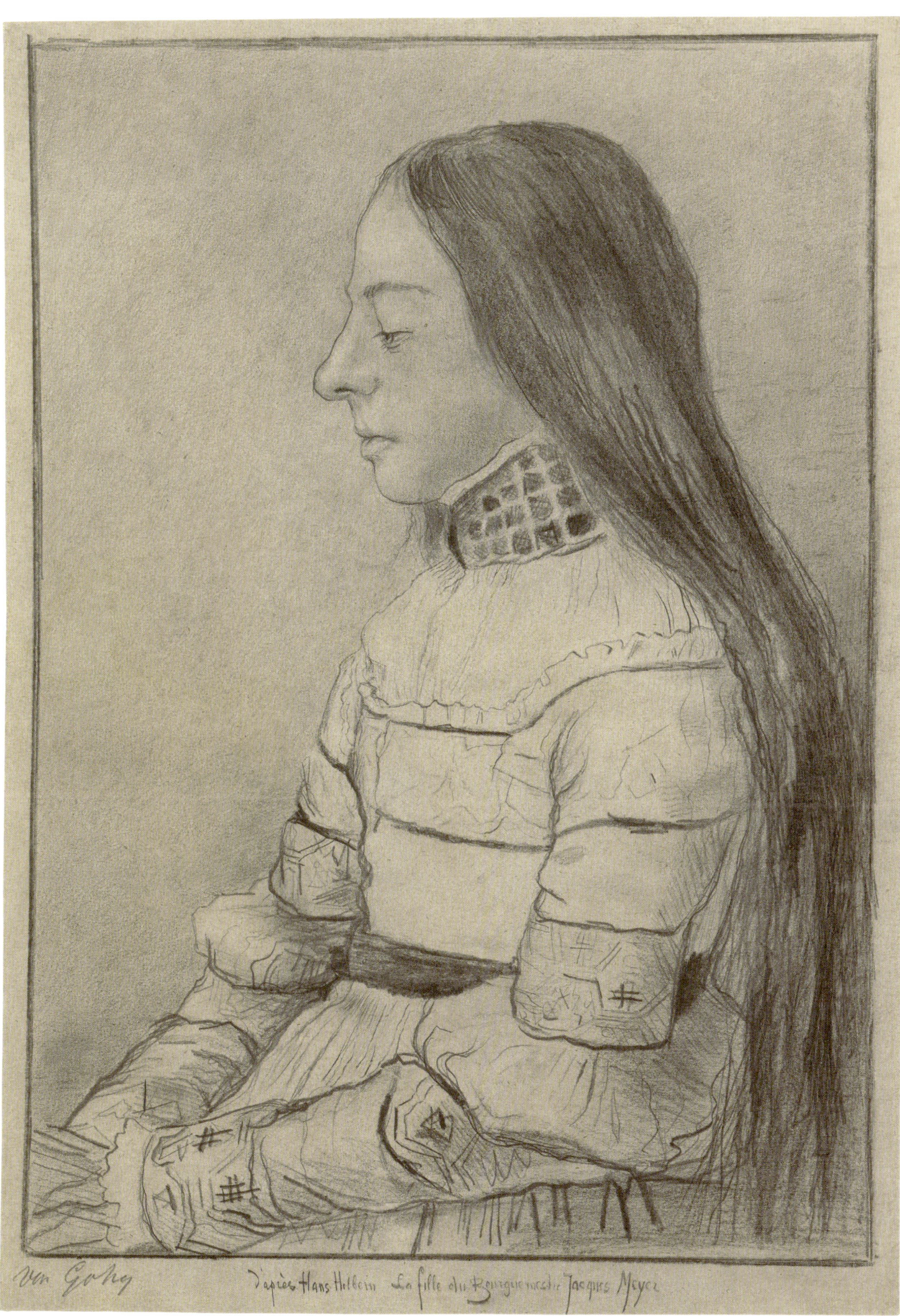

van Gogh
D'après Hans Holbein La fille du Bourguemestre Jacques Meyer

Cat. 3
Marsh with Water Lilies, Etten
Pen and India ink over graphite
on wove paper, 9 ¼ × 12 ⅜ inches
(23.5 × 31.43 cm)
Virginia Museum of Fine Arts,
Richmond, Collection
of Mr. and Mrs. Paul Mellon
85.777
F845

Provenance
Given to Miss. Wilhelmina van Gogh
(1862–1941), Dieren, Netherlands, from
her brother Vincent, 1881; J. P. Scholte,
Barchem, Netherlands, and Lochem,
Netherlands, 1956; Mrs. A. L. Scholte-
van Houten (daughter of Anna van
Gogh, the artist's sister); heirs of Mrs.
A.L. Scholte-van Houten collection;
Carl Pissarro collection; his sale,
London, Sotheby's, July 4, 1973, lot
214; purchased by Philippe Braum,
Galerie Hector Brame, Paris, 1973;
Mr. and Mrs. Paul Mellon, Upperville,
Virginia, July 1973–1985; given to
the Virginia Museum of Fine Arts,
Richmond, Virginia, December 1985.

Notes
1 Letter 160, Vincent van Gogh to Theo van Gogh, Brussels, November 1,
1880, and letter 164, Vincent van Gogh to Theo van Gogh, Brussels, April
2, 1881. Vincent van Gogh, *Portrait of Anthon van Rappard*, October 1884,
Nuenen, graphite on paper, Van Gogh Museum, Amsterdam (Vincent van
Gogh Foundation), do115V1962r.

2 Letter 165, Vincent van Gogh to Theo van Gogh, Brussels, April 12, 1881.

3 It is believed that Van Gogh used a reed pen for this drawing. However,
Sjraar van Heugten commented, "It is difficult to say exactly when he used
a reed, a quill, or a metal nib." See Ronald Pickvance, *Van Gogh in Arles*
(New York: Metropolitan Museum of Art, 1984), 54, and Sjraar van
Heugten, *Vincent van Gogh Drawings*, vol. 2, *Nuenen, 1883–1885, Van Gogh
Museum* (Amsterdam: Van Gogh Museum; London: Lund Humphries,
1997), 22.

4 Letter 168, Vincent van Gogh to Theo van Gogh, Etten, end of June 1881.

5 Anthon van Rappard, *Passievaart near Seppe,* June 1881, Van Gogh
Museum, Amsterdam. Van Gogh made another drawing of the marsh about
the same time: *The Swamp,* June 1881, pen and black ink over graphite on
laid paper, National Gallery of Canada, Ottawa [15461] (F 846). See Klaus
Albrecht Schröder, Heinz Widauer, Sjraar van Heugten, and Markije
Vellekoop, eds., *Heartfelt Lines: Van Gogh* (Vienna: Albertina Museum,
2008), 21–24, 116–19, cat. 1.

According to a letter to his brother Theo on November 1, 1880, Van Gogh met the artist Anthon van Rappard, who was studying at the Brussels Royal Academy of Fine Arts. They developed a friendship that lasted for about four years.[1] Van Gogh would work at times in Van Rappard's Brussels studio, and even after he left the city they remained in contact and continued to see each other regularly.

This drawing is from one of their artistic excursions together in the Dutch countryside. Van Gogh had returned to the Netherlands in April of 1881, living for a short time with his parents in Etten.[2] He persistently drew during this period, mainly practicing perspective, copying other artists or using models, and responding to nature. For the most part, he made these drawings by sketching with a pencil and then would elaborate on them with ink using a pen.[3] In June, Van Rappard stayed for twelve days in Etten, working in the surrounding countryside with Van Gogh, who wrote, "We went on a fair number of excursions together, several times to the heath at Seppe, among other places, and the so-called Passievaart, a huge marsh. . . . While he was painting I made a pen drawing of another spot in the marsh where many water lilies grow."[4]

Van Rappard and Van Gogh made drawings from the same vantage point, dividing the vast marsh into horizontal planes.[5] In Van Gogh's drawing, curved and straight lines delineate the aquatic plants, such as water lilies and tall reeds, in the immediate foreground. Broken horizontal lines of various lengths suggest water. Clumps of vegetation recede to a silhouetted town on the high horizon, and a lone bird glides over the wet, fertile landscape. Van Gogh implemented hatching and crosshatching instead of wash for tonal value, evoking the appearance of etched lines. Once he had completed the sheet, he signed it *Vincent*, added framing lines, and gave it to his sister, Wil, upon her move to Amsterdam. This superb early drawing is a precursor to the graphic sensibility of his late drawings from Arles. DMW

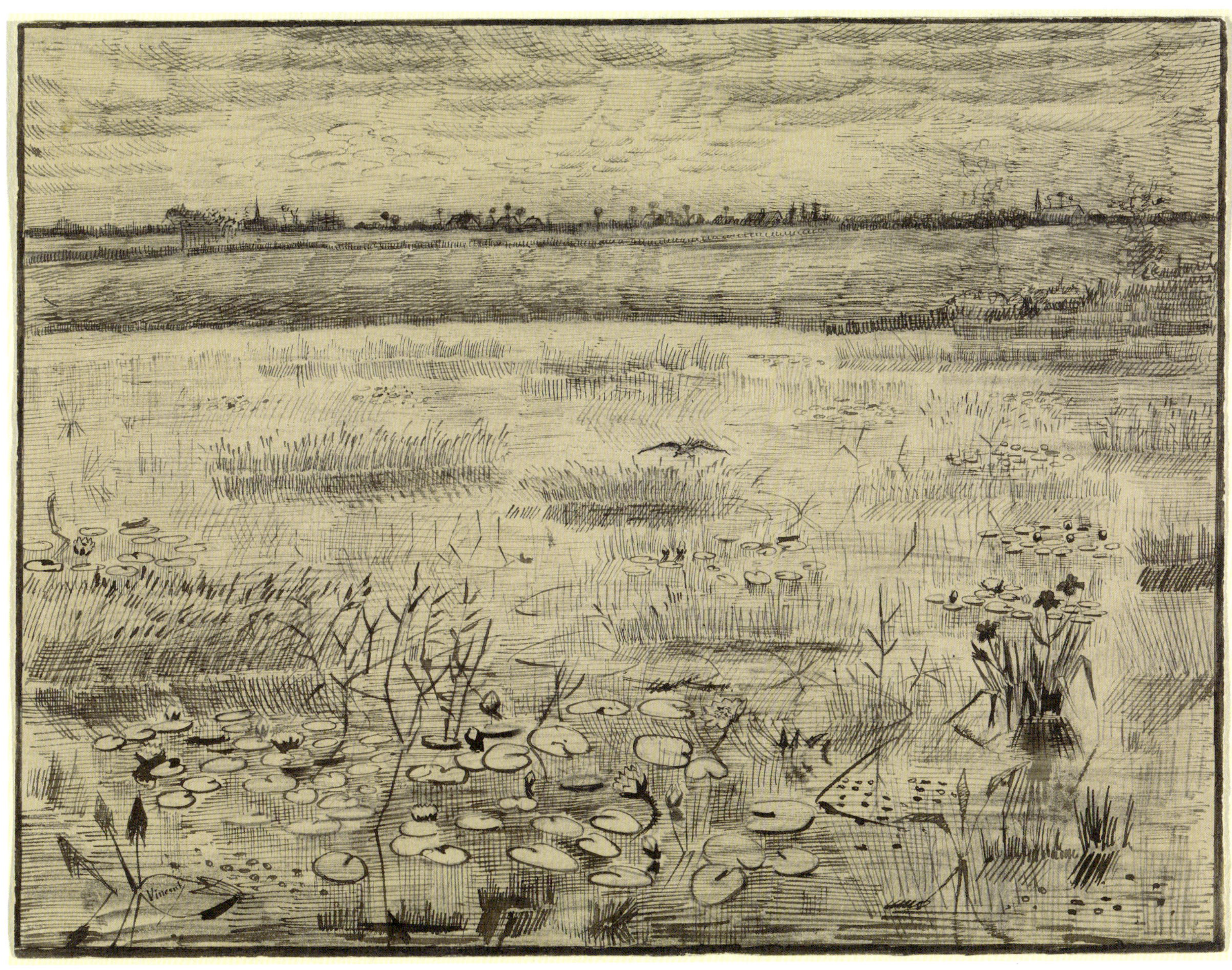
Vincent

September 1881
Etten

Cat. 4
Digger
Black chalk, wash, pen and
diluted ink, and opaque
watercolor, with traces of
charcoal on laid paper,
20 ¼ × 12 ¼ inches (51.5 × 31 cm)
Kröller-Müller Museum,
Otterlo
KM 121.662
F855

Provenance
Acquired by Hidde Nijland, Dordrecht,
before 1895; purchased from Hidde
Nijland by A. G. Kröller, The Hague,
July 1928; donated to the Kröller-
Müller Foundation by A. G. Kröller,
December 1928.

Van Gogh saw drawings and prints of peasant scenes by Jean-François Millet in exhibitions held in Paris after the painter's death in 1875.[1] About five years later, he embraced Millet's work to assist his early drawing attempts of similar subjects. They were lumbering at first but improved as his confidence and abilities grew. He maintained a strict routine in learning from drawing manuals and copying after prints. He moved to the artistically rich city of Brussels from the Borinage in October 1880, expanding his art education by enrolling in the Brussels Royal Academy of Fine Arts. Following the advice of the Dutch painter Willem Roelofs, whom he met in Brussels, the young artist sketched after three-dimensional antique models.

In April 1881, Van Gogh moved in with his parents in Etten, in the Brabant region where he was born. He expanded his drawing practice there by using live models in the rural countryside. In this drawing, the laborer arduously digs the firm ground with his shovel. His model was Piet Kaufmann, the Van Gogh family's gardener, who is believed to have posed for the artist between thirty and fifty times.[2]

At the outset of his training, Van Gogh worked with only a pencil and at times reinforced his images with pen lines. His artistic knowledge of papers and materials increased when he was in Brussels and began studying Armand Cassagne's *Traité d'aquarelle* (1875), exploring the possibilities of ink and watercolor.[3] In The Hague, Van Gogh had visited the painter Anton Mauve, who advised him to push beyond the use of ink and be more daring with his materials: "You must try it with charcoal and chalk and brush and stump."[4] DMW

Notes

1 Charles Pillet, *Catalogue des 95 dessins de Jean-François Millet: Composant la collection de M. Gavet et dont la vente aura lieu Hôtel Drouot, salles 8 et 9, les ven-dredi 11 et samedi 12 juin 1875, à deux heures* (Paris: Alcan-Lévy, 1875). See Frits Lugt, *Répertoire des catalogues de ventes publiques intéressant l'art ou la curiosité*, vol. 3, *Troisième période, 1861–1900* (The Hague: Martinus Nijhoff, 1964), no. 35754; Alexandre Piedagnel, *J.-F. Millet* (Paris: 1888), 73–83 (*Souvenirs de Barbizon*); and Paris, Galeries Durand-Ruel, exhibition of Millet's etchings (March 1876).

2 See Jos ten Berge, Teio Meedendorp, et al., *Drawings and Prints by Vincent van Gogh in the Collection of the Kröller-Müller Museum* (Amsfoort: ThiemeArt, 2007), 50.

3 See Armand T. Cassagne, *Traité d'aquarelle* (Paris: C. Fouraut et fils, 1875).

4 See Teun Berserik and Feico Hoekstra, *Vincent van Gogh: De vroege Jaren* (Amsterdam: Oog en Blik, De Bezige Bij, 2012); Fred Leeman and John Sillevis, *De Haagse School en de jonge Van Gogh* (Zwolle: Waanders, 2005); and Colta Ives, Susan Alyson Stein, Sjraar van Heugten, and Marije Vellekoop, *Vincent van Gogh: The Drawings* (New York: The Metropolitan Museum of Art; Amsterdam: Van Gogh Museum; New Haven and London: Yale University Press, 2005), 57, 66, 68.

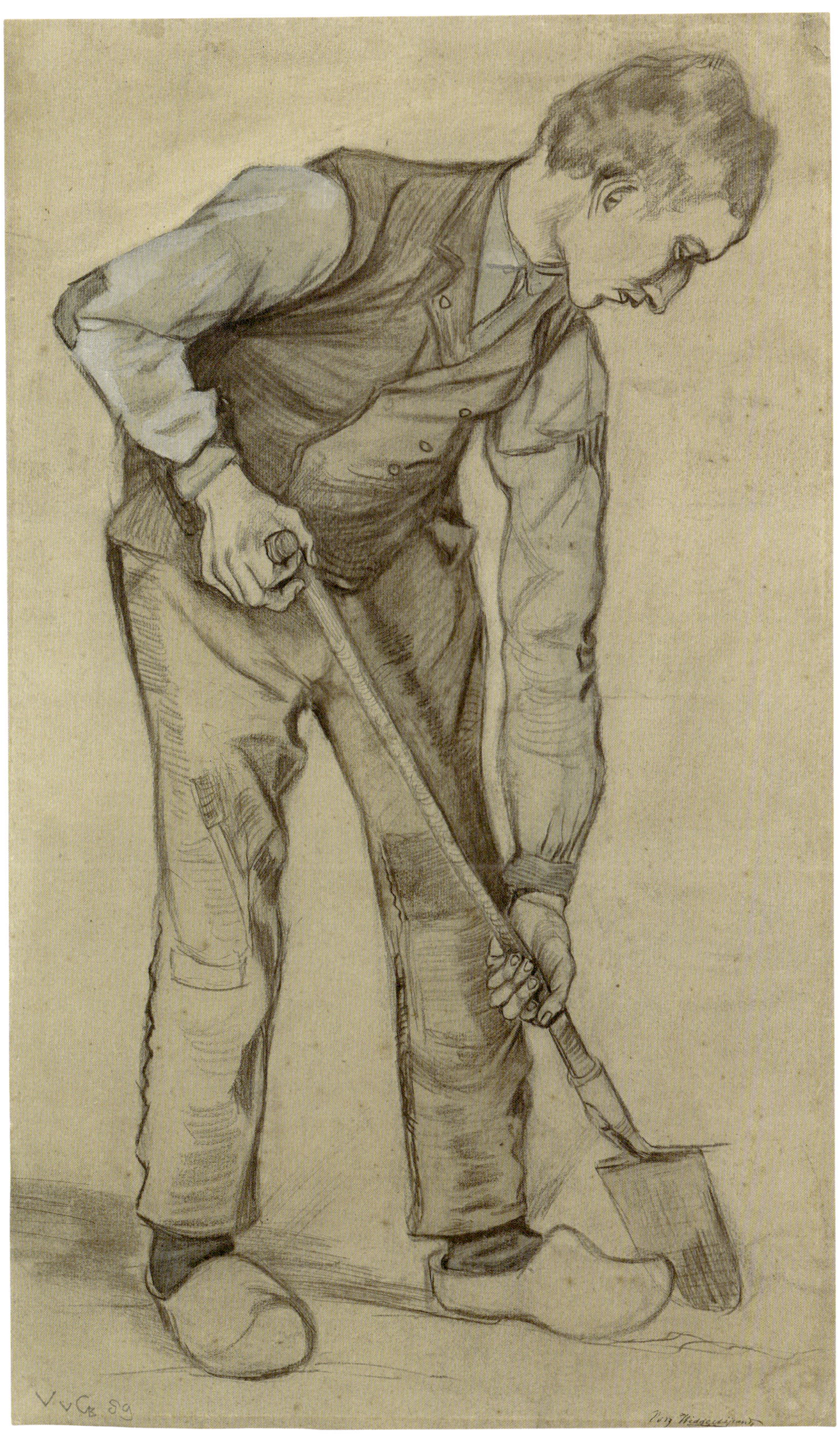

VvG 89

September 1881
Etten

Cat. 5
*Windmills near Dordrecht
(Weeskinderendijk)*
Graphite, black and green
chalk, pen and brush in ink,
and opaque watercolor
on laid paper,
10⅛ × 23½ inches
(25.7 × 59.8 cm)
Kröller-Müller Museum,
Otterlo
KM 126.249
F850

Provenance
L. C. Enthoven collection, Voorburg;
Enthoven collection sale, Amsterdam,
Frederik Muller & Cie, May 18, 1920,
lot 256, purchased from sale by H.
Kröller-Müller, 1920; donated to the
Kröller-Müller Foundation.

Van Gogh would excel in his treatment of landscapes while
working in France later in his career. His earliest explora-
tions in the genre, however, began in Holland, where he
rendered the panoramic, windswept plains and broad, open
skies. As he traveled in August 1881 to visit his mentor and
cousin by marriage, the painter Anton Mauve, Van Gogh
noticed the Weeskinderendijk windmills near Dordrecht.
On his return trip from The Hague to Etten, he exited the
train to capture them: "I was in The Hague until Thursday
morning. Then I went to Dordrecht, because I'd seen a spot
from the train that I wanted to draw. Namely the row of
windmills. I got it done even though it was raining, and so
at least I've brought home a souvenir from my outing."[1]

Mauve taught Van Gogh the fundamentals of watercolor
technique in his studio, but the younger artist also learned
from reading Armand Cassagne's *Traité d'aquarelle* in June
of 1881.[2] In this extended composition, Van Gogh used a
variety of materials to capture the broad field behind an
imposing, dilapidated white fence near a waterway crossing. A diminutive figure walks along a path, and various
windmills dot the horizon on a gray, cloudy day. Other small
buildings, chimney-topped factories, and ships with masts
and sails complete the scene in the distance. No doubt Van
Gogh worked out the details with chalk, ink, and watercolor when he was settled at home with more time to work.
He probably used a pencil only to jot down the main ideas
of the composition while in transit. Van Gogh typically used
an opaque watercolor, called gouache, that he would dilute
to achieve diverse consistencies, instead of the more trans-
parent version of the medium that has a fresh and luminous
appearance.[3] DMW

Notes
1 Letter 171, Vincent van Gogh to Theo van Gogh, Etten, August 26, 1881.

2 See Sjraar van Heugten, *Van Gogh Draughtsman: The Masterpieces* (Amsterdam:
Van Gogh Museum, 2005), 33.

3 See Siraar van Heugten, *Vincent van Gogh Drawings*, vol. 2, *Nuenen, 1883–1885,
Van Gogh Museum* (Amsterdam: Van Gogh Museum; London: Lund Humphries,
1997), 23.

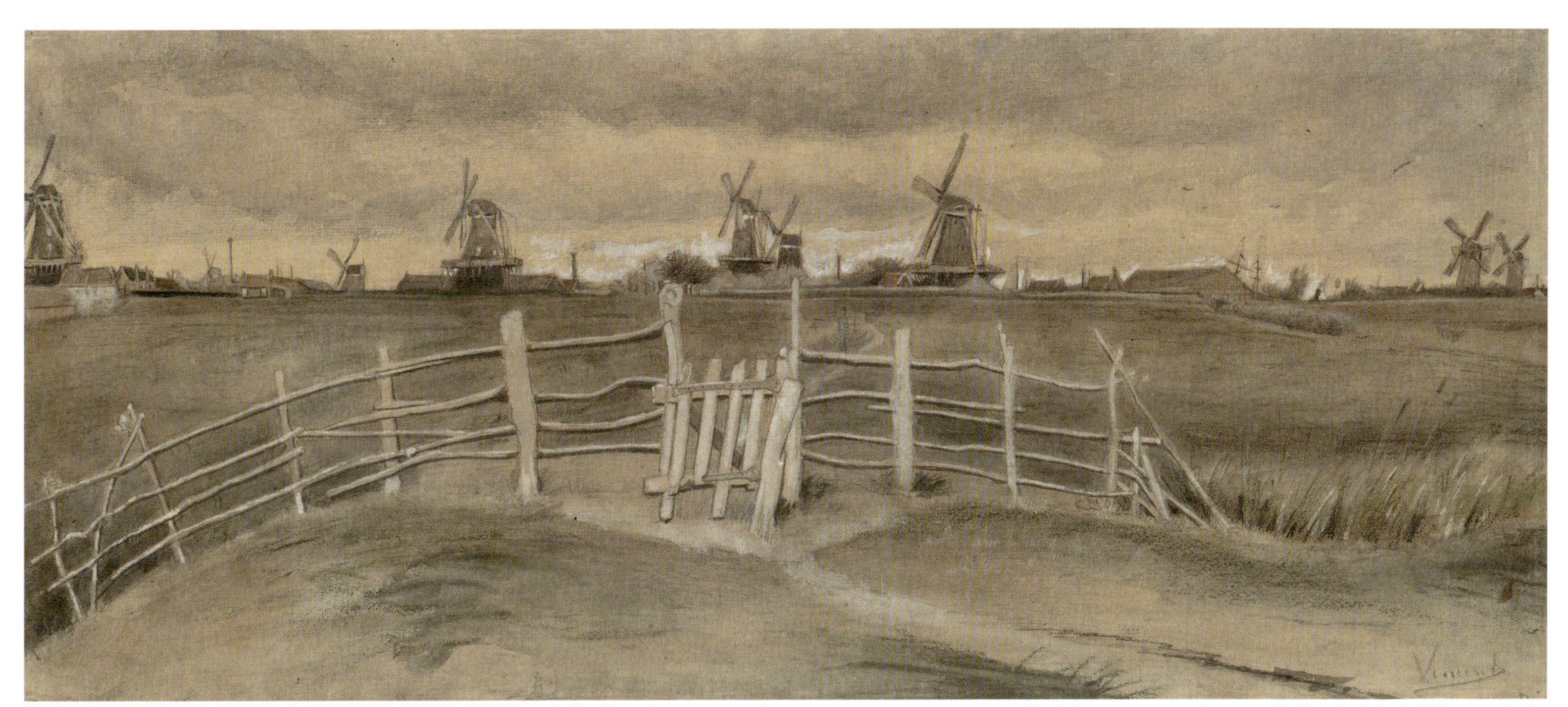

November–December 1881
Nuenen

Cat. 6
Still Life with Straw Hat
Oil on paper mounted
on canvas,
14 ⅜ × 21 ⅛ inches
(36.5 × 53.6 cm)
Kröller-Müller Museum,
Otterlo
KM 109.323
F62

Provenance
A. C. van Gogh-Carbentus, Nuenen/
Breda, November 1885/April 1886; A.
Schrauwen, Breda, 1886; J. C. and J. M.
Couvreur, Breda; W. van Bakel and
C. Mouwen, Breda, 1902; Oldenzeel, art
dealer, Rotterdam, 1903; L. C. Enthoven
coll., Voorburg; purchased by H. Kröller-
Müller at Enthoven sale, Amsterdam
(Frederik Muller), May 18, 1920, lot 222:
Nature morte.

This still life and another very similar work that features a pair of clogs instead of the straw hat are two of Van Gogh's earliest efforts in oil paint. They were painted under the tutelage of his cousin Anton Mauve, an accomplished landscapist working in The Hague, whom Vincent sought out at a moment of great personal unhappiness. Van Gogh's proposal of marriage had been turned down by Kee Vos, also a cousin, leaving him emotionally dejected.[1] He urgently wanted to pursue a career that would fulfill him spiritually and support him financially.

Mauve set his student a typical task for beginners: capture the different forms, shapes, and colors of a still life. This simple arrangement includes a white clay pipe, a white napkin, a bottle, a lidded red-brown ceramic pot with a brush or spoon poking out, a celadon-green ginger jar, and a box of matches all placed around a straw hat on a wooden table. The colors are muted, and the background is so dark that it is difficult to distinguish the object, perhaps a block of peat, placed at the far right.[2] But on the whole, Van Gogh, who up to this point had attempted only drawings, acquitted himself well, laying the oil paint on carefully to evoke the different textures of the objects and sensitively shading to give them three-dimensionality. Mauve was pleasantly surprised by Van Gogh's achievement, saying, "I always thought you were a bloody bore, but now I see that this isn't so."[3] Van Gogh, having failed in earlier attempts to find a profession, was elated. He wrote to his brother Theo about his latest works, "Of course they aren't masterpieces and yet I truly believe there's something sound and real in them, more at least than in what I've made up to now. And so I now consider myself to be at the beginning of making something serious."[4] Indeed, it was the beginning of the remarkable career of one of the greatest painters in the history of European art. HKA

Notes
1 Hildelies Balk, Jos ten Berge, et al., *The Paintings of Vincent van Gogh in the Collection of the Kröller-Müller Museum* (Otterlo: Kröller-Müller Museum, 2003), 27.

2 Ibid., 28.

3 Letter 191, Vincent van Gogh to Theo van Gogh, The Hague, between December 1 and 3, 1881.

4 Letter 193, Vincent van Gogh to Theo van Gogh, Etten, on or about December 23, 1881.

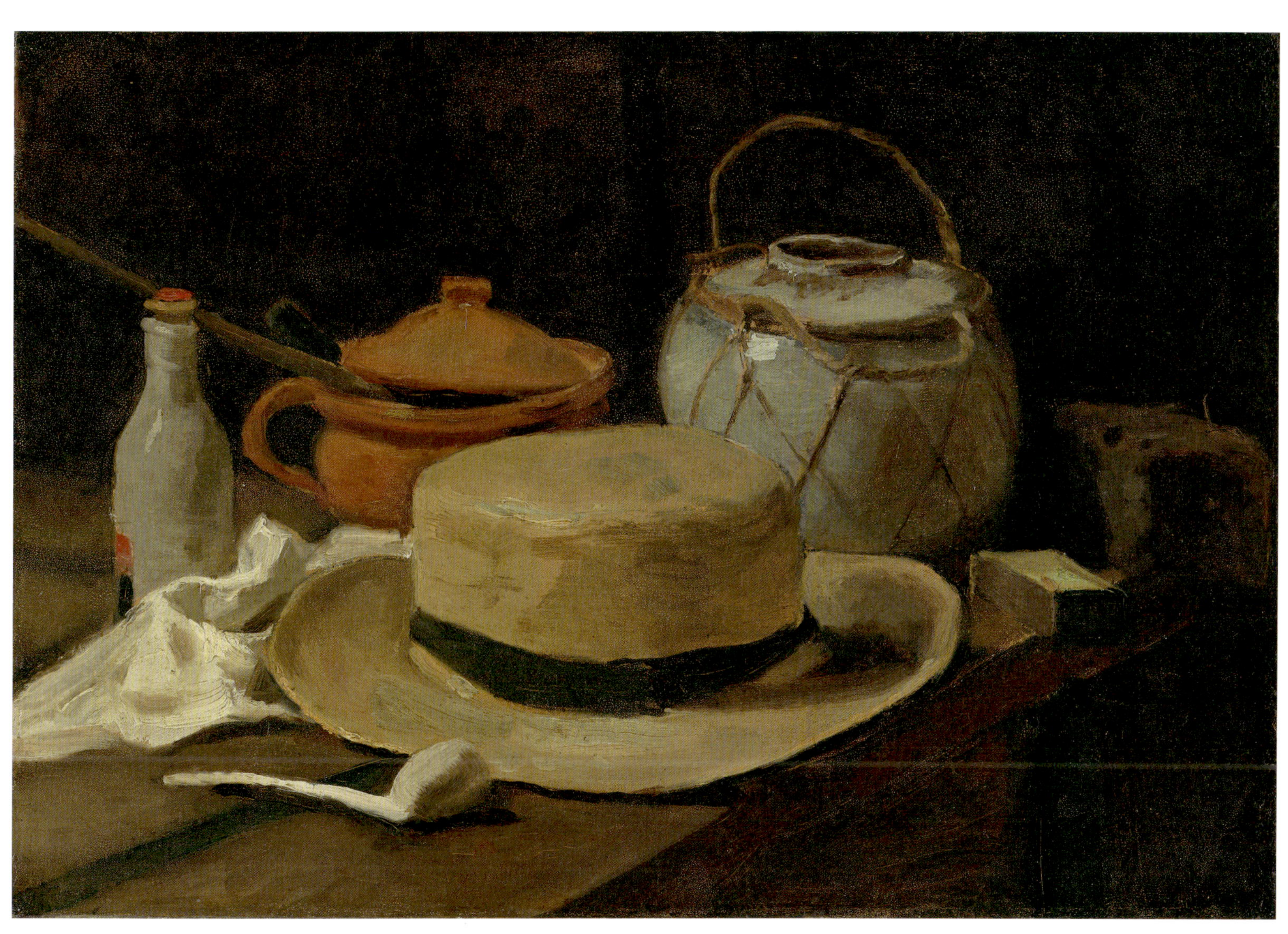

Cat. 7
Old Man in a Tailcoat
Graphite with scraping, traces
of fixative and squaring on
wove paper,
18 ⅝ × 10 ¼ inches (47.4 × 26 cm)
Van Gogh Museum,
Amsterdam
(Vincent van Gogh Foundation)
d380V1962
F960

Provenance
Theo van Gogh, Paris, after December
1882; Jo van Gogh-Bonger and Vincent
Willem van Gogh, Paris, January 25,
1891; administered by Jo van Gogh-
Bonger, Bussum/Amsterdam/Laren,
until September 2, 1925; on loan from
Vincent Willem van Gogh, Laren, to
the Stedelijk Museum, Amsterdam,
October 22, 1931; transferred to Vincent
van Gogh Foundation, Amsterdam,
July 10, 1962; agreement July 21, 1962,
entrusts collection to the State of the
Netherlands until realization of the
Rijksmuseum Vincent van Gogh,
Amsterdam; on loan to Stedelijk
Museum, Amsterdam, until opening
of Rijksmuseum Vincent van Gogh;
Rijksmuseum Vincent van Gogh,
Amsterdam, June 2, 1973; Van Gogh
Museum, Amsterdam, July 1, 1994.

When Van Gogh moved to The Hague in 1881, he focused on drawing from live models, both in his residence, capturing his mistress Clasina Maria ("Sien") Hoornik and her family members, and on the streets of the city. He also utilized as his models impoverished old men and women from the Dutch Reformed Home for the Elderly. One of his favorite subjects, whom he referred to as "orphan man," was Adrianus Jacobus Zuijderland, who posed for him on many occasions. A man in his seventies, Zuijderland was a war veteran who had fought in the Ten Days' Campaign of Holland against Belgium in 1831, as indicated by the Metal Cross he wears in several of the artist's drawings.[1]

In this sketch, Van Gogh shows the model with no hint of his surroundings. He has portrayed Zujiderland from the back in a long dark coat and with sideburns and untidy hair underneath a top hat. He holds a cane with a curved handle that is drawn only in outline. Top hats and tails are often equated with classy formal wear of the affluent, but during this period they were often associated with people who were reliant on castoffs or alms. This drawing was probably a study for an analogous watercolor of the beach at Scheveningen depicting a male figure with a woman rather than a walking stick on his arm.[2]

Van Gogh enjoyed drawing in graphite for its exactitude, and he liked to press firmly with his drawing tool, often onto coarse, thick sheets of paper. He used carpenter's pencils that enabled him to sketch wide and narrow lines from the same instrument, and he would sometimes fix his drawings with milk, making the graphite less shiny and more velvety black.[3] Scratching into the image produced lights and gave him the tonal gradation that he sought. DMW

Notes
1 See Wouter J. A. Visser, "Vincent van Gogh en Den Haag," *Jaarboek die Haghe* (1973): 62–65. The cross is in a drawing showing Zuiderland from the front. See *Old Man in a Tailcoat*, September–December 1882, graphite on wove paper with traces of squaring and fixative, 18 ⅝ × 9 ¼ inches (47.2 × 23.5 cm), Van Gogh Museum, Amsterdam, d65V1962.

2 Van Gogh, *Beach Scene*, 1882, watercolor, private collection (F982). See Siraar van Heugten, *Vincent van Gogh: Drawings*, vol. 1, *The Early Years, 1880–1883* (Amsterdam: Van Gogh Museum; London: Lund Humphries, 1996), 136, cat. 33.

3 See Sjraar van Heugten with Marije Vellekoop and Roelie Zwikker, *Van Gogh: Master Draughtsman* (New York: Harry N. Abrams, 2005), 39.

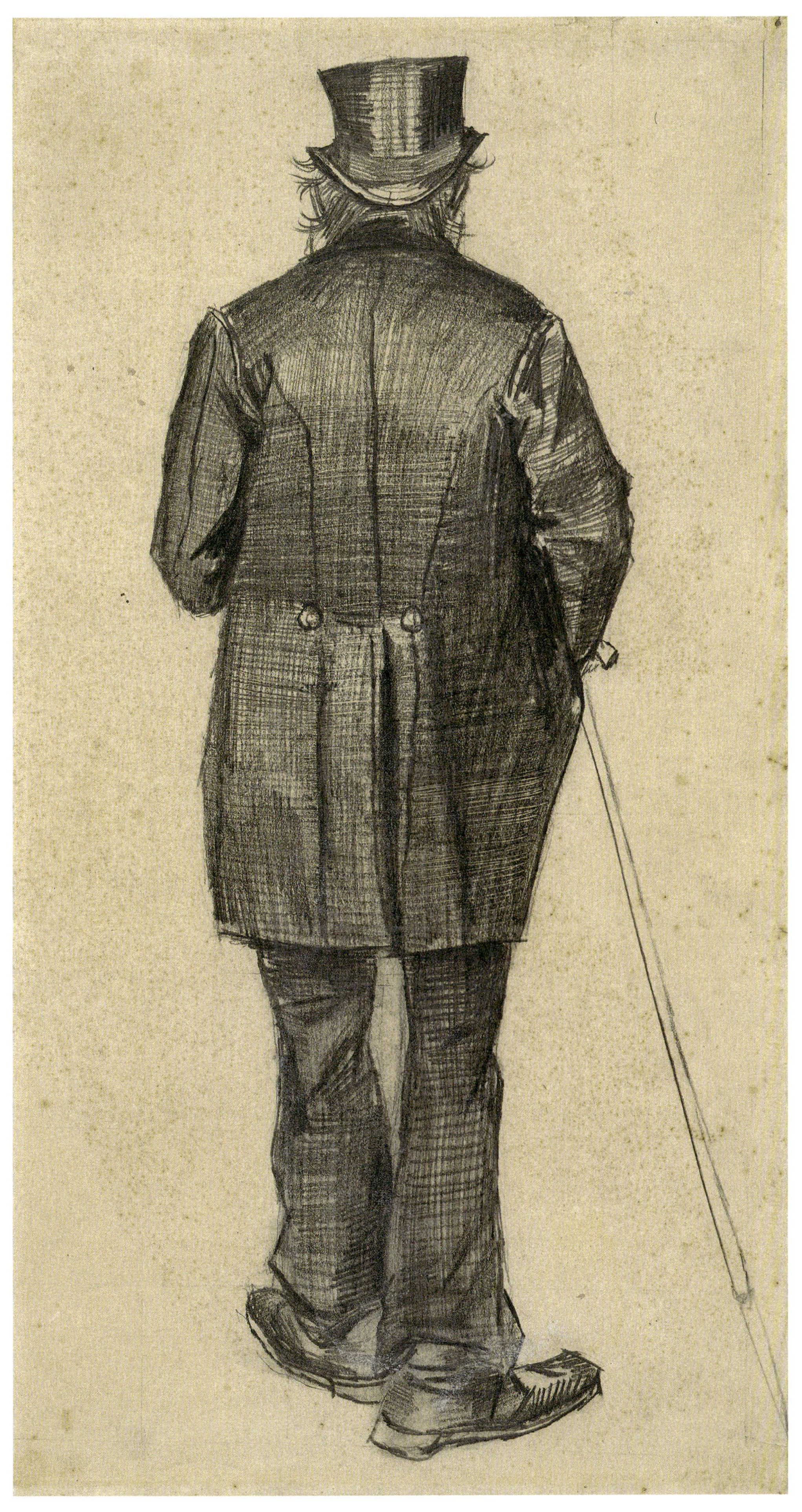

Cat. 8
Head of a Fisherman with a
Fringe of Beard and a Sou'wester
Graphite, black lithographic
crayon, brush and pen
in black ink, opaque white,
pink and reddish-brown
watercolor, and gray wash and
scraping on watercolor paper,
18 ⅝ × 11 ⅝ inches
(47.2 × 29.4 cm)
Van Gogh Museum,
Amsterdam
(Vincent van Gogh Foundation)
d70V1962
F1017

Provenance
Theo van Gogh, Paris, after January 1883;
Jo van Gogh-Bonger and Vincent Willem
van Gogh, Paris, January 25, 1891; trans-
ferred by Vincent Willem van Gogh,
Laren, July 10, 1962, to the Vincent van
Gogh Foundation, Amsterdam; agree-
ment July 21, 1962, entrusts collection to
the State of the Netherlands until reali-
zation of the Rijksmuseum Vincent van
Gogh, Amsterdam; on loan to Stedelijk
Museum, Amsterdam, until opening of
Rijksmuseum Vincent; Rijksmuseum
Vincent van Gogh, Amsterdam, June 2,
1973; Van Gogh Museum, Amsterdam,
July 1, 1994.

In November 1882, while living in The Hague, Van Gogh
began experimenting with lithography, a printmaking
technique that can produce drawn lines with a texture resem-
bling that of pencil or chalk. He could draw directly on the
stone or use transfer paper to print his drawings. Van Gogh
believed in making affordable prints for the people and
had hopes to work as an illustrator, having been influenced
heavily by the black-and-white imagery in English and
French magazines.[1] His experimentation with lithographic
materials also extended to his drawing practice. He liked
that the lithographic crayon was greasy, extremely black,
and could transfer his pencil's texture. He discussed using
a range of materials to increase tonal breadth in a letter to
Theo, calling the results "painting in black."[2] The lithographic crayon was a choice companion to his carpenter's
pencil, a brush or pen with lampblack, and white gouache
for the illuminated sections.

His penchant for diverse drawing materials extended to his
1883 project *Heads of the People,* influenced by wood engravings portraying the British working class published in the
English illustrated magazine *The Graphic.* His comparable
series was of six Dutch fishermen's heads with sou'westers,
collapsible waterproof rain hats utilized at sea. Van Gogh
received a previously owned, well-worn version of one of
these hats, about which he said that "many gales and seas
have swept over."[3] This highly finished drawing showcases
an old man with a fringed beard who is ready for stormy
weather in his neck-clasped jacket and sou'wester with ear-
flaps. Van Gogh used as his models men from the Dutch
Reformed Home for the Elderly. DMW

Notes
1 Letters 289, 290, and 291, Vincent van Gogh to Theo van Gogh, The Hague,
December 1, 1882, December 3, 1882, and between December 4 and 9, 1882,
respectively. See also Sjraar van Heugten and Fieke Pabst, *The Graphic Work of
Vincent van Gogh* (Zwolle: Waanders, 1995), 15–25; Sjraar van Heughten, *Van Gogh
Drawings: Influences and Innovations* (Arles: Actes Sud, 2015), 37–38.

2 "One puts into a drawing the depth of effect and the rich gradations of tone
that a painting should have.... One must be able to go from the highest lights to
the deepest shadows and do so with a few simple ingredients." See letter 297,
Vincent van Gogh to Theo van Gogh, The Hague, December 31, 1882, and January
2, 1883, 297.

3 See Teio Meedendorp, *Drawings and Prints by Vincent van Gogh in the Collection
of the Kröller-Müller Museum* (Otterlo: Kröller-Müller Museum, 2007), 182.
Van Gogh probably had been given this type of hat as a gift, and referred to them
in a letter, saying, "I'll be getting a *sou'wester* for the heads." See letter 301,
Vincent van Gogh to Theo van Gogh, The Hague, January 13, 1883.

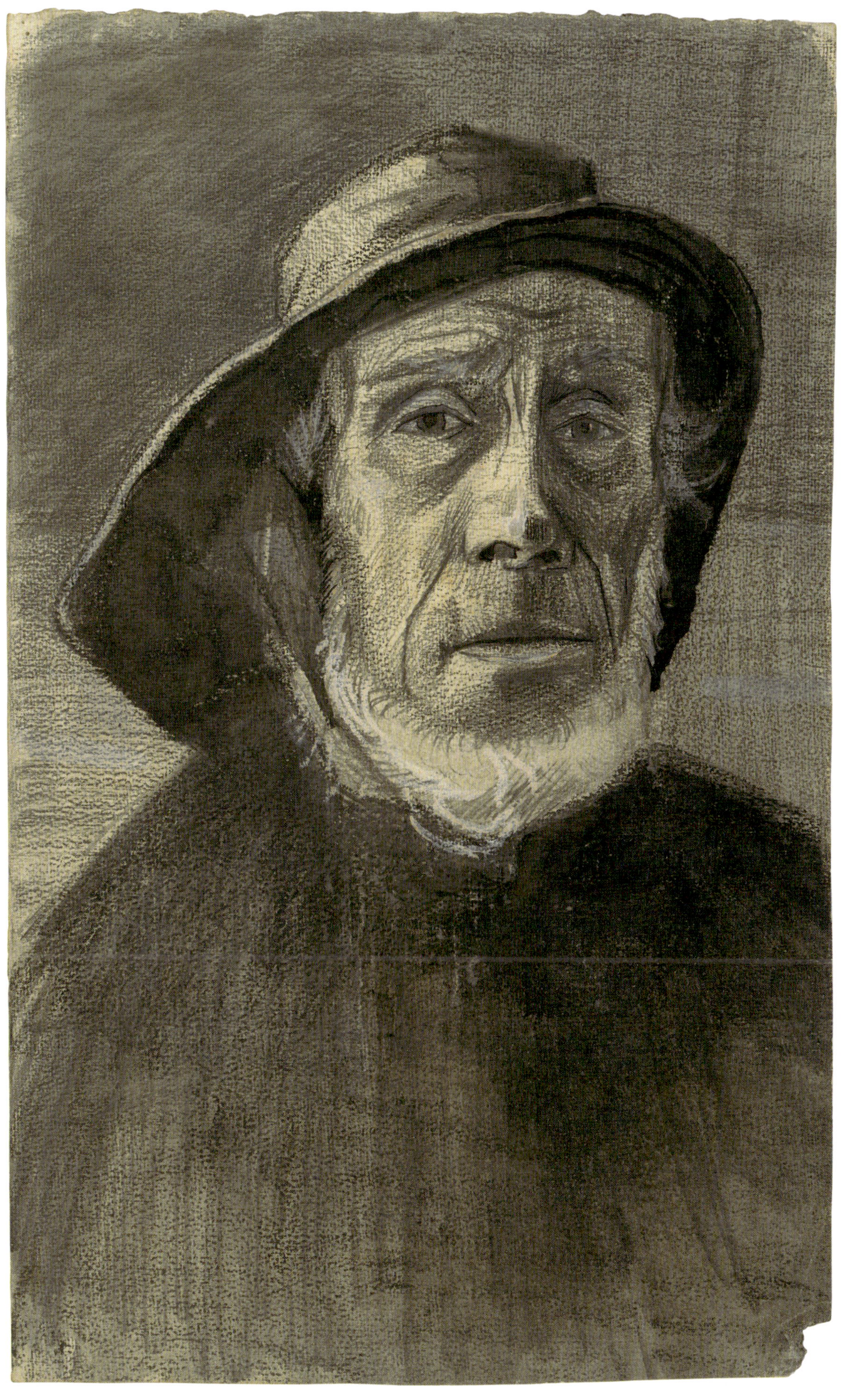

November 1884–May 1885
Nuenen

Cat. 9
Head of a Woman
Oil on canvas,
14 ⅞ × 11 ⅛ inches
(37.9 × 28.4 cm)
Kröller-Müller Museum,
Otterlo
KM 111.262
F74

Provenance
L. C. Enthoven coll., Voorburg; purchased by H. Kröller-Müller at Enthoven
sale, Amsterdam (Frederik Muller),
May 18, 1920, lot 214: *Portrait de vielle
paysanne.*

Studies of Heads (cats. 9–11)
At the end of 1883, Van Gogh moved back home to stay
with his parents, who had been living in the vicarage at
Nuenen since the previous year. In preparation for
what he anticipated as his career as a figure painter, he
executed many studies of heads — intending to paint
fifty, of which forty-seven are known. He began these
works in October 1884 during the visit of his friend and
fellow painter Anthon van Rappard, who was similarly
engaged in painting character heads, and he continued
until around the time of his father's death in the early spring
of 1885. The subjects of these studies were villagers in
Nuenen, whom Van Gogh depicted — some several times —
as primitive, coarse individuals, with almost animal-like
expressions. Most of them are unidentified, the notable
exception being Gordina de Groot (cat. 10). The paintings
are invariably dark in tone, roughly painted with broad
brushwork, wet-into-wet. About a third of these small
paintings were sent to his brother Theo in Paris.

With its uncompromising technique and direct stare,
this is one of the most arresting of Van Gogh's character
heads. The background varies from a slightly paler
green at left to an impenetrable dark tone at right, and
there is a sense of form and depth here that is unusual
in these studies. The shape of the bulky cap is well defined,
and the face is strikingly constructed in bold highlights
and sharp shadows, with the trademark catchlights in
the eyes. The textured brushstrokes consciously imitate
the wrinkles in the old woman's features.

In 1901 the critic Marie de Roode-Heijermans wrote of these
Nuenen head studies, "Most are painted simply, [they are]
well put together, grand and full of naive sincerity.... There
are some among them with such depth of understanding
and finesse in the reproduction of character that they equal
those of any modern Dutch portraitist."[1] DB

Note
1 Information for this work drawn from Hildelies Balk, Jos ten Berge, et al.,
The Paintings of Vincent van Gogh in the Collection of the Kröller-Müller Museum
(Otterlo: Kröller-Müller Museum, 2003), 86–87.

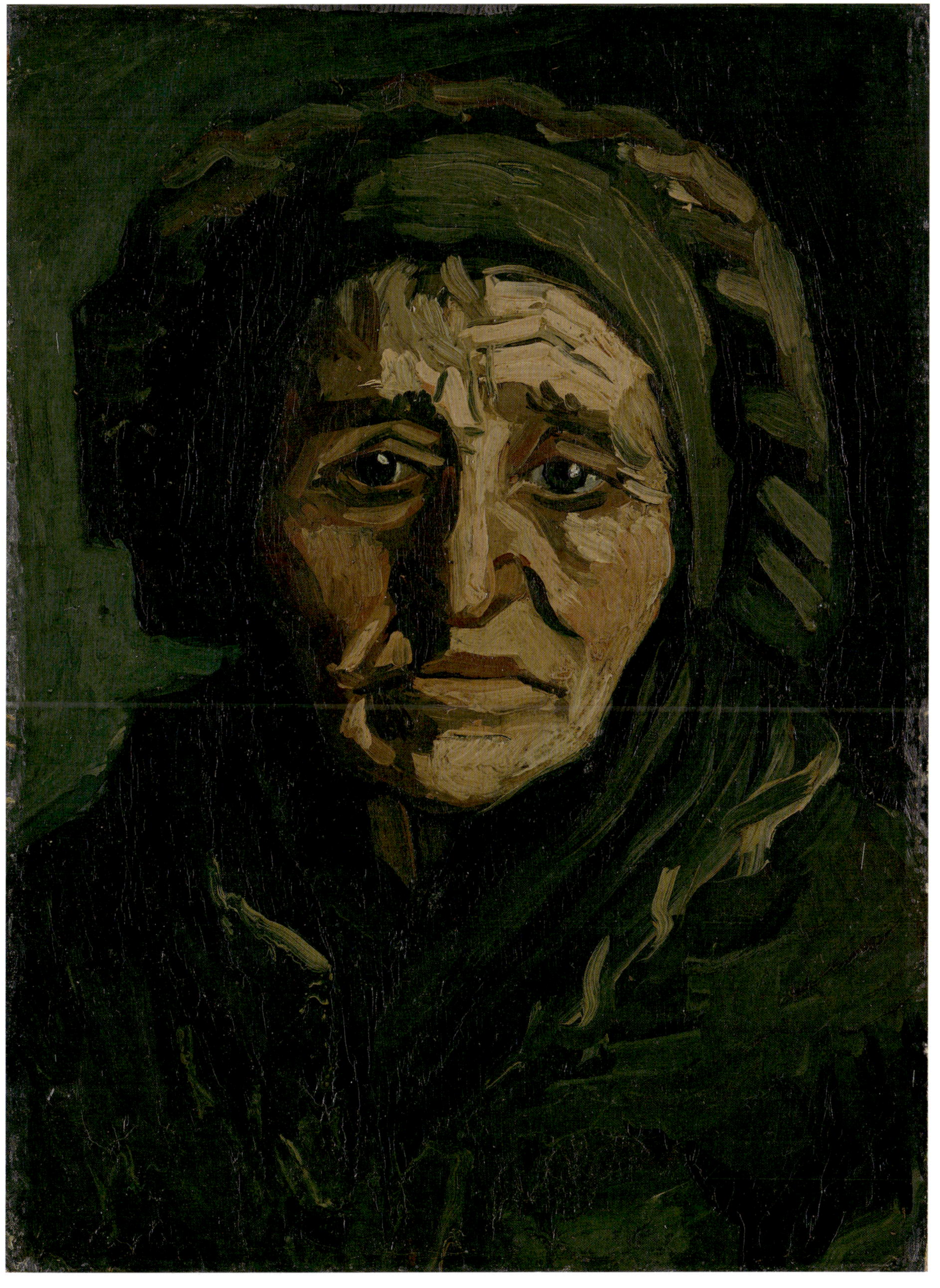

November 1884–May 1885
Nuenen

Cat. 10
Head of a Woman
Wearing a White Cap
Oil on canvas,
17 ⅜ × 14 ⅛ inches
(44 × 35.9 cm)
Kröller-Müller Museum,
Otterlo
KM 100.285
F85

Provenance
Theo van Gogh, Paris, May 5–6, 1885;
A. Aurier coll., Paris; S. Williame-Aurier
coll., Châteauroux, October 5, 1892;
purchased by H. P. Bremmer from J.
Williame, Châteauroux, June 1914;
purchased by H. Kröller-Müller from H.
P. Bremmer, The Hague, April 11, 1917.

This study highlights one of the characteristic white gauze caps worn by the women of Nuenen: usually a dark inner cap protected the head and set off the pattern of the white fabric of the outer cap. Referring to these details, Van Gogh wrote to Anton Kerssemakers, a painting student in Nuenen: "the heads of these women here with the white caps—it's difficult—but it's so eternally beautiful. It's precisely the chiaroscuro—the white and the part of the face in shadow, that has such a fine tone."[1]

The sitter is Gordina de Groot, daughter of a Nuenen farming family. The De Groots were captured in Van Gogh's first masterpiece, *The Potato Eaters*, painted during April 1885 in their dark house at 4 Gerwenseweg (see page 15, fig. 2). He wrote that a long period of preparation was necessary to realize the painting: "it's taken a whole winter of painting studies of heads and hands."[2] He painted Gordina several times, and she is clearly the woman at the left in the final picture. At this moment she was pregnant, which caused difficulties for Van Gogh. When she gave birth, rumors circulated that he was the father of her baby: "A girl that I had frequently painted was about to have a baby and they suspected me, though I had nothing to do with it."[3] The local Catholic priest forbade any of his congregants to pose again for the artist, despite the fact that it soon became known that the father was, in fact, another member of the congregation.

The painting of the cap is detailed and careful, with precise parallel strokes for the pleating of the headband and more animated strokes suggesting the bulk of the outer and upper folds of the material. The rest of the study is painted freely, wet-in-wet, with bold shadows and white highlights on the face and brilliant catchlights in the eyes. The paint surface bears the marks of other canvases, perhaps pressed together when Van Gogh sent the painting, with others from Nuenen, to Theo in Paris around May 5–6, 1885.[4] DB

Notes
1 Letter 478, Vincent van Gogh to Anton Kerssemakers, Nuenen, between January 1 and 8, 1885.

2 Letter 497, Vincent van Gogh to Theo van Gogh, Nuenen, April 30, 1885.

3 Letter 531, Vincent van Gogh to Theo van Gogh, Nuenen, on or about September 2, 1885.

4 See Hildelies Balk, Jos ten Berge, et al., *The Paintings of Vincent van Gogh in the Collection of the Kröller-Müller Museum* (Otterlo: Kröller-Müller Museum, 2003), 88–91.

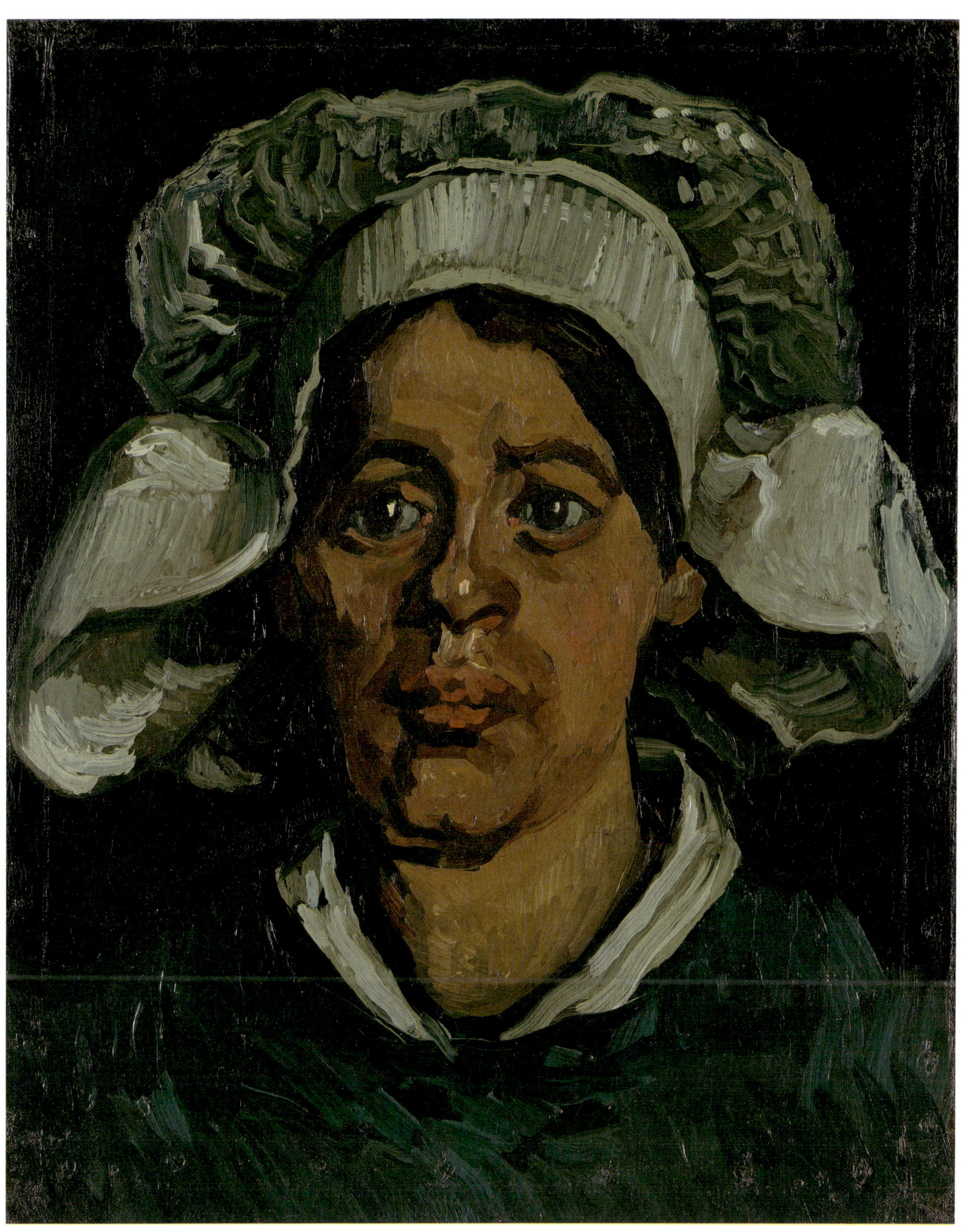

Cat. 11
Head of a Woman
Oil on canvas on panel,
9 ⅞ × 7 ½ inches
(25.1 × 19 cm)
Kröller-Müller Museum,
Otterlo
KM 107.308
F153

Provenance
A. C. van Gogh-Carbentus, Nuenen/
Breda, November 1885/April 1886; A.
Schrauwen, Breda, 1886; J. C. and J. M.
Covreur, Breda; W. van Bakel and C.
Mouwen, Breda, 1902; Oldenzeel, art
dealer, Rotterdam; W. H. C. Bolleurs,
Rotterdam; purchased by H. Kröller-
Müller at sale of several provenances
(the widow of M. C. Calkoen,
Amsterdam, dowager Jhr. A. W. Witsen,
The Hague), Amsterdam (Frederik
Muller), November 25–26, 1913, lot 119.

In early March 1885, Van Gogh wrote to Theo that he was concentrating on the effects of light and particularly "figures against the light of a window."[1] This seems to be one of those studies, an exercise in managing detail in dark tones against a light background. In the same letter to Theo, Vincent also wrote, "It's not redundant to point out that one of the most important achievements of the painters of this century has been to paint a darkness that is nonetheless color."[2]

Van Gogh painted this woman several times, although her name is not recorded. Here, she is wearing an under-cap, similar to the one below the white gauze in the Gordina de Groot study (cat. 10). The painting is very rapidly worked, with the head laid in quickly with pinkish accents, and the light background painted around it. The lighter line along the edge of the face and cap is caused by the buildup of pale paint as Van Gogh moved his loaded brush around the profile. Some odd details are left uncorrected, such as the too-narrow neck rendered in light tones. Van Gogh valued a spontaneous touch and avoided reworking such studies.[3] He would later say about another group of works, "If I keep them here too long, I'm bound to start working on them again, and I think it's better you should receive them, as it were, straight from the field."[4] DB

Notes
1 Letter 495, Vincent van Gogh to Theo van Gogh, Nuenen, April 21, 1885.

2 Ibid.

3 See Hildelies Balk, Jos ten Berge, et al., *The Paintings of Vincent van Gogh in the Collection of the Kröller-Müller Museum* (Otterlo: Kröller-Müller Museum, 2003), 94–95.

4 Letter 515, Vincent van Gogh to Theo van Gogh, Nuenen, on or about July 14, 1885.

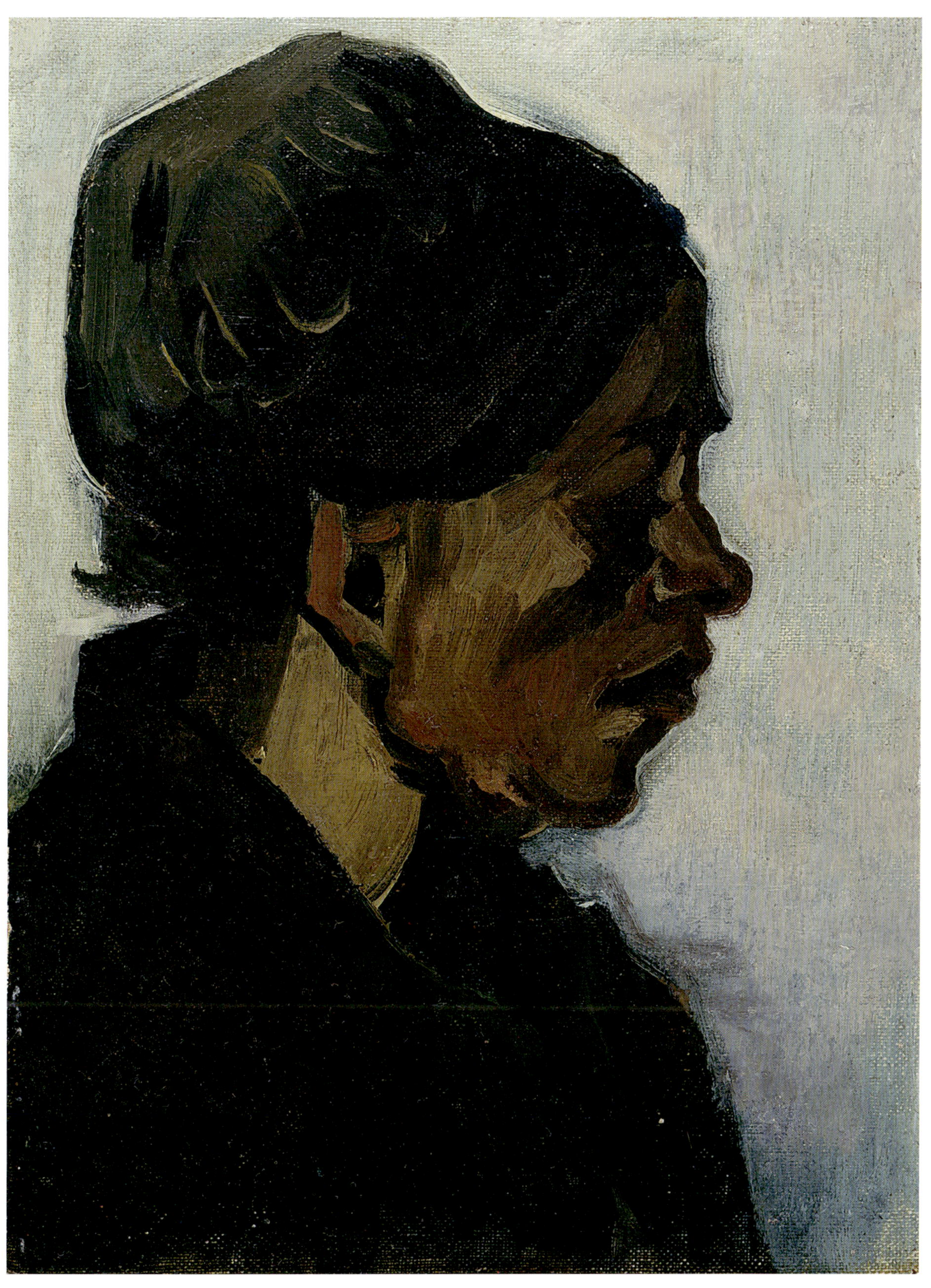

**Late May–early June 1885
Nuenen**

Cat. 12
*The Old Church Tower at Nuenen
("The Peasants' Churchyard")*
Oil on canvas,
25 ⅝ × 31 ½ inches (65 × 80 cm)
Van Gogh Museum,
Amsterdam
(Vincent van Gogh Foundation)
s2V1962
F84

Provenance
Sent by the artist to Theo van Gogh,
Paris, early June 1885; Jo van Gogh-
Bonger and Vincent Willem van Gogh,
Paris, January 25, 1891; administered
by Jo van Gogh-Bonger, Bussum/
Amsterdam/Laren, until September 2,
1925; on loan to the Rijksmuseum,
Amsterdam, 1917–19; on loan from
Vincent Willem van Gogh, Laren,
to the Stedelijk Museum, Amsterdam,
December 16, 1930; transferred to
the Vincent van Gogh Foundation,
Amsterdam, July 10, 1962; agreement
July 21, 1962, entrusts collection to
the State of the Netherlands until
realization of the Rijksmuseum Vincent
van Gogh, Amsterdam; on loan to
Stedelijk Museum, Amsterdam, until
opening of Rijksmuseum Vincent
van Gogh; Rijksmuseum Vincent van
Gogh, Amsterdam, June 2, 1973; Van
Gogh Museum, Amsterdam, July 1, 1994.

The old medieval church, just outside the village of Nuenen, could be seen from the vicarage where Van Gogh's parents lived. When he arrived, it was already being demolished but still had its spire and part of the churchyard wall, which he recorded in earlier studies in 1884. By the time he painted this picture, both of those had gone, and the tower itself was about to be torn down. At the beginning of June, he wrote, "The old church tower will be pulled down next week! The spire is already gone — I'm working on a painting of it."[1] By the end of June, the demolition was complete. He began to depict the tower from the other side, but, since this angle did not work, he scraped it down and returned to the vantage point he had taken in his earlier study; traces of the scraped-down composition are visible below the surface of the present painting.

This was one of Van Gogh's first major paintings, concentrating, like the slightly earlier *Potato Eaters*, on the remote, primitive peasant world that fascinated him. He described his thoughts on the symbolism of the painting:

I wanted to say how that ruin shows that for centuries peasants have been laid to rest in the same fields in which they toil during their life — I wanted to express how perfectly simple death and burial is, as simple as the falling of the autumn leaves — just some earth dug up — a little wooden cross. The fields around — they make a final line against the horizon, where the grass of the churchyard ends — like the horizon of a sea. And now this ruin tells me how a creed and a religion have moldered away, even though they were so well established — how, nevertheless, the life and death of the peasants is and remains the same: always sprouting and withering like the grass and the flowers that are growing in this graveyard.[2]

The "peasants' churchyard" had special significance for Van Gogh: his own father, Theodorus van Gogh, had been buried there on March 30, 1885, just before the painting of this picture.[3] DB

Notes

1 Letter 506, Vincent van Gogh to Theo van Gogh, Nuenen, on or about June 2, 1885.

2 Letter 507, Vincent van Gogh to Theo van Gogh, Nuenen, on or about June 9, 1885.

3 See Louis van Tilborgh and Marije Vellekoop, *Vincent van Gogh Paintings*, vol. 1, *Dutch Period 1881–1885, Van Gogh Museum* (Amsterdam and Blaricum: Van Gogh Museum/V+R Publishing, 1999), 152–59, cat. 28.

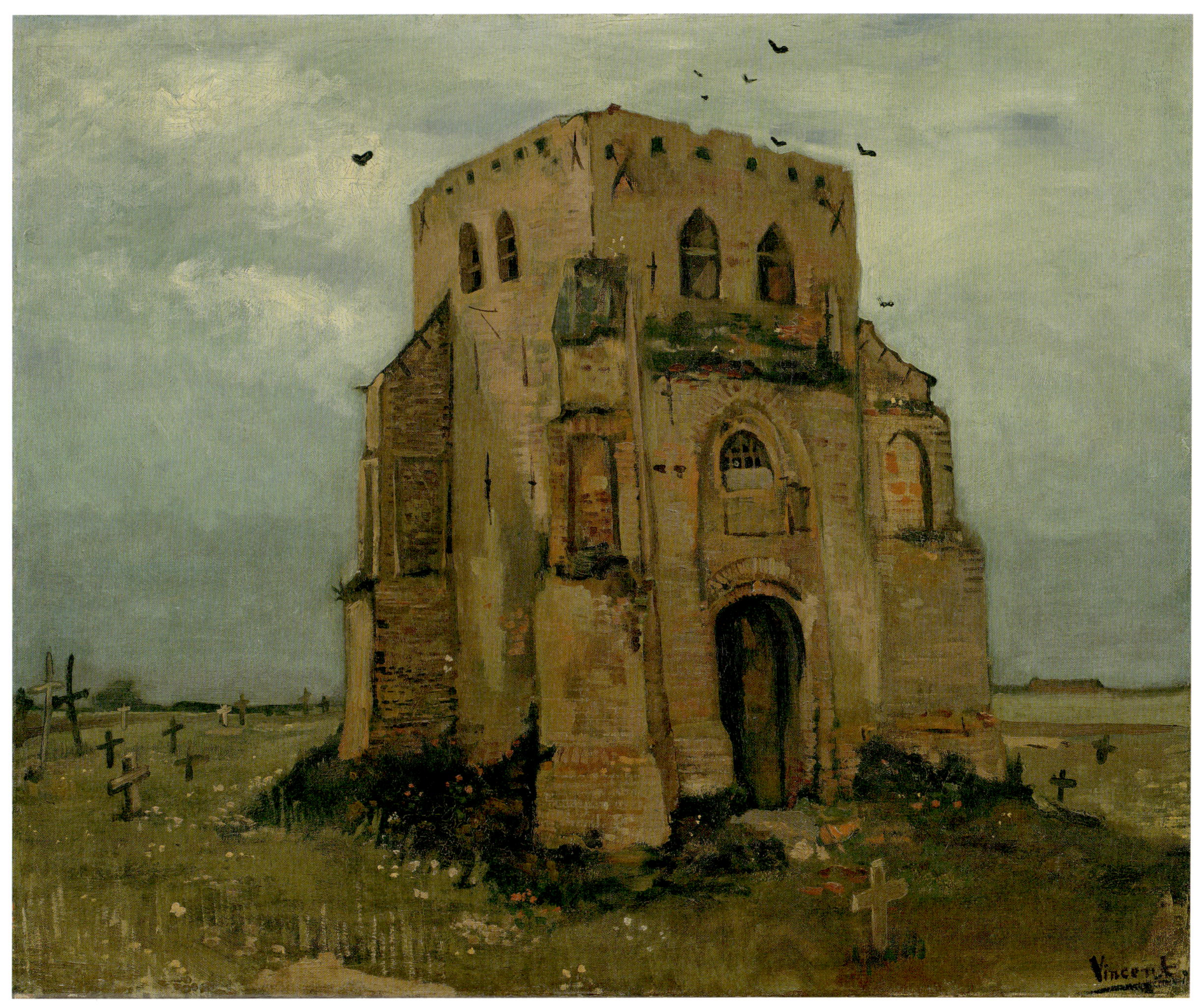

June 1885
Nuenen

Cat. 13
Cottage
Oil on canvas, 13 ⅞ × 26 ⅜ inches
(35.5 × 67 cm)
Private collection, Houston
F91

Provenance
Private collection since at least 1990.

Vincent van Gogh's father was appointed pastor of the Reformed Church in Nuenen, a village in North Brabant in 1882. Known today as Van Gogh Village Nuenen, it became a significant site in Van Gogh's artistic development.[1] With all previous attempts at finding a suitable career having ended in failure, he was forced to accept living there with his parents in late 1883. Although his relationship with his father was particularly fraught, his living arrangements did allow him the opportunity to devote himself entirely to painting, and his output of 195 paintings, 313 drawings, and 25 watercolors produced during the two years at Nuenen is considerable. Many of his paintings depict peasants, including *Head of a Woman Wearing a White Cap* (cat. 10) and two heads of older women (cats. 9 and 11). His efforts to capture their simple lives culminated in his early masterpiece, *The Potato Eaters*, dated 1885 and today in the Van Gogh Museum, Amsterdam (see page 15, fig. 2). He felt strongly that, like his role model Jean-François Millet, "one must paint the peasants as if one were one of them, as feeling, thinking as they do themselves. . . . I so often think that the peasants are a world in themselves, so much better in many respects than the civilized world."[2]

Van Gogh painted at least fourteen different sites of Nuenen, including its churches, his father's rectory, the churchyard, as well as many of its cottages. Some of the cottages are quite impressive, but this one is a simple, low building whose whitewashed wall is punctuated by two windows and a door. A short chimney stack rises a little above the thatched roof, a material typical of Dutch cottages of this period. The viewpoint Van Gogh chose allows a part of the farmyard to be visible in the foreground as well as space to either side of the cottage. Eleven trees, some very young and with little foliage, are rhythmically spaced from left to right, enlivening the entire canvas. The tonality is quite muted, typical for Van Gogh's works from Nuenen, in which browns and earth colors dominate, evoking an Old-Masterly air.
HKA

Notes
1 www.vangoghvillagenuenen.nl/van-gogh_eng/van-gogh-in-nuenen_eng.aspx.

2 Letter 497, Vincent van Gogh to Theo van Gogh, Nuenen, April 30, 1885.

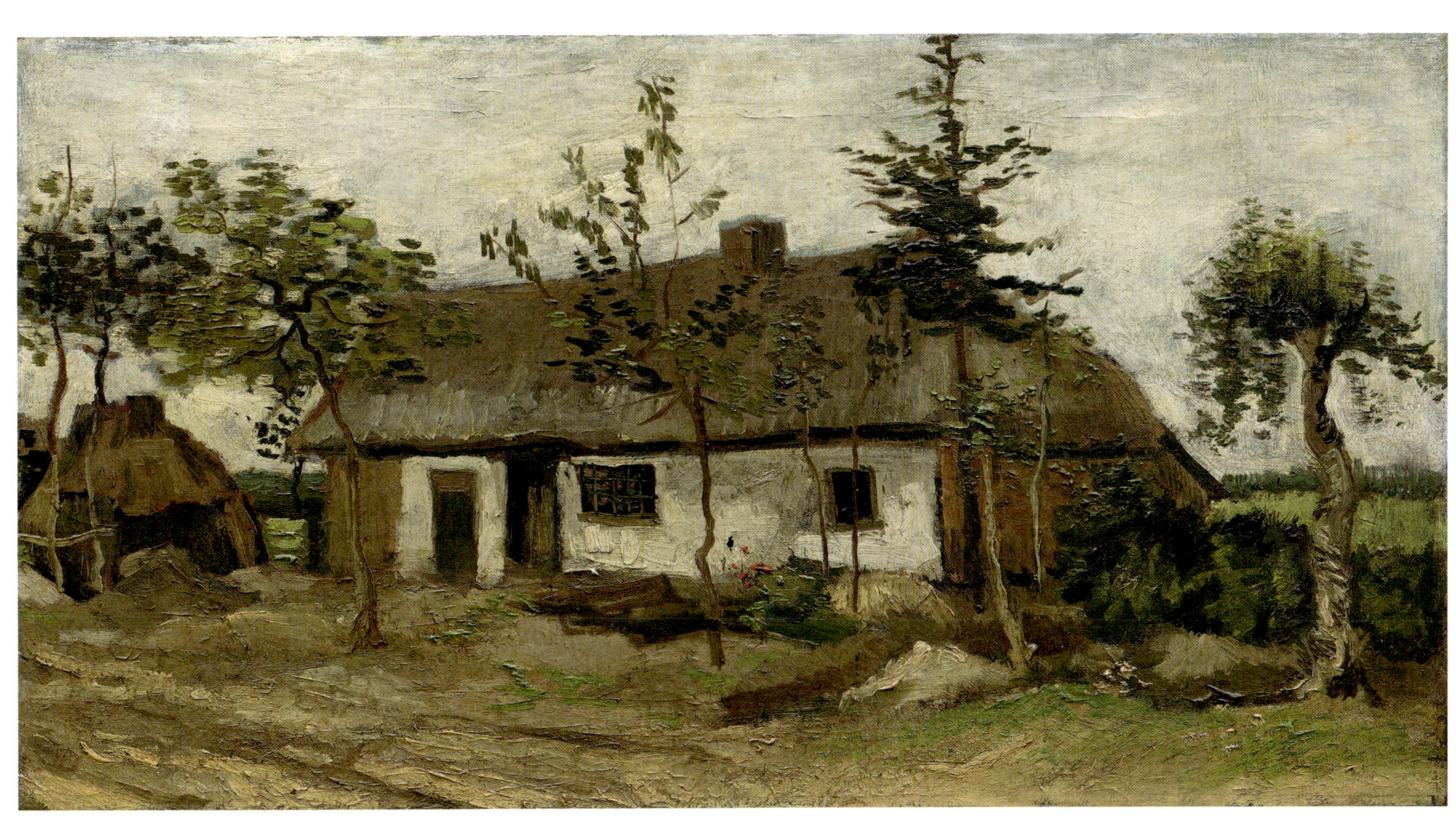

July–August 1885
Nuenen

Cat. 14
Reaper
Black chalk and grayish
white opaque watercolor on
wove paper,
22⅛ × 14⅞ inches
(56.2 × 37.8 cm)
Kröller-Müller Museum,
Otterlo
KM 121.581
F1313

Provenance
Acquired by Hidde Nijland, Dordrecht,
before 1904; purchased from Hidde
Nijland by A. G. Kröller, the Hague, July
1928; donated to the Kröller-Müller
Foundation by A. G. Kröller, December
1928.

In 1884, one year before he made this drawing, Van Gogh wrote to his brother Theo, "To me, *Millet*, not Manet, is that essential modern painter who opened the horizon to many."[1] He continued to follow in the footsteps of Jean-François Millet while living in rural Nuenen, where he had moved to live with his parents in December 1883 after residing in The Hague and in the eastern province of Drenthe. The artist was excited to draw the subjects of the harvest there: he would have his models pose for him at his home or studio as if engaging in their myriad undertakings, and he would then go into the fields to personally experience and participate in these activities, including reaping and gleaning. He intended not only to use these as preparatory drawings for paintings but also to create a series of all the laborers of the field, possibly connecting them to the twelve months of the year. Van Gogh may have taken his inspiration from a twelve-month series of rustic scenes by another French Realist painter, Léon-Augustin Lhermitte.[2]

He looked to the drawings of the Romantic artist Eugène Delacroix for instruction, wanting his figures to be less flat and linear and more volumetric.[3] This large-scale figure is drawn with thick strokes of black chalk. He is harvesting wheat using a reaping hook to gather the stalks and then cut them with a short-handled scythe. Van Gogh considered reaping wheat to be "certainly almost the most beautiful of all."[4] *Reaper* was the counterpart to *Sower* in his oeuvre. Whereas the sower disseminated the seeds to propagate the earth, the reaper was viewed as the figure of death, and the corn that he gleans represented humanity. DMW

Notes
1 Letter 428, Vincent van Gogh to Theo van Gogh, Nuenen, on or about February 3, 1884.

2 See Sjraar van Heugten, *Vincent van Gogh: Drawings*, vol. 2, *Nuenen, 1883–1885, Van Gogh Museum* (Amsterdam and Zwolle: Van Gogh Museum/Waanders, 1997), 237–39.

3 See Sjraar van Heugten with Marije Vellekoop and Roelie Zwikker, *Van Gogh: Master Draughtsman* (New York: Harry N. Abrams, 2005), 68–71.

4 See letter 522, Vincent van Gogh to Theo van Gogh, Nuenen, July 29, 1885; Teio Meedendorp, *Drawings and Prints by Vincent van Gogh in the Collection of the Kröller-Müller Museum* (Otterlo: Kröller-Müller Museum, 2007), 312.

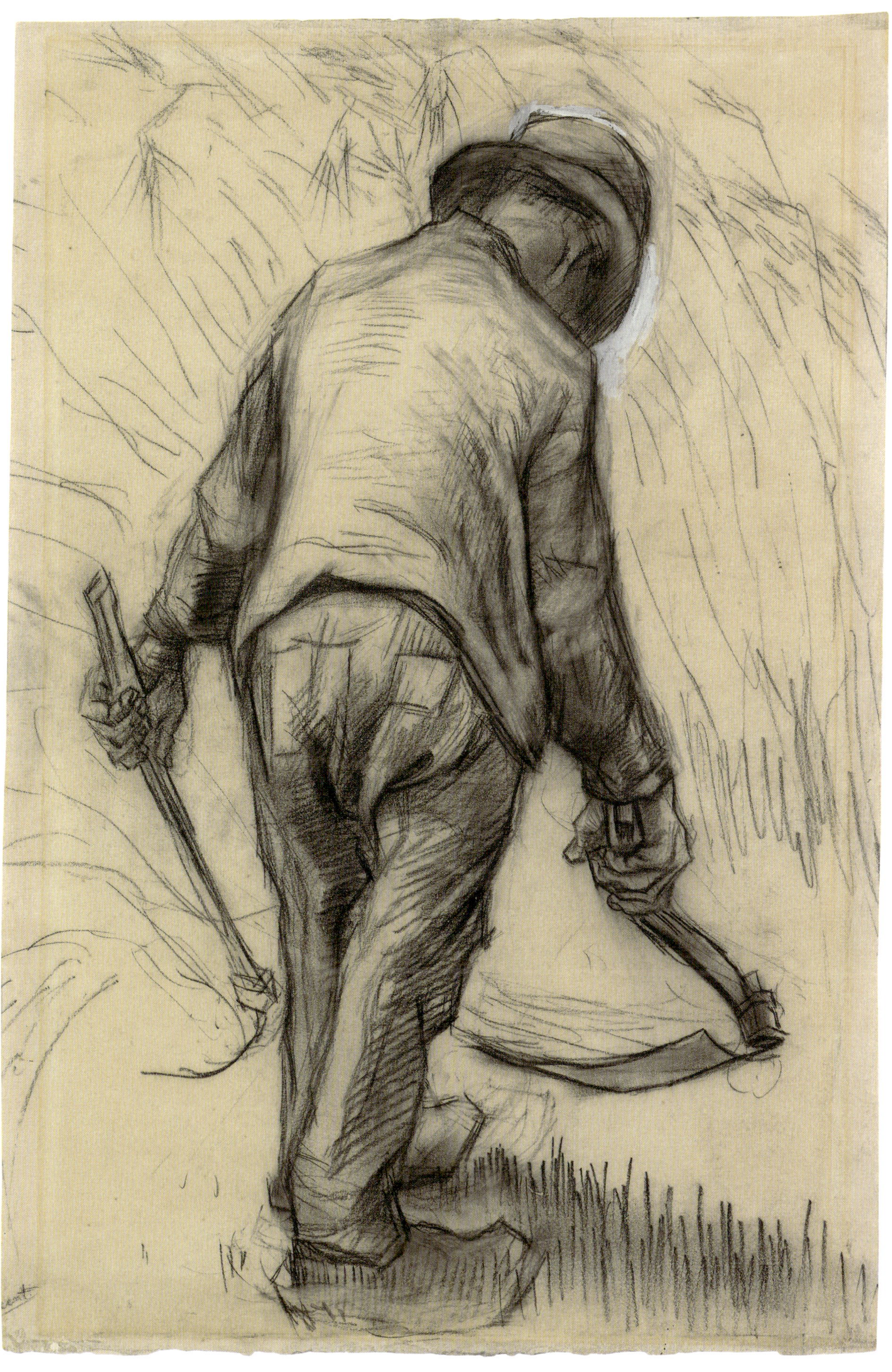

July–August 1885
Nuenen

Cat. 15
Peasant Woman Cleaning a Pot
Black chalk with traces
of fixative (splashed on)
on wove paper,
21 ⅜ × 17 ¼ inches
(54.5 × 43.8 cm)
Kröller-Müller Museum,
Otterlo
KM 117.859
F1282

Provenance
Acquired by Hidde Nijland, Dordrecht,
before 1904; purchased from Hidde
Nijland by A. G. Kröller, The Hague, July
1928; donated to the Kröller-Muller
Foundation by A. G. Kröller, December
1928.

Notes
1 Letter 515, Vincent van Gogh to Theo van Gogh, Nuenen, on or about
July 14, 1885; see Siraar van Heugten, *Vincent van Gogh: Drawings*, vol. 2,
Nuenen 1883–1885, Van Gogh Museum (Amsterdam: Van Gogh Museum;
London: Lund Humphries, 1997), 11.

2 See Sjraar van Heugten with Marije Vellekoop and Roelie Zwikker,
Van Gogh: Master Draughtsman (New York: Harry N. Abrams, 2005), 21;
and Teio Meedendorp, *Drawings and Prints by Vincent van Gogh in the
Collection of the Kröller-Müller Museum*, 2nd ed. (Amsterdam: University
Press, 2009), 340.

3 Some of Van Gogh's graphite drawings from 1884–85 were known to
have been treated with milk to make the images darker and more matte
as well as to fix them. See Van Heugten, *Vincent van Gogh Drawings*, vol. 2,
23, 239.

4 See letters 160, 164, 166, and 168, Vincent van Gogh to Theo van Gogh,
Brussels, November 1, 1880, and April 2, 1881, and Etten, on or about
April 30 or May 1, 1881, and end of June 1881, respectively. See also Armand
T. Cassagne, *Traité d'aquarelle* (1875), and John Gage, *Color and Culture:
Practice and Meaning from Antiquity to Abstraction* (Berkeley and Los
Angeles: University of California Press, 1993), 205.

5 See Lee Hendrix, ed., *Noir: The Romance of Black in 19th-Century French
Drawings and Prints* (Los Angeles: The J. Paul Getty Museum, 2016),
51–66.

Van Gogh recorded peasant life while in Nuenen, where he painted his famed *Potato Eaters* (1885), and he believed that his contribution to modern art was "showing the figure of the peasant in action."[1] This included representing not only people working in the fields but also indoor activities such as weaving and women occupied with household chores. Anton Mauve had taught him to not focus on specifics — faces, hands, clothing — arguing that would be too distracting. Instead, he wanted Van Gogh to step back and assess the figures' proportions, giving a more general view.[2]

Van Gogh used strokes of black chalk to draw this peasant woman bending over to clean the lid of a pot. A kettle and basket are summarily sketched beside her. Although Van Gogh commonly used a pencil for drawing early in his career, he had begun sketching by 1885 in black chalk. Its gestural ease and the ability to produce thin as well as broad, soft lines appealed to his freer, spontaneous style. As in this example, he would use fixative on his drawings to better preserve them, prevent them from smudging, and at times increase the darkness of the lines.[3]

In the early 1880s, the artist Anthon van Rappard, who shared his Brussels studio with Van Gogh for a short while, introduced him to Armand Cassagne's handbook *Traité d'aquarelle* (1875). For Cassagne, black was "the most fundamental color in nature," and the three primary colors could form an infinite array of grays, which were an important aspect of Van Gogh's palette in Holland.[4] Black also evoked the rusticity and poverty of the rural existence, furthering Van Gogh's kinship to the Realist tradition and his influencers, Jean-François Millet and the prominent *fusainiste* Léon-Augustin Lhermitte.[5] DMW

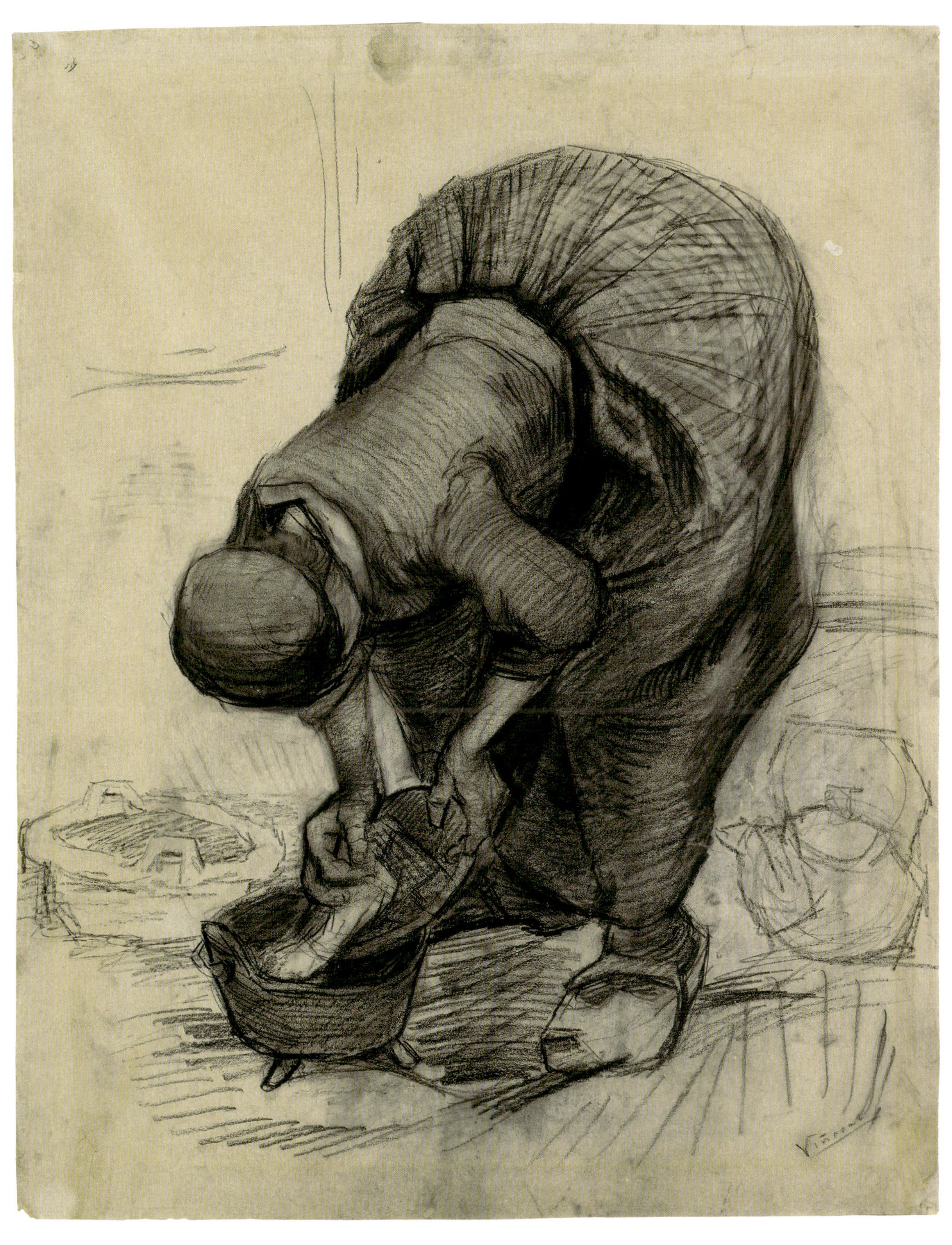

Cat. 16
Portrait of a Prostitute
Oil on canvas,
18 ¼ × 15 ⅛ inches
(46.3 × 38.5 cm)
Van Gogh Museum,
Amsterdam
(Vincent van Gogh Foundation)
s143V1962
F207a

Provenance
Theo van Gogh, Paris, after December
1885; Jo van Gogh-Bonger and Vincent
Willem van Gogh, Paris, January 25,
1891; administered by Jo van Gogh-
Bonger, Bussum/Amsterdam/Laren,
until September 2, 1925; donated by
Vincent Willem van Gogh to the (first)
Vincent van Gogh Foundation, Laren,
March 11, 1952; transferred to the
Theo van Gogh Foundation, Laren,
December 28, 1960; agreement July 21,
1962, entrusts collection to the State of
the Netherlands until realization of
the Rijksmuseum Vincent van Gogh,
Amsterdam; donated July 21, 1962,
by the Theo van Gogh Foundation
to the (second) Vincent van Gogh
Foundation; on loan to Stedelijk
Museum, Amsterdam, until opening
of Rijksmuseum Vincent van Gogh;
Rijksmuseum Vincent van Gogh,
Amsterdam, June 2, 1973; Van Gogh
Museum, Amsterdam, July 1, 1994.

Both the subject matter and the lighter tonality of this portrait would seem to indicate that it was made during Van Gogh's time in Paris, 1886–88. However, this work in fact dates to his earlier period in Antwerp, where he had arrived in November 1885, and was probably painted shortly there-after.[1] Van Gogh actively sought out models among the city's prostitutes. He explained his multiple reasons for doing so to his brother Theo: he lacked the funds to hire proper mod-els, but also he felt that painting these "working girls" would give him a chance to practice portraiture, "to get a whore's expression when I paint whores," and furthermore would allow him to posit himself among the Realist painters.[2] These explanations seem somewhat disingenuous given that Van Gogh, while living in The Hague between 1882 and 1883, had had a long affair with a former prostitute named Sien Hoornik, whom he had drawn and painted repeatedly.[3]

There is no obvious indication that the woman portrayed here in three-quarter profile, wearing a light blue dress with a modest décolleté, a small cross on a gold chain around her neck, and a little dangling earring, is a prostitute. Her hair is worn in a chignon in a very proper fashion, and her ex-pression, though somewhat puzzled, is not wanton. Only her bright red lips and her painted eyelids, unthinkable at this time for "decent" women, point to her "fallen" state.

The painting has all the hallmarks of having been executed very swiftly, wet-in-wet, probably within a matter of hours.[4] Van Gogh's new predilection for cobalt blue is evident, as the color dominates the background and recurs in a lighter tone in the woman's dress. The brushstrokes are energetic and the impasto heavy, especially in the flesh tones of the head and neck. The face is rendered with great sympathy for this woman, very characteristic of Van Gogh's deep-seated empathy for the lowest and the poorest, which had informed his love for Sien as well as his ministry among the miners of the Borinage in Belgium. HKA

Notes
1 Louis van Tilborgh and Ella Hendriks, *Vincent van Gogh Paintings*, vol. 2, *Antwerp and Paris, 1885–1888, Van Gogh Museum* (Amsterdam and Zwolle: Van Gogh Museum/Waanders, 2011), 171, cat. 47.

2 Letter 550, Vincent van Gogh to Theo van Gogh, Antwerp, December 28, 1885.

3 Steven W. Naifeh and Gregory White Smith, *Van Gogh: The Life* (New York: Random House, 2011), 278–303.

4 Van Tilborgh and Hendriks, *Vincent van Gogh Paintings*, vol. 2, 174.

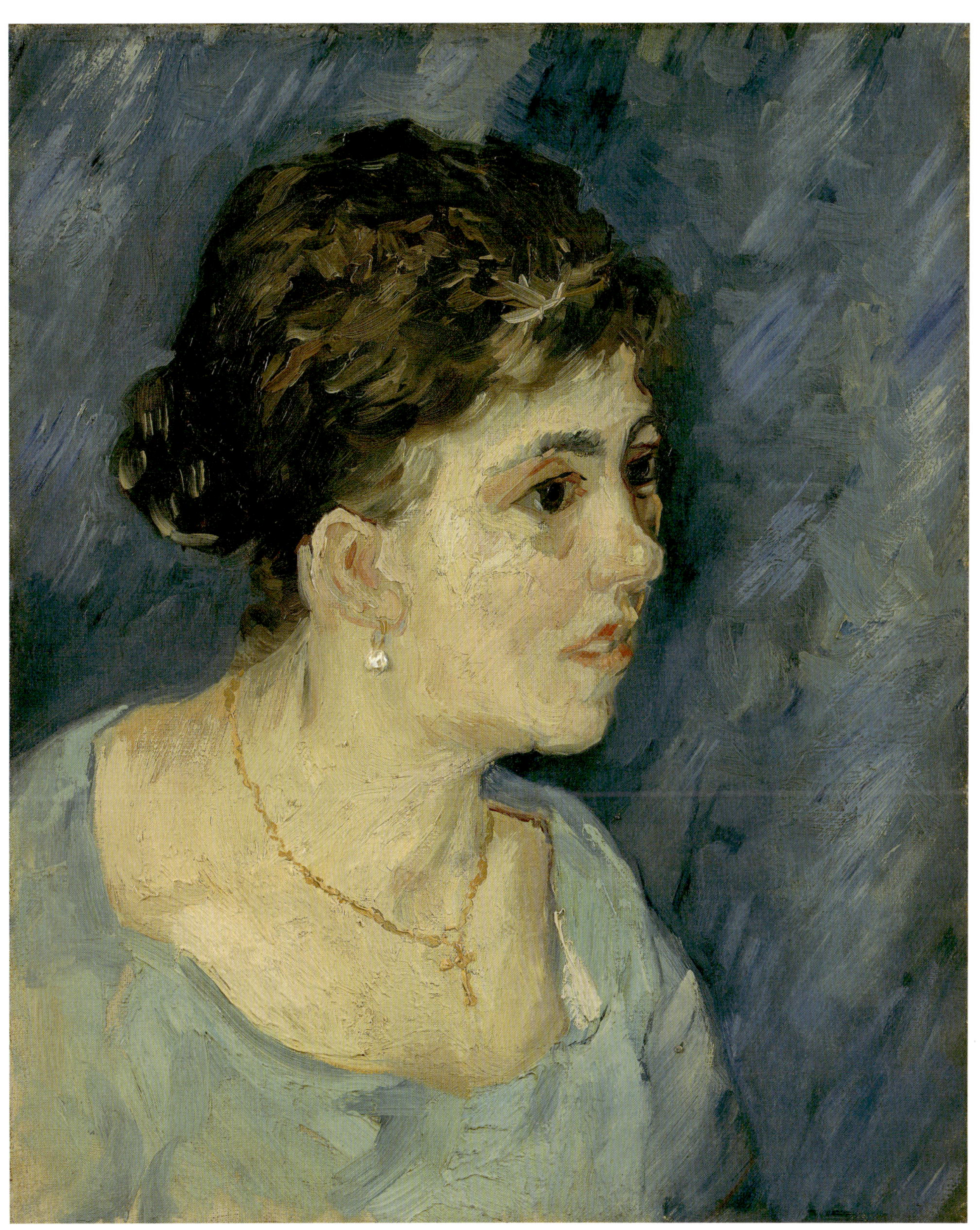

April–May 1886
Paris

Cat. 17
The Hill of Montmartre
Oil on canvas,
15 × 24 inches (38.1 × 61.1 cm)
Kröller-Müller Museum,
Otterlo
KM 109.824
F266

Provenance
Eugène Blot, art dealer, Paris; purchased
by H. Kröller-Müller at Blot, art dealer,
1912.

1886
Paris

Cat. 18
The Hill of Montmartre
Black chalk with a brown tinge
on laid paper,
15 × 18 ¾ inches (31.8 × 47.8 cm)
Van Gogh Museum,
Amsterdam
(Vincent van Gogh Foundation)
d151V1962
F1398

Provenance
Left by the artist at the apartment of Theo
van Gogh, Paris, sometime between March
and April 1886; Jo van Gogh-Bonger, and
Vincent Willem van Gogh, Paris, January
25, 1891; administered by Jo van Gogh-
Bonger, Bussum/Amsterdam/Laren, until
September 2, 1925; transferred by Vincent
Willem van Gogh, Laren, to the Vincent
van Gogh Foundation, Amsterdam, July 10,
1962; agreement July 21, 1962, entrusts collection to the State of the Netherlands until
realization of the Rijksmuseum Vincent
van Gogh, Amsterdam; on loan to Stedelijk
Museum, Amsterdam, until opening of
Rijksmuseum Vincent van Gogh; Rijksmuseum Vincent van Gogh, Amsterdam, June
2, 1973; Van Gogh Museum, Amsterdam,
July 1, 1994.

Van Gogh arrived in Paris from Antwerp on February 28, 1885. He stayed with Theo, first in a small apartment on the rue Laval and then, a few months later, in larger accommodations on the rue Lepic, halfway up the hill of Montmartre. He had lived in Montmartre ten years before, when working for the fine art and print dealers Goupil & Cie, but during that period he spent most of his time in his room reading the Bible. Now, he frequented the bars and cafés, socializing with fellow artists, and drawing and painting the city around him. On the fourth floor of the building, the new apartment commanded splendid views of Paris, which Van Gogh painted in a colorful impressionistic style. In the other direction, he would often walk around the hill to the northern slope, where he would see this view of vegetable gardens, the long building of the Ferme Debray, and the three windmills along the skyline: from left to right, the Radet, the Moulin à Poivre, and the Blute-Fin (also known as the Moulin de la Galette and owned by the Debray family since 1809).

The windmills of Montmartre had been a popular subject for artists for decades before Van Gogh saw them. In 1840 Camille Corot painted *Moulin de la Galette à Montmartre*. Vincent said to Theo that he wanted to use his Paris stay to study the "technique and coloration of Millet, Delacroix, Corot and others," and Corot's quiet, measured style seems to have been a major influence in the painting of this picture, with its Barbizon tonality and autumnal feel.[1] Van Gogh also owned a series of nine views of Montmartre by the engraver Auguste Delâtre, published in the journal *L'Artiste* in 1886, which are said to have been his direct source of inspiration.

He depicted this side of Montmartre several times from different vantage points in both paintings and drawings. The present drawing was once considered a later copy of the painting, but recent research has connected it to a newly dis-covered drawing in identical style that was in the collection of Theo and his wife, Jo van Gogh-Bonger. It is now securely attributed to Van Gogh's hand and is clearly a detailed pre-liminary study for the painting.[2] DB

Notes
1 Letter 506, Vincent van Gogh to Theo van Gogh, Nuenen, on or about June 2, 1885.

2 See Hildelies Balk, Jos ten Berge, et al., *The Paintings of Vincent van Gogh in the Collection of the Kröller-Müller Museum* (Otterlo: Kröller-Müller Museum, 2003), 140–42, and Sjraar van Heugten and Marije Vellekoop, *Vincent van Gogh Drawings*, vol. 3, *Antwerp and Paris, 1885–1888, Van Gogh Museum* (Amsterdam: Van Gogh Museum; London: Lund Humphries, 2001), 327–29 (listed as a rejected work).

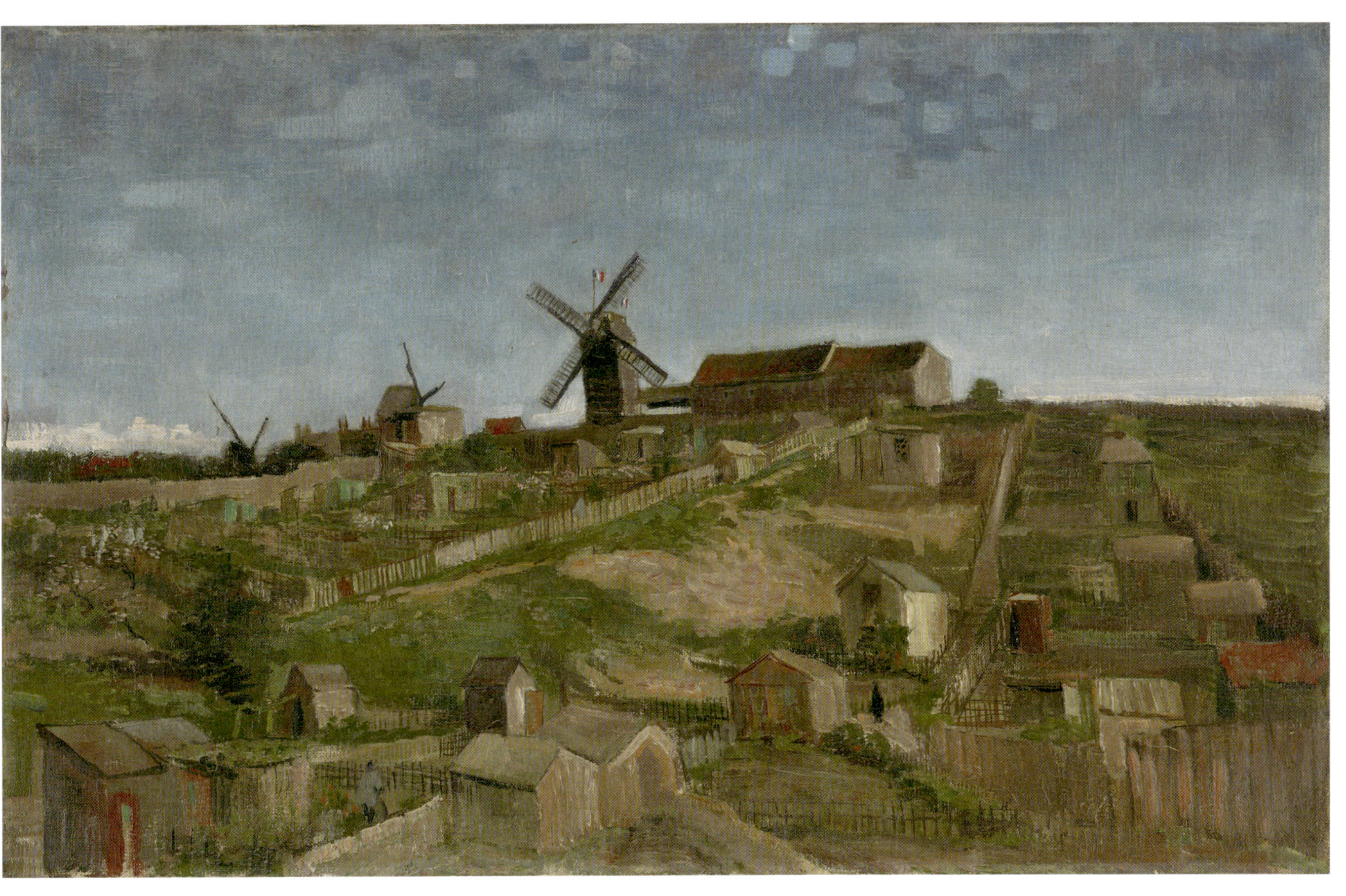

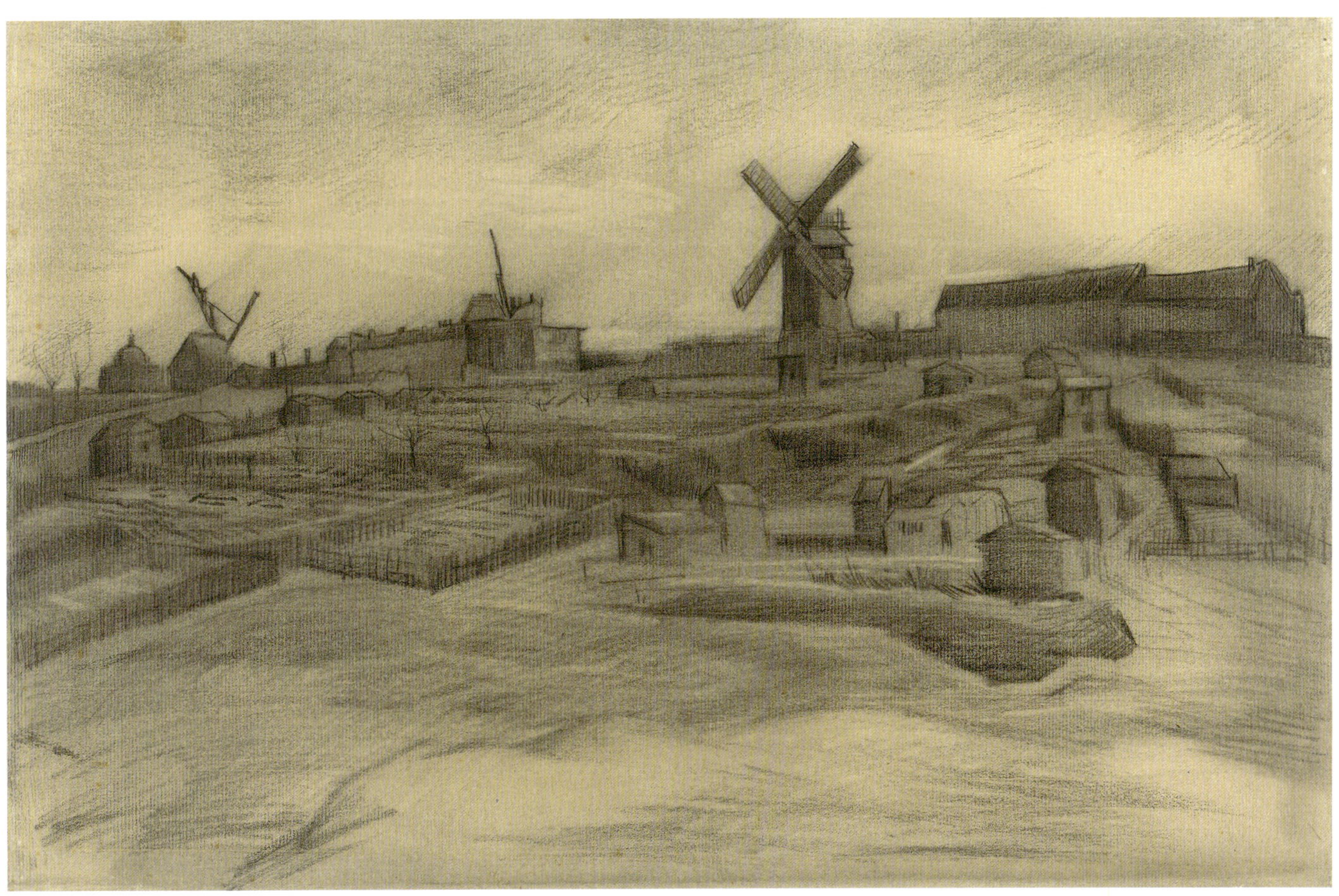

June 1886
Paris

Cat. 19
Roses and Peonies
Oil on canvas,
23 ½ × 28 ½ inches
(59.8 × 72.5 cm)
Kröller-Müller Museum,
Otterlo
KM 109.371
F249

Provenance
A. C. van Gogh-Carbentus; heirs A. C. van Gogh-Carbentus (kept by Jo van Gogh-Bonger, Amsterdam), April 29, 1907; purchased by A. G. Kröller at sale Frederik Muller; Amsterdam, possibly c. 1909; purchased by Kröller-Müller Museum from A. G. Kröller's estate, May 14, 1941.

Flower still lifes played a decisive role in the pivotal change that Van Gogh's style underwent during his years in Paris, 1886–88. His production could be described as feverish — he painted at least thirty of these works during the summer of 1886 alone — and this painting is believed to be one of the earliest of that group.[1] As his brother Theo wrote to their mother in July of that year, he strongly hoped that, by painting these still lifes, Vincent would "make his works fresher in color."[2] By this date, a general appreciation of the lighter palettes of the Impressionists had set in, and the dark tones of his early works seemed old-fashioned and out of step with the avant-garde. Van Gogh's first exposure to works by the Impressionists and Pointillists dates to this period, but rather than just imitating them, he delved into the field of color theory, focusing in particular on the ideas of Charles Blanc, which informed their works.[3] However, Van Gogh was also aware of the importance of the theories developed by Eugène Delacroix, whom he admired as a great colorist.

This lovely bouquet of roses and peonies is an outstanding example of Van Gogh's reaction to these theories. Red and green, the opposites on the color wheel of primary and secondary colors, dominate this composition. The dark red background and cool green of the tabletop echo the colors of the flowers and the earthenware jug. Unfortunately, the red of the blossoms, probably executed with red lake pigments made of organic dyes, has faded considerably, mitigating the resounding color contrasts that had been so typical of Delacroix's works. This still life, as well as three others, document Adolphe Monticelli's powerful influence on Van Gogh, who highly regarded the works of that little-known and probably mad painter. In particular, he imitated Monticelli's heavy use of impasto, developing it into his own characteristic style. The high ridges of paint and the sculptural quality of his brushwork would eventually become a hallmark of his painting. HKA

Notes
1 Hildelies Balk, Jos ten Berge, et al., *The Paintings of Vincent van Gogh in the Collection of the Kröller-Müller Museum* (Otterlo: Kröller-Müller Museum, 2003), 143.

2 Jan Hulsker, *Van Gogh in Close-Up* (Amsterdam: Meulenhoff, 1993), 81.

3 Charles Blanc, *Grammaire des arts du dessin, architecture, sculpture, peinture* (Paris: Librairie Renouard, 1876).

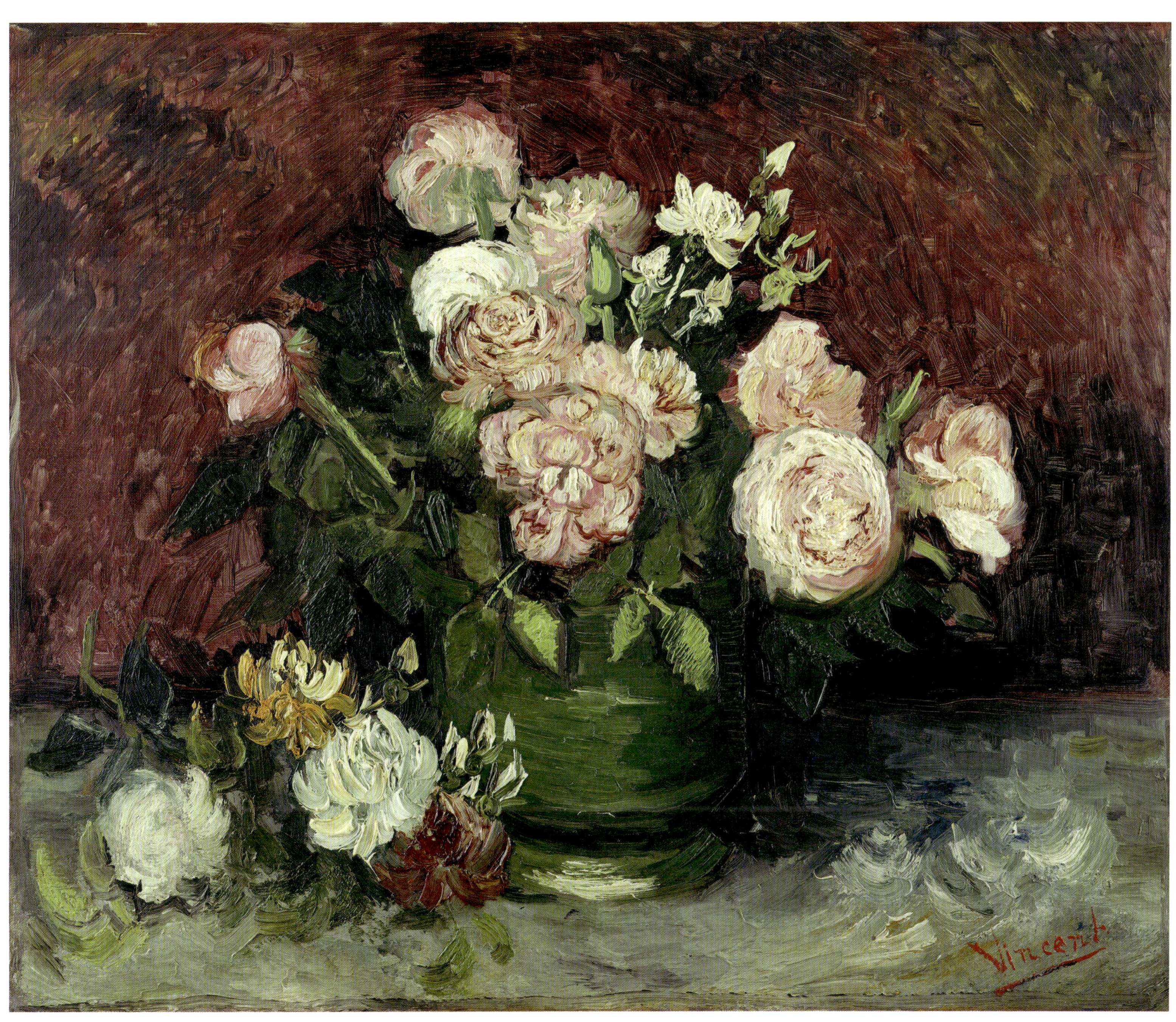

Cat. 20
*Vase with Gladioli and
Chinese Asters*
Oil on canvas,
18 ¼ × 15 ⅛ inches
(46.5 × 38.4 cm)
Van Gogh Museum,
Amsterdam
(Vincent van Gogh Foundation)
s144V1962
F248a

Provenance
Left by the artist at the apartment of
Theo van Gogh, Paris, sometime between
August–mid-September 1886; Jo van
Gogh-Bonger, and Vincent Willem van
Gogh, Paris, January 25, 1891; adminis-
tered by Jo van Gogh-Bonger, Bussum/
Amsterdam/Laren; Vincent Willem van
Gogh, September 2, 1925; loaned to the
Rijksmuseum, Amsterdam, 1917–19;
loaned to Mesdag Museum, The Hague,
1926; transferred by Vincent Willem
van Gogh, Laren, to Vincent van Gogh
Foundation, Amsterdam, July 10, 1962;
agreement July 21, 1962, entrusts col-
lection to the State of the Netherlands
until realization of the Rijksmuseum
Vincent van Gogh, Amsterdam; on loan
to Stedelijk Museum, Amsterdam,
until opening of Rijksmuseum Vincent
van Gogh; Rijksmuseum Vincent van
Gogh, Amsterdam, June 2, 1973; Van
Gogh Museum, Amsterdam, July 1, 1994.

Painted just a few months later than *Roses and Peonies* (cat. 19), this still life represents a major step forward for Van Gogh. The darker tonality, still dominant in the earlier painting despite his efforts to "make his works fresher in colors," is now replaced with an overall light palette, both in the background and in the flowers.[1] For the background, Van Gogh used his favorite cobalt blue already found in the background of *Portrait of a Prostitute* (cat. 16). In comparison, the brushstrokes here are less agitated, giving the impression of a monochrome, flecked wallpaper. This background serves as a cool foil to the exuberant whites, pinks, reds, and yellow of the flowers. The ground, on the other hand, is painted in a soft pink-brown that harmonizes with the pink and red gladioli placed upon it on either side of the simple vase, whose decor is difficult to decipher. Already in these early flower still lifes, Van Gogh shows his predilection for a shallow picture space, a characteristic that also informs his celebrated bouquets of roses, sunflowers, and irises (cat. 48).

Unlike the bouquet of roses and peonies, here the flowers are arranged loosely, giving ample room to each individual stalk. Despite the relative sparsity, this bouquet takes up the entire picture space, fanning out from left to right and reaching from top to bottom of the canvas. Three pinkish white gladioli, all turned to the left, dominate the left side; on the right originally only the large red and smaller pink gladioli and the two aster blooms were depicted. Not satisfied with this concept, Van Gogh changed it decisively by adding the yellow stalk. This was clearly an afterthought, since unlike the rest of the bouquet the yellow flowers are painted on top of the blue of the background, as documented by the blue pigment dragged into the yellow by his brush.[2] It was a stroke of brilliance. Instead of leaving a void at the center of the composition, Van Gogh allows it to rotate around this stalk of dazzling yellow flowers. HKA

Notes
1 Jan Hulsker, *Van Gogh in Close-Up* (Amsterdam: Meulenhoff, 1993), 81.

2 Louis van Tilborgh and Ella Hendriks, *Vincent van Gogh Paintings*, vol. 2, *Antwerp and Paris, 1885–1888, Van Gogh Museum* (Amsterdam and Zwolle: Van Gogh Museum/Waanders, 2011), 246–47.

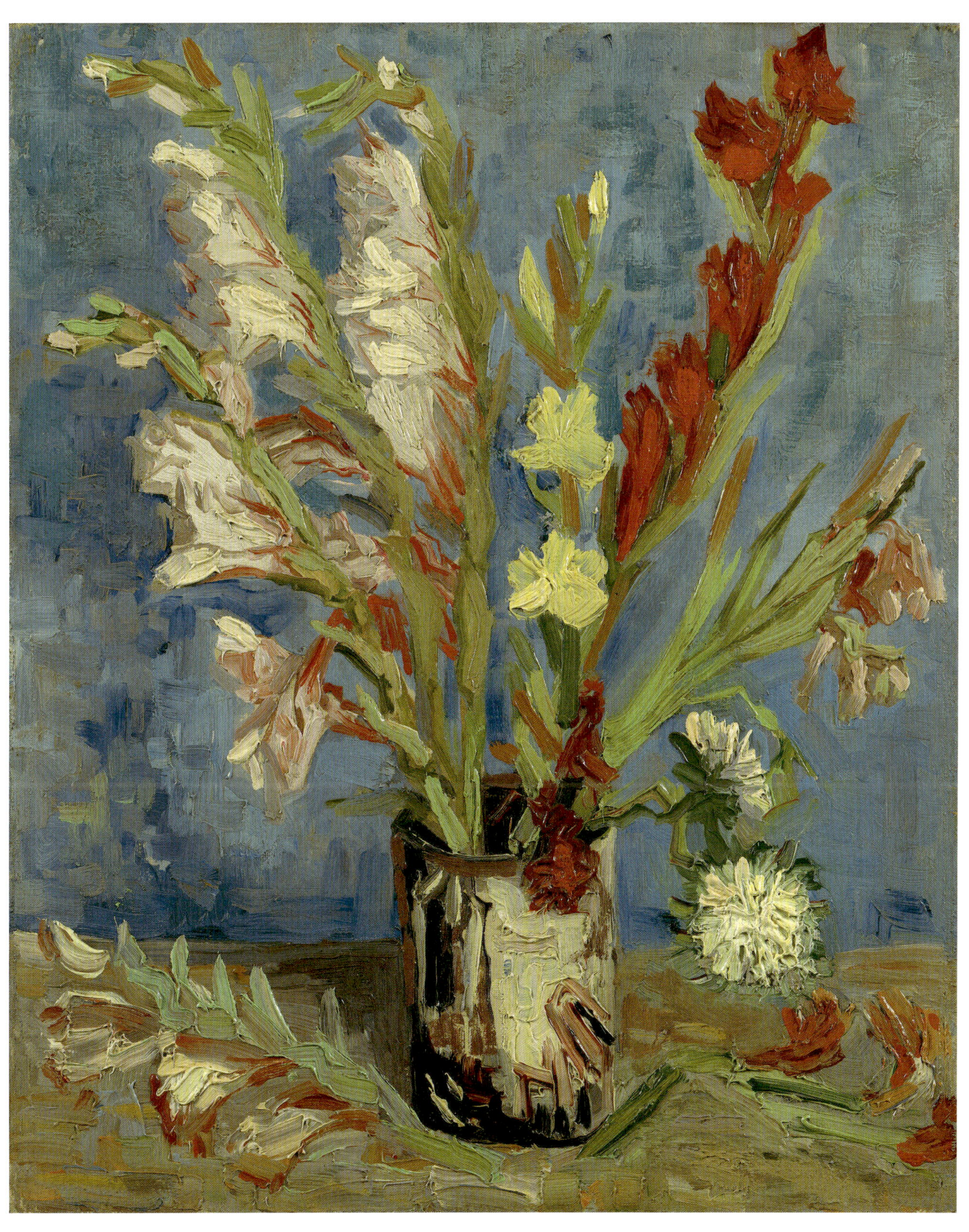

Cat. 21
*In the Café: Agostina Segatori in
Le Tambourin*
Oil on canvas,
21 ⅞ × 18 ½ inches (55.5 × 47 cm)
Van Gogh Museum,
Amsterdam
(Vincent van Gogh Foundation)
s17V1962
F370

Provenance
Left by the artist at the apartment of
Theo van Gogh, Paris, sometime be-
tween January and March 1887; Jo van
Gogh-Bonger and Vincent Willem van
Gogh, Paris, January 25, 1891; adminis-
tered by Jo van Gogh-Bonger, Bussum/
Amsterdam/Laren, until September 2,
1925; on loan from Vincent Willem van
Gogh, Laren, to the Stedelijk Museum,
Amsterdam, October 22, 1931; trans-
ferred to Vincent van Gogh Foundation,
Amsterdam, July 10, 1962; agreement
July 21, 1962, entrusts collection to the
State of the Netherlands until real-
ization of the Rijksmuseum Vincent
van Gogh, Amsterdam; on loan to
Stedelijk Museum, Amsterdam, until
opening of Rijksmuseum Vincent van
Gogh; Rijksmuseum Vincent van Gogh,
Amsterdam, June 2, 1973; Van Gogh
Museum, Amsterdam, July 1, 1994.

Agostina Segatori was the Italian owner of Le Tambourin café, a restaurant and cabaret that she had opened at 62 Boulevard de Clichy in 1885. She was a famous former painters' model who had posed for Camille Corot, Jean-Léon Gérôme, Eugène Delacroix, and Edouard Manet and, at the time this was painted, she was Van Gogh's lover. She is shown with arms crossed, a cigarette, and a glass of beer (her second, judging by the two saucers underneath); she sits at a tambourine-shaped table with tambourine-shaped stools, the trademark furnishings of the establishment, and plates, lamps, and paintings on the wall echo the theme. She is fashionably dressed in a gray-green jacket and polka-dotted blue-black skirt. Her hair is swept up into a spectacular hat with red feathered plumes, and a parasol lies on the stool next to her.

Agostina allowed Van Gogh to exhibit his works in the café, where he presented, among others, an exhibition of floral paintings. He also exhibited his collection of Japanese prints for sale, some of which are visible in the steeply receding background here: the nearest one is of two geishas. Despite the initial intensity of their love affair (attested to by Paul Gauguin), the relationship became troubled and stormy, and they agreed to separate in July 1887. Van Gogh tried to retrieve his paintings and prints (exactly how many is not known), but Agostina kept them until she was forced to sell them along with Le Tambourin after it went bankrupt.

The painting is interesting technically. Conservation studies reveal a scraped-off bust-length portrait of a woman beneath the painting of Agostina, to which it is unrelated. The canvas may even be an old one that Van Gogh had started in Antwerp and brought with him to Paris. The technique of Agostina's portrait is remarkable for the variety of handling, with brushstrokes of stiff and fluid paint, some short, some long, some narrow, some broad, and areas of deliberate rubbing and scratching. The face is different again: in the lighter parts a pattern of short, curved strokes done in stiff paint with a small, hard brush has left the paint raised in relief. This appears to be a unique method of handling in Van Gogh's work.[1] DB

Note
1 See Louis van Tilborgh and Ella Hendriks, *Vincent van Gogh Paintings*, vol. 2, *Antwerp and Paris, 1885–1888, Van Gogh Museum* (Amsterdam and Zwolle: Van Gogh Museum/Waanders, 2011), 299–305, cat. 84.

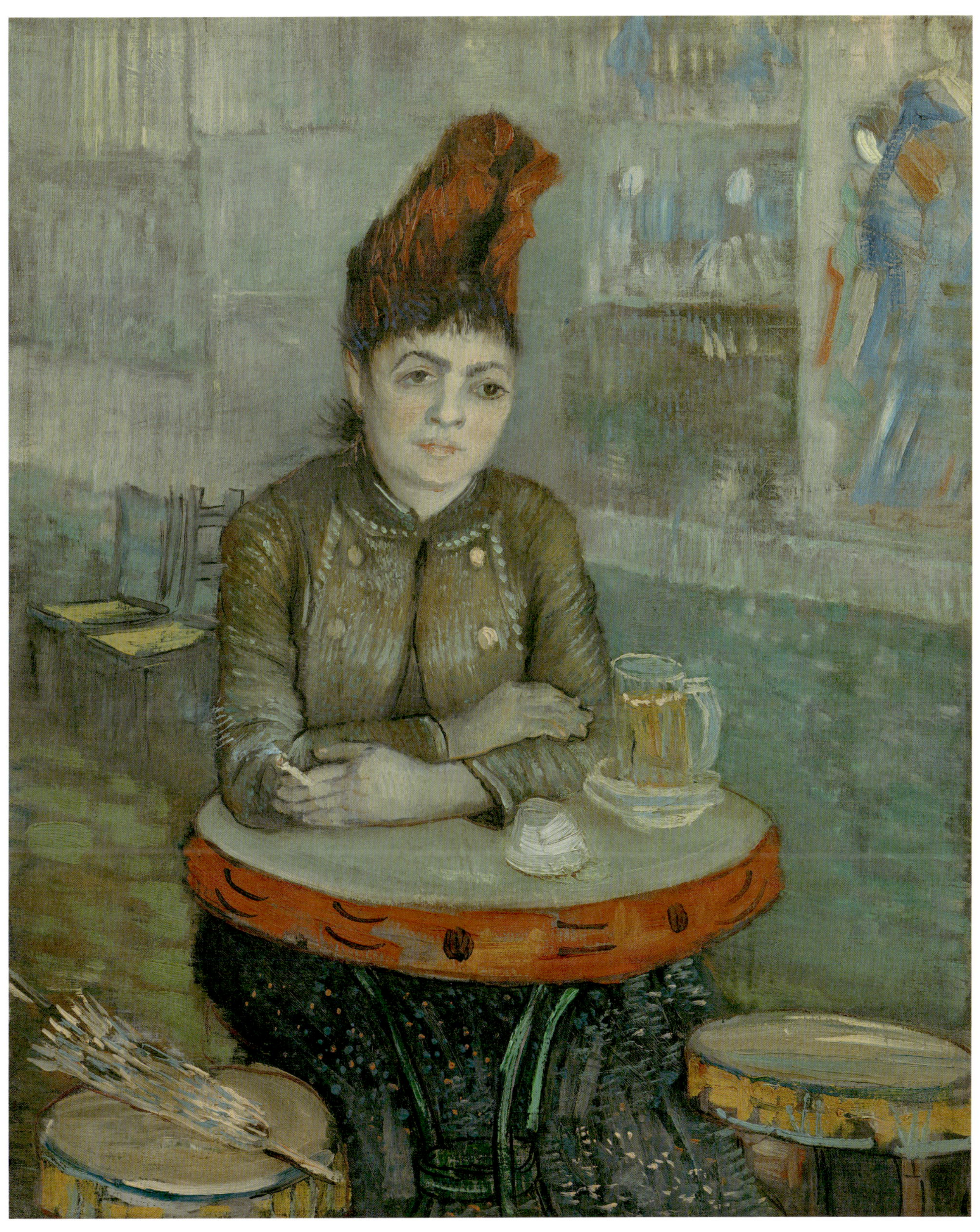

January–April 1887
Paris

Cat. 22
Head of a Man
(Possibly Theo van Gogh)
Chalk and watercolor on paper,
13 ¾ × 10 ⅛ inches
(34.9 × 25.8 cm)
Van Gogh Museum,
Amsterdam
(Vincent van Gogh Foundation)
d17V1962r
F1244dr

Provenance
Left by the artist at the apartment of
Theo van Gogh, Paris, sometime
between January and April 1887; Jo van
Gogh-Bonger and Vincent Willem van
Gogh, Paris, January 25, 1891; adminis-
tered by Jo van Gogh-Bonger, Bussum/
Amsterdam/Laren, until September 2,
1925; on loan from Vincent Willem van
Gogh, Laren, to the Stedelijk Museum,
Amsterdam, October 22, 1931; trans-
ferred to Vincent van Gogh Foundation,
Amsterdam, July 10, 1962; agreement
July 21, 1962, entrusts collection to the
State of the Netherlands until reali-
zation of the Rijksmuseum Vincent
van Gogh, Amsterdam; on loan to
Stedelijk Museum, Amsterdam, until
opening of Rijksmuseum Vincent van
Gogh; Rijksmuseum Vincent van Gogh,
Amsterdam, June 2, 1973; Van Gogh
Museum, Amsterdam, July 1, 1994.

Carried out in black, blue, orange, and red chalks with white watercolor, this vibrant study of a man's head in profile is popularly identified as a portrait of Theo van Gogh. It certainly bears a striking resemblance to him when compared with contemporary photographs: the large curved nose with prominent nostrils, the mustache, the shape of the ears, and the reddish hair all match closely. The only difference is that, in photographs, Theo's hair is curly and brushed back, whereas here it is straight and combed forward. Although the identification cannot be made with complete certainty, this is undoubtedly a careful, posed portrait rather than a random sketch, and Theo remains the most likely candidate.

The bright tonality is consistent with Van Gogh's discovery of color in Paris, and the technique is confident and bold with pronounced diagonal hatching. The head is given its outline and color in firm strokes of black and orange chalk. The collar has been filled in with white watercolor. The sheet of paper has been used twice: on the verso is a sketchy head of a man in a top hat, done in black and green chalk and drawn with the paper at right angles to the present composition. Both compositions are datable to the first three or four months of 1887.[1] DB

Note
1 Sjraar van Heugten and Marije Vellekoop, *Vincent van Gogh Drawings*, vol. 3, *Antwerp and Paris, 1885–1888, Van Gogh Museum* (Amsterdam: Van Gogh Museum; London: Lund Humphries, 2001), 241–45.

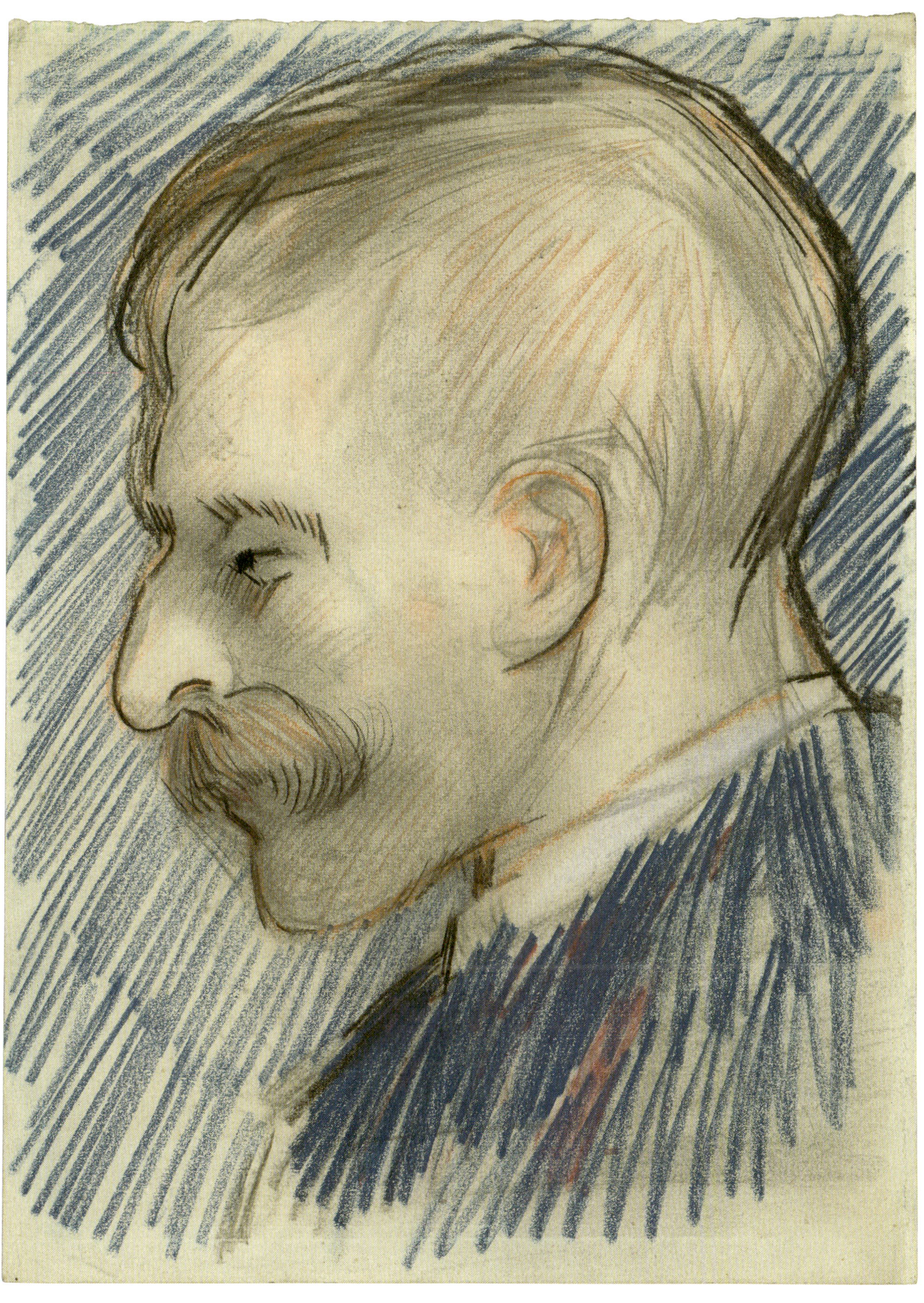

Late February–mid-April 1887
Paris

Cat. 23
Impasse des Deux Frères
Oil on canvas,
13 ¾ × 25 ¾ inches (35 × 65.3 cm)
Van Gogh Museum,
Amsterdam
(Vincent van Gogh Foundation)
s14V1962
F347

Provenance
Left by the artist at the apartment
of Theo van Gogh, Paris, sometime
between late February and mid-April
1887; Jo van Gogh-Bonger and Vincent
Willem van Gogh, Paris, January
25, 1891; administered by Jo van
Gogh-Bonger, Bussum/Amsterdam/
Laren, until September 2, 1925;
loaned by Vincent Willem van Gogh,
Laren, to Rijksmuseum, Amsterdam,
1927–30; loaned to Stedelijk Museum,
Amsterdam, October 22, 1931; trans-
ferred to Vincent van Gogh Foundation,
Amsterdam, July 10, 1962; agreement
July 21, 1962, entrusts collection to the
State of the Netherlands until reali-
zation of the Rijksmuseum Vincent
van Gogh, Amsterdam; on loan to
Stedelijk Museum, Amsterdam, until
opening of Rijksmuseum Vincent van
Gogh; Rijksmuseum Vincent van Gogh,
Amsterdam, June 2, 1973; Van Gogh
Museum, Amsterdam, July 1, 1994.

The Impasse des Deux Frères was an east-west lane
that linked the three windmills on the top of the hill of
Montmartre. In this view looking west, the Radet and
Blute-Fin windmills are out of sight to the south, although
the entrance to the latter and its belvedere are visible at
left. The Poivre mill appears on the right side of the road,
its sails facing west. Its entrance is decorated with four
flags. Just to the right, two large posts, each bearing a flag,
mark the gateway to the Debray family's garden, where
food and dancing were on offer. Next to the gateway is an
advertisement in the form of a wheeled model of a wind-
mill. The lane is unpaved, with stone gutters shown as
blue lines in the painting. The trees are leafless, although
people are strolling and sitting out at tables, suggesting
that it may be an early spring day.

Vincent and Theo lived on the rue Lepic, just a street away.
The Impasse was a regular walk for them, and Van Gogh
sketched and painted these surroundings a number of times.
The lightness of touch and bright, fresh tonality in the
painting are hallmarks of the more impressionistic and colorful style that Van Gogh adopted in Paris. There are traces
of another composition underneath — a fairly common
occurrence in his work of this period — scraped down and
blanked-out with a thick layer of white paint. X-rays are
not wholly conclusive, but the underlying picture may have
been one of the tall, narrow flower still-life studies that he
was painting around this time. Close examination also suggests that Van Gogh used a perspective frame of stretched
wires to sketch out the central part of the composition: faint
horizontal and vertical lines are visible, especially with
technical photography. The receding street to the left fell
outside the perspective frame and was drawn separately
with a vanishing point near the left edge of the canvas, the
two viewpoints giving the impression of a wide-angle lens.[1]
DB

Note
1 See Louis van Tilborgh and Ella Hendriks, *Vincent van Gogh Paintings*, vol. 2,
Antwerp and Paris, 1885–1888, Van Gogh Museum (Amsterdam and Zwolle: Van
Gogh Museum/Waanders, 2011), 328–34, cat. 92.

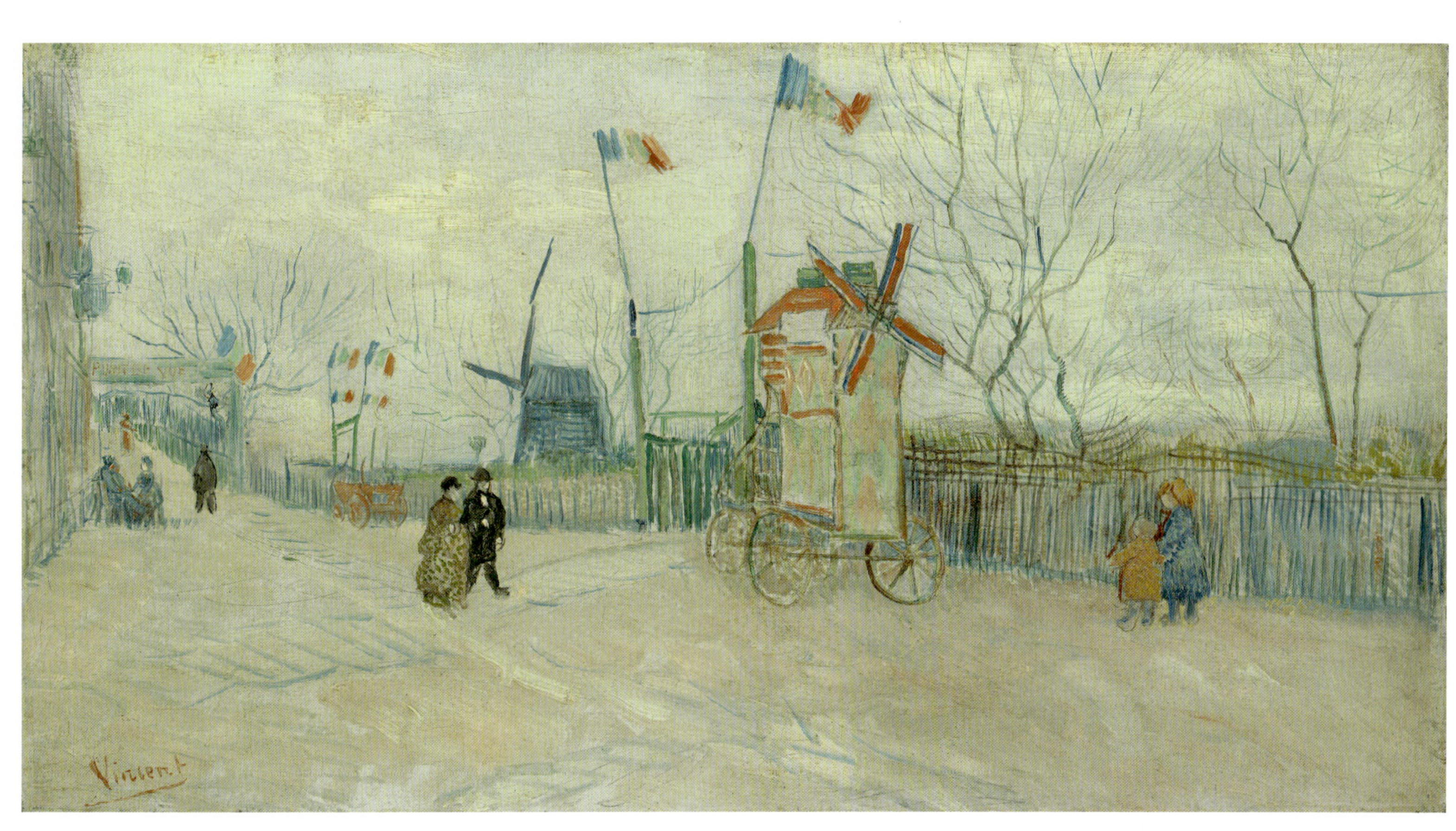

Cat. 24
Self-Portrait
Oil on cardboard,
16 ⅛ × 13 inches (41 × 33 cm)
Van Gogh Museum,
Amsterdam
(Vincent van Gogh Foundation)
s17V1962
F356

Provenance
Left by the artist at the apartment
of Theo van Gogh, Paris, sometime
between March and June 1887; Jo van
Gogh-Bonger and Vincent Willem van
Gogh, Paris, January 25, 1891; adminis-
tered by Jo van Gogh-Bonger, Bussum/
Amsterdam/Laren, until September 2,
1925; on loan from Vincent Willem van
Gogh, Laren, to the Stedelijk Museum,
Amsterdam, October 22, 1931; trans-
ferred to Vincent van Gogh Foundation,
Amsterdam, July 10, 1962; agreement
July 21, 1962, entrusts collection to the
State of the Netherlands until real-
ization of the Rijksmuseum Vincent
van Gogh, Amsterdam; on loan to
Stedelijk Museum, Amsterdam, until
opening of Rijksmuseum Vincent van
Gogh; Rijksmuseum Vincent van Gogh,
Amsterdam, June 2, 1973; Van Gogh
Museum, Amsterdam, July 1, 1994.

Vincent van Gogh was very much aware of the achieve-ments in the field of self-portraiture by his Dutch seventeenth-century predecessor Rembrandt van Rijn. Rembrandt produced more than sixty self-portraits over the span of his long career, and these works have been celebrated as both psychological studies and mas-terpieces of painting. Inevitably, Van Gogh would have compared his efforts to those of the master; to paint his own image must have been a somewhat daunting under-taking. Although Van Gogh made numerous portraits in the very early part of his career, he did not attempt any self-portraits before his time in Paris. However, once he embarked on this genre, he proceeded in an almost frenzied manner, painting twenty-seven self-portraits between the fall of 1886 and 1888.[1]

This painting was probably carried out in the spring of 1887, under the direct influence of Pointillism. Pointillist or Divisionist paintings had been featured in the last Impressionist exhibition in the spring of 1886 and made a significant impact on the art world. Van Gogh knew Paul Signac, one of the finest representatives of this style, personally.[2] This self-portrait, as well as one in the Art Institute of Chicago, also from 1887, clearly documents Van Gogh's very personal interpretation of Pointillism, using not dots but very short brushstrokes.

Van Gogh shows himself in the classic three-quarter profile, wearing the same brown jacket with blue-green trim found in several of his self-portraits of this period that distinguishes him as a bourgeois gentleman. The phys-iognomy of his gaunt face, receding hairline, red beard, and green eyes are entirely consistent with his other self-portraits. While fine, densely applied brushstrokes make up the face, much broader and loosely applied strokes are seen on the jacket. A halo of light blue dabs enliven the neutral background around the head and upper shoulders. This effect, however, was not Van Gogh's intention, but resulted from the fading of a purple underlayer of cochineal. A black-and-white photograph from 1908 shows the densely painted canvas, but fading had changed the image to its present state by 1949, as documented by a photograph from that year.[3] HKA

Notes
1 Louis van Tilborgh and Ella Hendriks, *Vincent van Gogh Paintings*, vol. 2, *Antwerp and Paris, 1885–1888, Van Gogh Museum* (Amsterdam and Zwolle: Van Gogh Museum/Waanders, 2011), 264.

2 Françoise Cachin, *Signac: Catalogue raisonné de l'œuvre peint* (Paris: Gallimard, 2000), 32–33.

3 Van Tilborgh and Hendriks, *Vincent van Gogh Paintings*, vol. 2, 361.

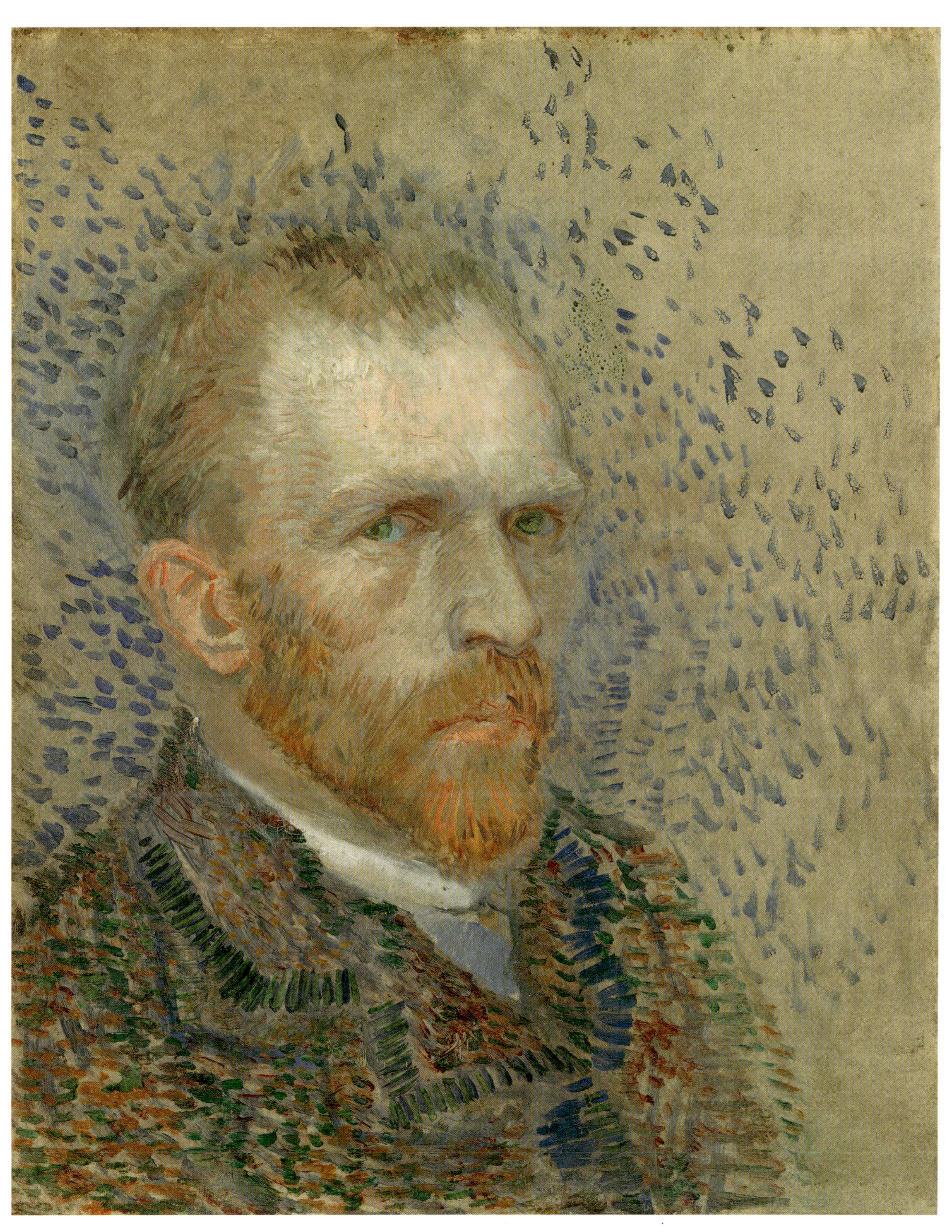

Cat. 25
Trees and Undergrowth
Oil on canvas,
18 ⅛ × 21 ¾ inches
(46.1 × 55.2 cm)
Van Gogh Museum,
Amsterdam
(Vincent van Gogh Foundation)
s66V1962
F309a

Provenance
Left by the artist at the apartment
of Theo van Gogh, Paris, second half
of July 1887; Jo van Gogh-Bonger
and Vincent Willem van Gogh, Paris,
January 25, 1891; probably sold to
Henri Bonger, Amsterdam, after 1905;
Betsy Bonger, Amsterdam, May
17, 1929; Vincent Willem van Gogh,
Laren, January 17, 1944; transferred
to Vincent van Gogh Foundation,
Amsterdam, July 10, 1962; agreement
July 21, 1962, entrusts collection to
the State of the Netherlands until
realization of the Rijksmuseum Vincent
van Gogh, Amsterdam; on loan to
Stedelijk Museum, Amsterdam, until
opening of Rijksmuseum Vincent van
Gogh; Rijksmuseum Vincent van Gogh,
Amsterdam, June 2, 1973; Van Gogh
Museum, Amsterdam, July 1, 1994.

In 1887 Van Gogh began to venture farther afield from the apartment on the rue Lepic, exploring the territory of the Impressionists, out along the banks of the Seine. Throughout the spring and summer, he returned often to Asnières, where he painted scenes of bourgeois leisure, including boats on the river and the famous Restaurant de la Sirène. He also painted six woodland scenes, including the present work, full of the sort of brushwork that he had observed in Impressionist paintings.

The canvas for *Trees and Undergrowth* was much reused. On the back, found during lining in 1969, is a landscape of trees and a lake painted in a vertical format by some other artist entirely. Van Gogh appropriated the painting, re-mounted it on the stretcher back-to-front, and primed the exposed raw canvas for his own use. The visible composition is not his first painting on this canvas: it covers an earlier work, undoubtedly also by him, whose subject cannot be deciphered.

As with other works, Van Gogh used a perspective frame to fix the main elements of the scene. Traces of the associated horizontals, verticals, diagonals, and edges have been detected by technical photography. The vertical tree trunk at the right runs up the inner edge of the frame, and the center falls just above the patch of sunlight on the floor of the wood. The painting is a faithful exercise in Impressionist technique: the variety of brushstrokes — including a sprinkling of Pointillist dots — and the complementary colors of red-green and yellow-violet attest to Van Gogh's eagerness to embrace current developments in the Parisian art world.[1] DB

Note
1 See Louis van Tilborgh and Ella Hendriks, *Vincent van Gogh Paintings*, vol. 2, *Antwerp and Paris, 1885–1888, Van Gogh Museum* (Amsterdam and Zwolle: Van Gogh Museum/Waanders, 2011), 410–15, cat. 112.

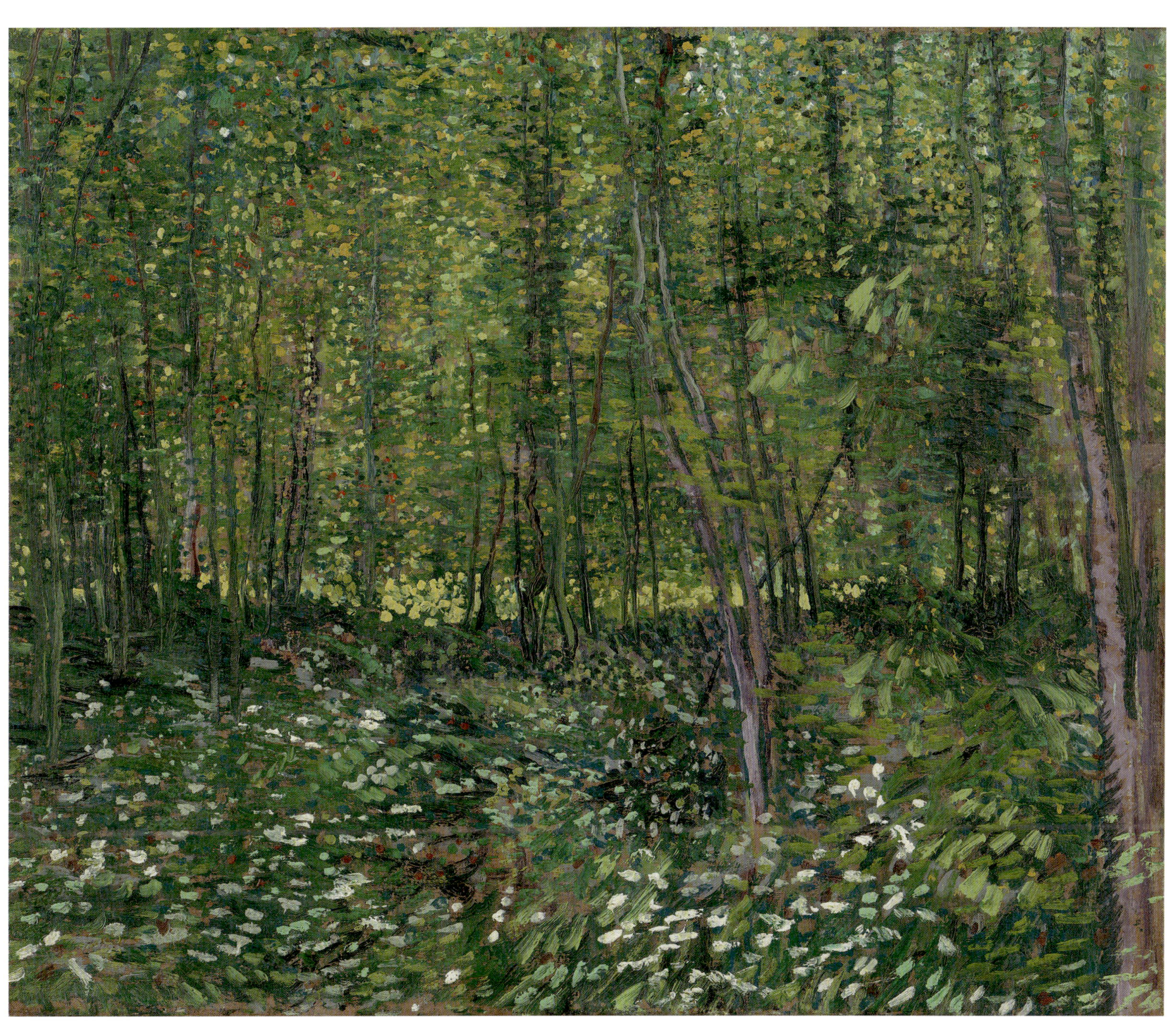

Summer 1887
Paris

Cat. 26
*Le restaurant de la Sirène a
Asnières (The Restaurant de la
Sirène at Asnières)*
Oil on canvas,
21 ½ × 25 ¾ inches (54.5 × 65.5 cm)
Musée d'Orsay, Paris,
Joseph Reinach bequest, 1921
RF 2325
F 313

Provenance
Jo van Gogh-Bonger, Amsterdam; A.
Schuffenecker, Clamart until 1921;
Joseph Reinach, 1921; Louvre Museum,
Paris, accepted by the state as a legacy
of Joseph Reinach, May 26, 1921; Musée
du Luxembourg, Paris, 1923; Louvre
Museum, 1929; Louvre Museum, Galerie
nationale du Jeu de Paume, Paris, 1947;
Musée d'Orsay, Paris, 1986.

In the spring and summer of 1887, Van Gogh, following
in the footsteps of the Impressionists, traveled often from
the center of Paris to paint motifs along the banks of the
Seine. A favorite destination was the riverside town of
Asnières, just downriver from one of the Impressionists'
habitual locations, the island of La Grande Jatte. In and
around the town, he painted canvases of tourist sights and
landmarks, including views of bridges and the famous
Restaurant de la Sirène, a large Victorian establishment with
long verandas packed with day-trippers from the city,
and spectators watching regattas and events on the river.

Van Gogh's development, both in style and subject, is clearly
indebted to Impressionism, and the complex calligraphy
of brilliant hatched brushstrokes is characteristic of his Paris
paintings. Unlike his fellow painters, however, he was
more concerned with depicting the building than in showing the convivial people inside at leisure or at play. The
street scene is sparsely populated but conveys life and energy
through its use of animated horizontal brushwork and
distinctive color. Accents of red punctuate the composition —
culminating in the crimson wall at the near right — set off
by stripes of green foliage, all surrounded by a yellow haze
of afternoon light.

Van Gogh and the painter Émile Bernard spent time together
in Asnières; the only known photograph of Van Gogh as
an adult was taken sitting with Bernard by the water's edge.
Bernard was presumably alluding to a depiction of the
Restaurant de la Sirène when he recounted to the art dealer
Ambroise Vollard that some of the works Van Gogh produced in Paris featured "smart restaurants decorated with
colored awnings and oleanders."[1] DB

Note
1 See "Vincent Van Gogh: The Restaurant de la Sirène," Musée d'Orsay, http://
www.musee-orsay.fr/en/collections/works-in-focus/painting/commentaire_id/the-
restaurant-de-la-sirene-15390.html?tx_commentaire_pi1%5BpidLi%5D=509&tx_
commentaire_pi1%5Bfrom%5D=841&cHash=057cc2a0e4.

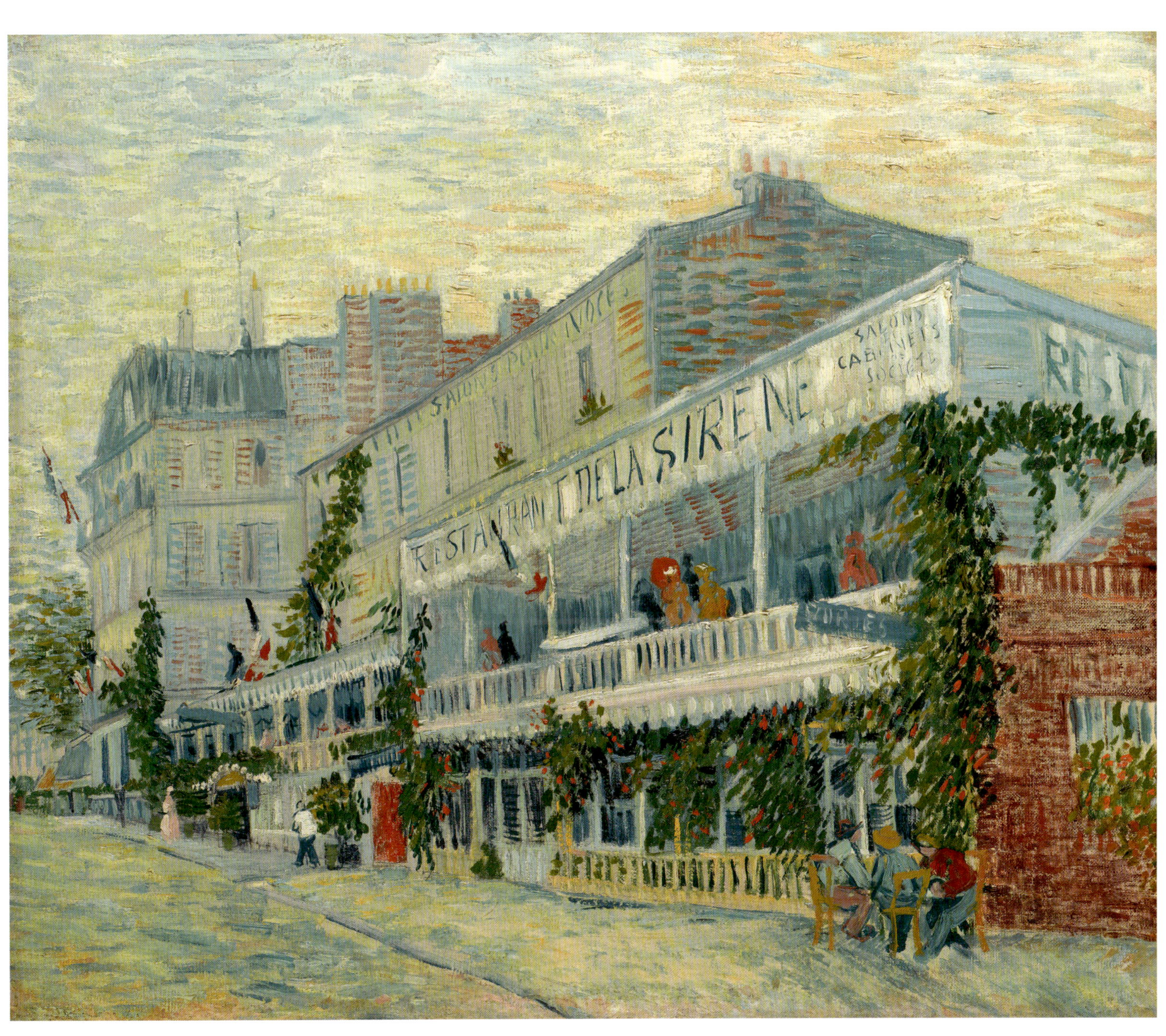

SALON CABINETS SOCIÉTÉ
RESTAURANT DE LA SIRÈNE

**February 1888
Arles**

Cat. 27
An Old Woman of Arles
Oil on canvas,
22 ⅞ × 16 ½ inches (58 × 42 cm)
Van Gogh Museum,
Amsterdam
(Vincent van Gogh Foundation)
s145V1962
F390

Provenance
Sent by artist to Theo van Gogh, Paris,
early May 1888; Jo van Gogh-Bonger
and Vincent Willem van Gogh, Paris,
January 25, 1891; administered by Jo
van Gogh-Bonger, Bussum/Amsterdam/
Laren, until September 2, 1925; trans-
ferred by Vincent Willem van Gogh
to the Vincent van Gogh Foundation,
Amsterdam, July 10, 1962; agreement
July 21, 1962, entrusts collection to the
State of the Netherlands until real-
ization of the Rijksmuseum Vincent
van Gogh, Amsterdam; on loan to
Stedelijk Museum, Amsterdam, until
opening of Rijksmuseum Vincent van
Gogh; Rijksmuseum Vincent van Gogh,
Amsterdam, June 2, 1973; Van Gogh
Museum, Amsterdam, July 1, 1994.

Van Gogh traveled from Paris to Arles in February 1888, arriving on Monday, the 20th, to find heavy snowfall and the coldest February in the region since 1860. He lodged at the Hôtel-Restaurant Carrel, 30 rue Cavalerie, not far from the northern edge of town. The same week, he bought canvases and paints and painted three studies. As he wrote to Theo in one of his first letters from Provence, these included "an old woman of Arles, a landscape with snow, a view of a stretch of pavement with a butcher's shop. The women really are beautiful here, it's no joke — on the other hand, the Arles museum is dreadful."[1] The present portrait of the "old woman of Arles" that he mentions is probably of Elisabeth Garcin, the hotel owner's mother-in-law, who was sixty-eight years old at the time. The knotted black kerchief on her head was a typical part of a widow's mourning dress, and wisps of gray hair project above her ringed ears. She wears a white blouse and is draped in a voluminous blue dress. Part of a bed can be seen in the background.

It was in Arles that Van Gogh finally realized the goal he set in Nuenen of becoming a portrait and figure painter. The contrast between this portrait and the dark character heads of peasants of 1884–85 could not be more profound. As in some of those earlier studies, the sitter is shown head-on, steadily and calmly regarding the viewer, but she is bathed in the cool light of a brilliant Provençal winter day. Here, the brightness and fragmented touch of the Parisian palette has given way to something altogether richer and stronger. The influence and inspiration of Japanese prints is clearly evident in the outlines and structure of the old Arlésienne. The great transformation in technique and intensity that Van Gogh's Arles sojourn would bring about had already begun.[2] DB

Notes
1 Letter 578, Vincent van Gogh to Theo van Gogh, Arles, on or about February 24, 1888.

2 See Ronald Pickvance, *Van Gogh in Arles* (New York: The Metropolitan Museum of Art, 1984), 41.

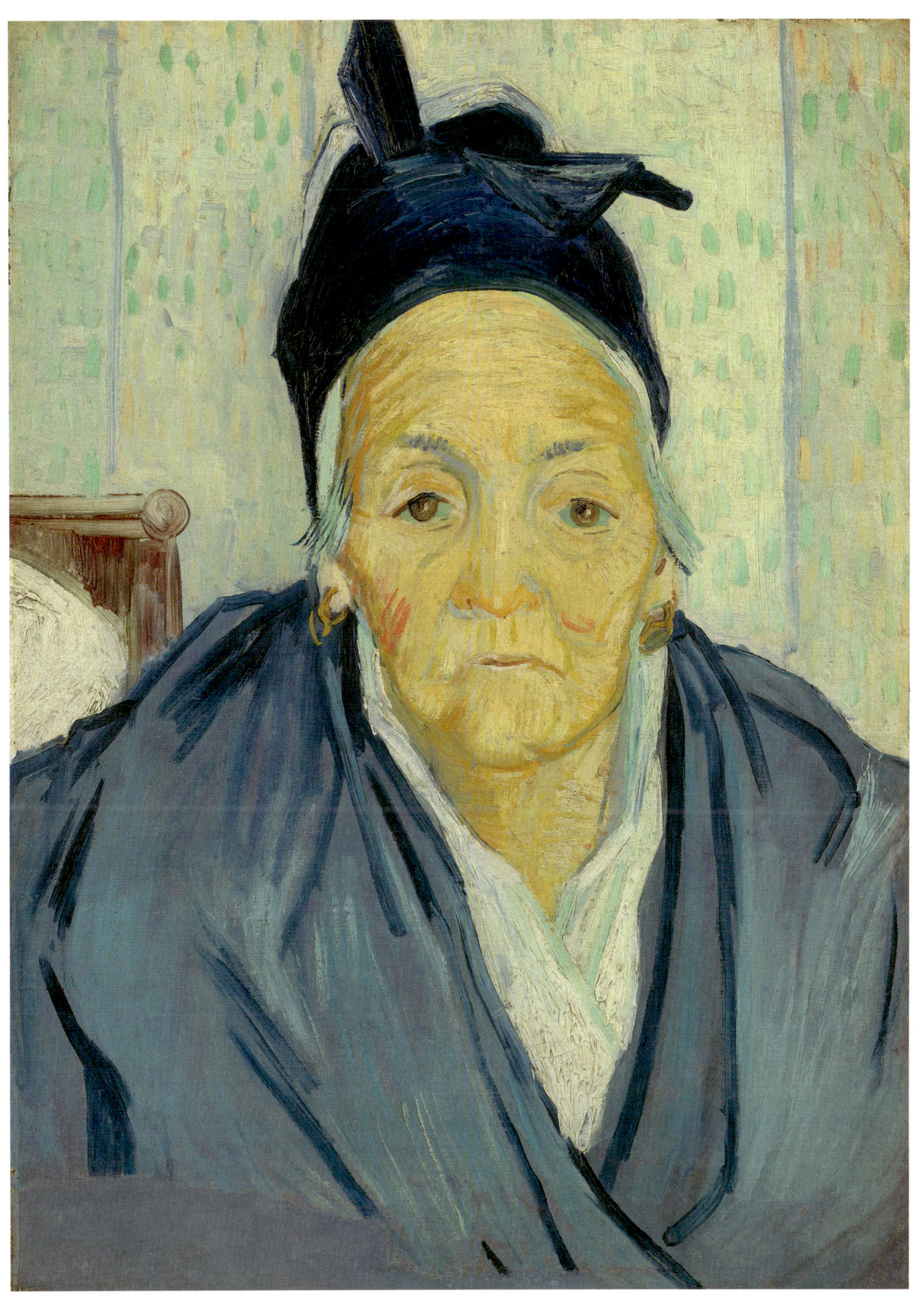

Cat. 28
Basket of Lemons and Bottle
Oil on canvas,
21 ⅛ × 25 ⅜ inches
(53.8 × 64.3 cm)
Kröller-Müller Museum,
Otterlo
KM 111.196
F384

Provenance
Jo van Gogh-Bonger, Amsterdam; M. M.
van Valkenburg coll., Laren (R 1904);
purchased by H. Kröller-Müller at M. M.
van Valkenburg sale, Rotterdam (A. M.
Reckers, art dealer), March 1, 1909.

The color yellow held a particular fascination for Vincent van Gogh. Experiencing the intense sunlight of southern France, he famously wrote to his brother Theo in Paris, "Sunshine, a light which, for want of a better word I can only call yellow — pale sulphur yellow, pale lemon, gold. How beautiful yellow is!"[1] The outside of his house in Arles was painted yellow, and he created a number of his celebrated still lifes of sunflowers in August 1888 to decorate it. This color, which elicited an intense feeling of warmth and happiness in Van Gogh, dominates this still life of lemons in a basket to such a degree that it can be seen as an experiment in painting yellow on yellow.

This was not the first still life of lemons by Van Gogh, and in fact lemons had aroused his interest several times already. A year earlier, he had painted *Still Life with Decanter and Lemons on a Plate* and *Still Life with Lemons on a Plate* (both 1887, Van Gogh Museum, Amsterdam). However, these compositions are much more traditional in their insistence on color contrasts. In order to distinguish the fruit from the basket and the tablecloth, he not only painted each element with differentiated brushstrokes but also employed different shades of yellow. The lemons are actually quite a dark shade, the two at left almost orange. Van Gogh further shaded the lemons and basket in light blue to set them off from the yellow tablecloth. The background in soft green, stippled with white and yellow, forms a color contrast, but a much more muted one than in the earlier works. Unfortunately, a number of recent technical studies have shown that some of the yellow pigments that Van Gogh used have faded or are beginning to fade.[2] Inevitably, the fading affects, or will affect, the expressive power of the paintings. HKA

Notes
1 Letter 659, Vincent van Gogh to Theo van Gogh, Arles, on or about August 12, 1888.

2 Sarah Everts, "Van Gogh's Fading Colors Inspire Scientific Inquiry," *Chemical & Engineering News* 94, no. 5 (February 1, 2016): 32–33, https://cen.acs.org/articles/94/i5/Van-Goghs-Fading-Colors-Inspire.html.

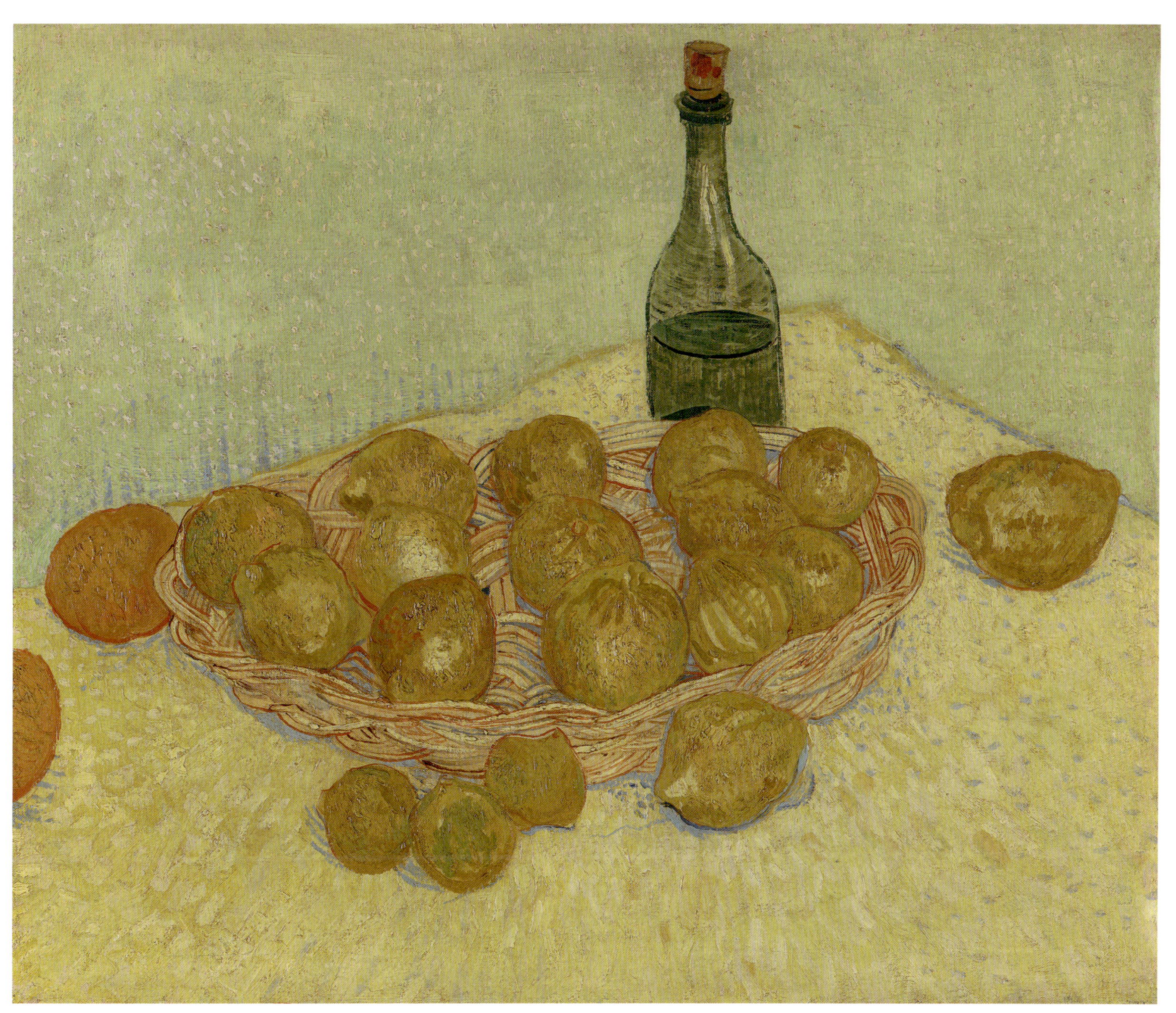

Cat. 29
The Langlois Bridge at Arles
Oil on canvas,
19 ½ × 25 inches (49.5 × 64 cm)
Wallraf-Richartz-Museum &
Fondation Corboud, Cologne
WRM 1197
F570

Provenance
Family of the artist; [Lucien Moline, Paris,
December 1895?]; Jos Hessel, Paris,
probably by 1904, at the latest by 1909;
Bernheim-Jeune, Paris; Paul Cassirer,
Berlin, May 1910–June 8, 1911; acquired
by the Wallraf-Richartz-Museum in
June 1911.

Notes
1 Ingo Walter and Rainer Metzger, *Vincent van Gogh, The Complete
Paintings*, vol. 2, *Arles, February 1888–Auvers-sur-Oise, July 1890* (Cologne:
Benedikt Taschen, 1990), 323–25, 343. The four earlier versions are
The Langlois Bridge at Arles with Women Washing, March 1888, Kröller-
Müller Museum, Otterlo, F397; *The Langlois Bridge at Arles with Road
alongside the Canal,* March 1888, Van Gogh Museum (Vincent van Gogh
Foundation), Amsterdam, F400; *The Langlois Bridge at Arles,* April 1888,
private collection, F1480; *The Langlois Bridge at Arles,* April 1888, private
collection, Paris, F571.

2 This struggle with perspective is most noticeable in the bridge paintings:
The Seine Bridge at Asnières, summer 1887, Collection Dominique de Menil,
Houston, F240; and *The Seine with the Pont de la Grande Jatte,* summer 1887,
Van Gogh Museum, Amsterdam (Vincent van Gogh Foundation).

3 Letter 585, Vincent van Gogh to Theo van Gogh, Arles, on or about March
16, 1888.

4 Wallraf-Richartz-Museum website, www.wallraf.museum/
sammlungen/19-Jahrhundert/meisterwerke (accessed October 11, 2018).

Drawbridges must have been a motif deeply embedded
in Van Gogh's childhood memories, yet he did not paint any
before his sojourn in the South of France. There, the modest drawbridge over a small canal on the outskirts of Arles
became the subject of four paintings and one watercolor,
all carried out between March and May 1888.[1] This version is
the last of the group and the only one in which the bridge
is seen from the right side of the canal. In three of the earlier
versions, Van Gogh pays close attention to a group of
women washing at the riverbank just below the bridge, but
here he has reduced this anecdotal motif to a single figure.
Instead of a horse-drawn cart, as seen in the other paintings,
a woman with a parasol traverses the bridge. Her rounded
shape contrasts with the grid of verticals and diagonals of
the drawbridge's mechanism. The brushstrokes are wide
and directional, schematically evoking plants, bricks, the
surface of the water, and the lightly clouded sky.

The four paintings of the drawbridge can be considered a
series, but unlike Claude Monet, Van Gogh was uninterested
in depicting a particular motif under different atmospheric
conditions. Instead, the constantly sunny atmosphere of the
South is the defining element and is reflected in his bright
palette. Having struggled with perspective in his paintings
in the past,[2] Van Gogh used a perspective frame, as he often
had in Paris. This Old Master tool facilitated the correct
drawing of the lines, especially those of the drawbridge's
complicated superstructure. Van Gogh mentioned the frame
in a letter describing his drawbridge works to his brother
Theo,[3] and a grid of pencil lines has been detected under the
paint through modern technology.[4] Far from working in
the spontaneous manner often ascribed to him, Van Gogh
carefully planned this composition. Nevertheless, the un-
mixed colors applied directly in front of the motif are typical
of his famously rapid and emotive working method. HKA

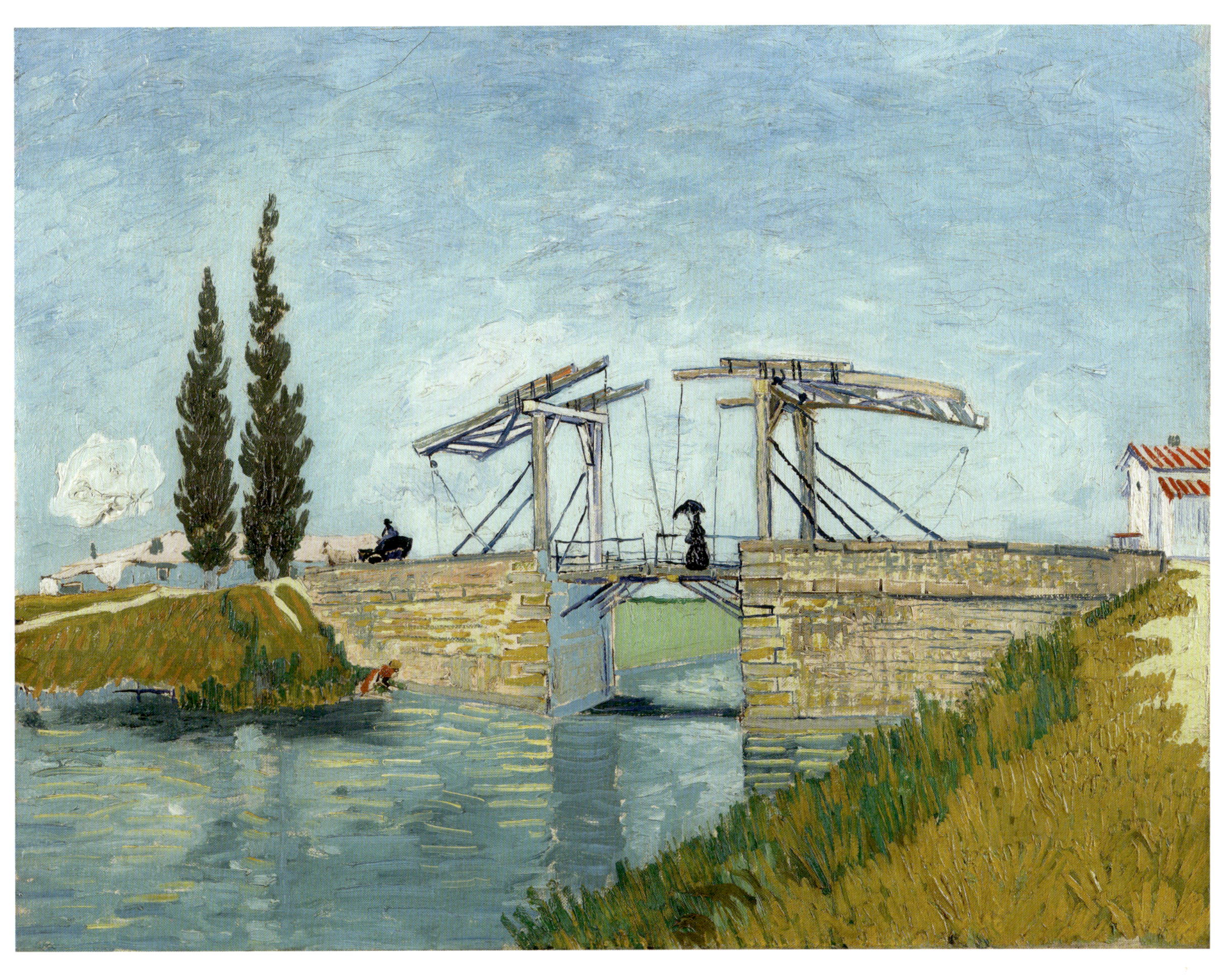

May 1888
Arles

Cat. 30
Field with Poppies
Oil on canvas,
9 ½ × 13 ¾ inches (24 × 35 cm)
Van Gogh Museum,
Amsterdam
(Vincent van Gogh Foundation)
s33V1962
F576

Provenance
Given by the artist to Paul Eugène
Milliet to take to Theo van Gogh, Paris,
mid-August 1888; Jo van Gogh-Bonger
and Vincent Willem van Gogh, Paris,
January 25, 1891; sold to Kunstzalen
Oldenzeel, Rotterdam, May 1896; sold
to Henri Bonger, Amsterdam, after
1896; Betsy Bonger, Amsterdam, May
17, 1929; Vincent Willem van Gogh,
Laren, January 17, 1944; donated to the
(first) Vincent van Gogh Foundation,
Laren, March 11, 1952; transferred to
the Theo van Gogh Foundation, Laren,
December 28, 1960; agreement July 21,
1962, entrusts collection to the State
of the Netherlands until realization
of the Rijksmuseum Vincent van Gogh,
Amsterdam; donated by the Theo van
Gogh Foundation to the (second) Vincent
van Gogh Foundation, July 21, 1962; on
loan to Stedelijk Museum, Amsterdam,
until opening of Rijksmuseum Vincent
van Gogh; Rijksmuseum Vincent van
Gogh, Amsterdam, June 2, 1973; Van
Gogh Museum, Amsterdam, July 1, 1994.

Van Gogh had traveled to Provence seeking warmth and bright sunshine, so he was quite taken aback by the snow-covered landscape that he found when he arrived in Arles on February 20, 1888.[1] It took some effort on his part to acclimate to his new home, but when the usual mild Mediterranean temperatures returned, he explored his environs. During the months of March and April, he painted a series of ravishingly beautiful flowering trees, and by May he started to devote his attention to the verdant fields on the immediate outskirts of the city. Despite his early passion for depicting peasants performing their chores indoors as well as out-of-doors, Van Gogh had shown virtually no interest in fields as a topic during his years in Holland. The first canvases devoted entirely to this subject, *Wheat Field with a Lark* (1887, Rijksmuseum, Amsterdam) and *Pasture in Bloom* (1887, Kröller-Müller Museum, Otterlo) date from his years in Paris.

In this painting, he reprises the stark horizon to divide the canvas in equal halves, as he had in *Wheat Field with a Lark*. A cluster of farmhouses under trees at the right and two smaller outcroppings of houses at left enliven the composition. Indicative of the stronger southern light, the colors are more saturated here than in the earlier work. The red poppies — each a single dab of the brush — contrast sharply with the dark greens of the unripened wheat as this field stretches out under the intense blue of the Mediterranean sky.

Van Gogh saw his efforts to capture the landscape near Arles in direct competition with Paul Cézanne's mastery of the Provençal landscape around his native Aix. Referring to his own landscapes painted just one month later, he wrote to Theo, "If, coming home with my canvas, I say to myself: look, I've arrived precisely at *père* Cézanne's tones. . . . Goes without saying that seen together they'd hold their own, but there would be no resemblance."[2] Indeed they do, but sadly Van Gogh never had the opportunity to see his works alongside those of Cézanne. HKA

Notes
1 Martin Bailey, *Studio of the South: Van Gogh in Provence* (London: Frances Lincoln, 2016), 21.

2 Letter 624, Vincent van Gogh to Theo van Gogh, Saint-Rémy-de-Provence, January 31, 1890.

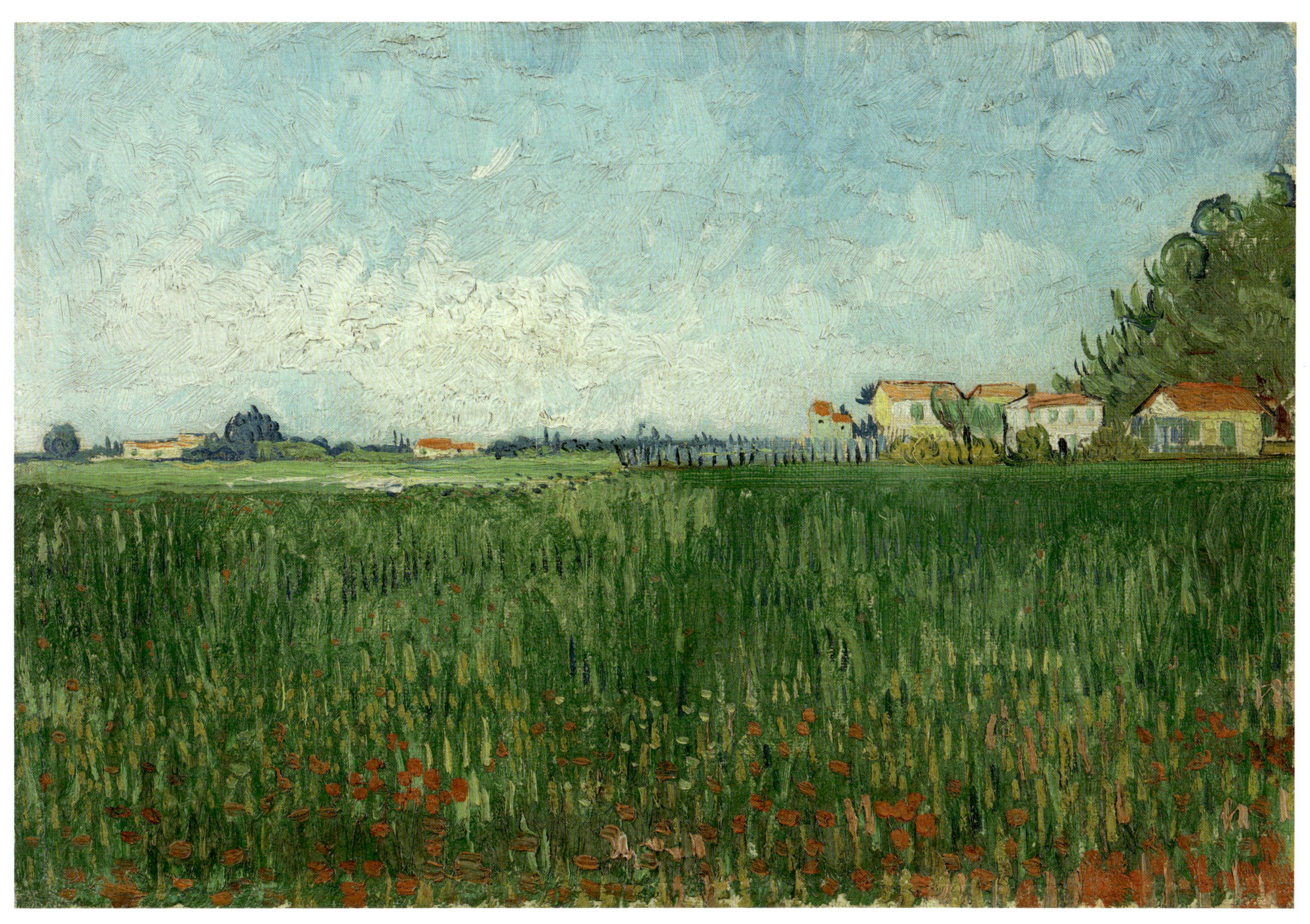

Cat. 31
View of Saintes-Maries-de-la-Mer
Oil on canvas,
25 ¼ × 20 ⅞ inches (64.2 × 53 cm)
Kröller-Müller Museum,
Otterlo
KM 106.327
F416

Provenance
C. Hoogendijk coll., The Hague (probably
purchased between late August 1897
and early December 1899); purchased by
H. Kröller-Müller at C. Hoogendijk sale,
Amsterdam (Frederik Muller), May 21,
1912, lot 25: *Arles.*

Van Gogh traveled south by coach from Arles to Saintes-Maries-de-la-Mer, a seaside town on the Mediterranean, and stayed for three days from May 30 or 31 to June 4 or 5, 1888. Saintes-Maries was famously Catholic, containing the relics of two saints, and it appealed to Van Gogh's residual religious fervor as well as to his conviction that the landscape of southern Provence was very much like Japan. He took three blank canvases with him, and this is one of the resulting paintings; the other two are seascapes. Elated, he described the color of the sea to Theo as being "like mackerel, in other words, changing — you don't always know if it's green or purple — you don't always know if it's blue — because a second later, its changing reflection has taken on a pink or gray hue."[1]

This superb landscape depicts the northern view of the town. Rows of purple-blue bushes — perhaps a little less purple than they had been originally because of fading of the red pigment in the mixture — lead the eye toward the central church. The painting is dominated by the "green blue of the sky heated white-hot," as the artist described the light of Provence in one of his letters.[2] The composition is a geometric construction of blues and oranges, complementary colors, and reminiscent of Paul Cézanne, whom Van Gogh was beginning to admire. He also made a drawing of the same view, but it is fairly certain that the painting, as well as the drawing, were both made on the spot.

What happened to the three paintings that he made on his trip south is something of a mystery. He wrote that he would leave them behind "because of course they are not dry enough to be subjected to five hours of jolting in a carriage."[3] Whether he did in fact take them or had them sent on is not known. He might have intended to collect them on a subsequent visit, but he never went back.[4] DB

Notes
1 Letter 619, Vincent van Gogh to Theo van Gogh, Saintes-Maries-de-la-Mer, on or about June 3 or 4, 1888.

2 Letter 624, Vincent van Gogh to Theo van Gogh, Arles, June 12 or 13, 1888.

3 Letter 619.

4 See Hildelies Balk, Jos ten Berge, et al., *The Paintings of Vincent van Gogh in the Collection of the Kröller-Müller Museum* (Otterlo: Kröller-Müller Museum, 2003), 221–23.

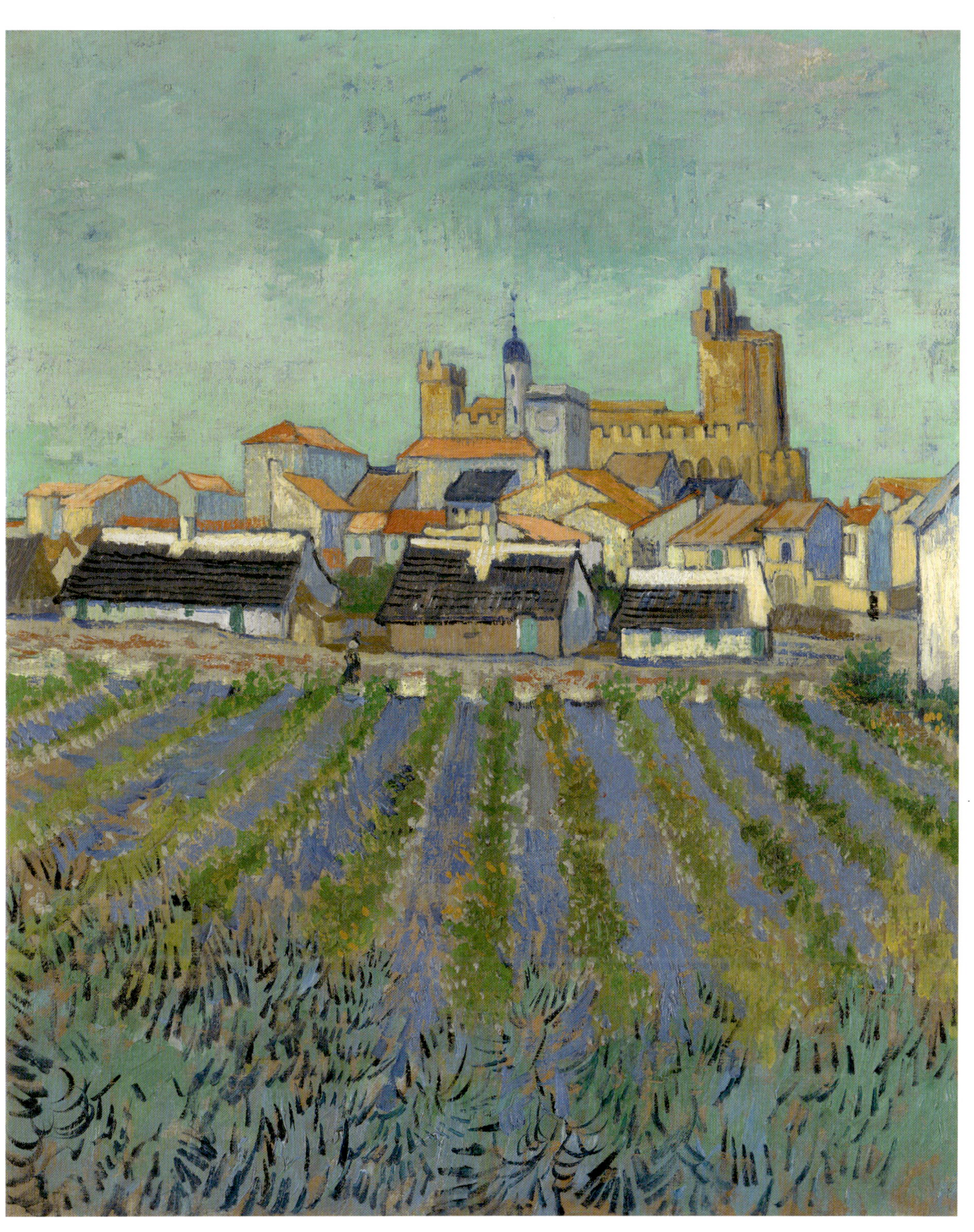

July 1888
Arles

Cat. 32
Les Rochers (The Rocks)
Oil on canvas,
21 ¼ × 25 ½ inches (54 × 64.8 cm)
The Museum of Fine Arts,
Houston, gift of Mrs. Audrey
Jones Beck
74.139
F466

Provenance
Theo van Gogh, Paris, 1888; Mrs.
Johanna van Gogh-Bonger, Amsterdam
and Laren, the Netherlands; [Paul
Cassirer, Berlin]; Mrs. Margarete
Mauthner, Berlin; Josef Stransky, New
York, [Wildenstein and Company, New
York]; Sir A. Chester Beatty, London;
Miss Edith Beatty, London; [Arthur
Tooth & Sons, London, 1962]; Mr. and
Mrs. John A. Beck, Houston, 1964;
gift of Mrs. Audrey Jones Beck to the
Museum of Fine Arts, Houston, 1974.

The Rocks, painted in early July 1888 near the town of Arles in southern France, depicts a lone oak tree, bent and twisted by the mistral winds, standing on an outcropping of rocks. The tree, whose trunk consists only of zigzagging green lines, while its foliage is indicated by simple dabs in a variety of greens, rises against an empty but subtly colored sky. The lack of landmarks makes it impossible to assign an exact location to this landscape, but it was probably painted in the vicinity of Montmajour. The rocky terrain around this ancient monastery fascinated Van Gogh, who repeatedly explored this region, not far from his base in Arles.

"Yesterday, at sunset, I was on a stony heath where very small, twisted oaks grow, in the background a ruin on the hill, and wheat fields in the valley," he wrote to his brother Theo on July 5, 1888.[1] Just three days later, he wrote that he had two large drawings ready to be sent to Paris, one of them presumably the pencil, pen, reed pen, and ink drawing *The Rock of Montmajour with Pine Trees* (July 1888, see page 19, fig. 6), which relates closely to this painting. The drawing, made from a slightly different angle, includes more trees, but the rocky outcropping is very similar. Van Gogh employed the same dark outline of the individual rocks in the painting as in the drawing. These emphatic lines add a calligraphic element to this work, painted with very heavy impasto. Some areas are so built up that they seem three-dimensional, almost sculptural.

In the quintessential Impressionist manner, Van Gogh painted out-of-doors, directly in front of the motif, and he struggled with all sorts of difficulties inherent in *plein air* work. In a letter to Theo, dated July 13, 1888, he famously complained, "How I'd make a painting of it if there wasn't this bloody wind! That's the thing that's annoying here when you plant your easel somewhere. And it's definitely for that reason that the painted studies aren't as finished as the drawings. The canvas shakes all the time."[2] Despite the wind and the added annoyance of mosquitoes, Van Gogh battled on, creating some of the most iconic images of the Provençal landscape. HKA

Notes
1 Letter 636, Vincent van Gogh to Theo van Gogh, Arles, July 5, 1888.

2 Letter 639, Vincent van Gogh to Theo van Gogh, Arles, on or about July 13, 1888.

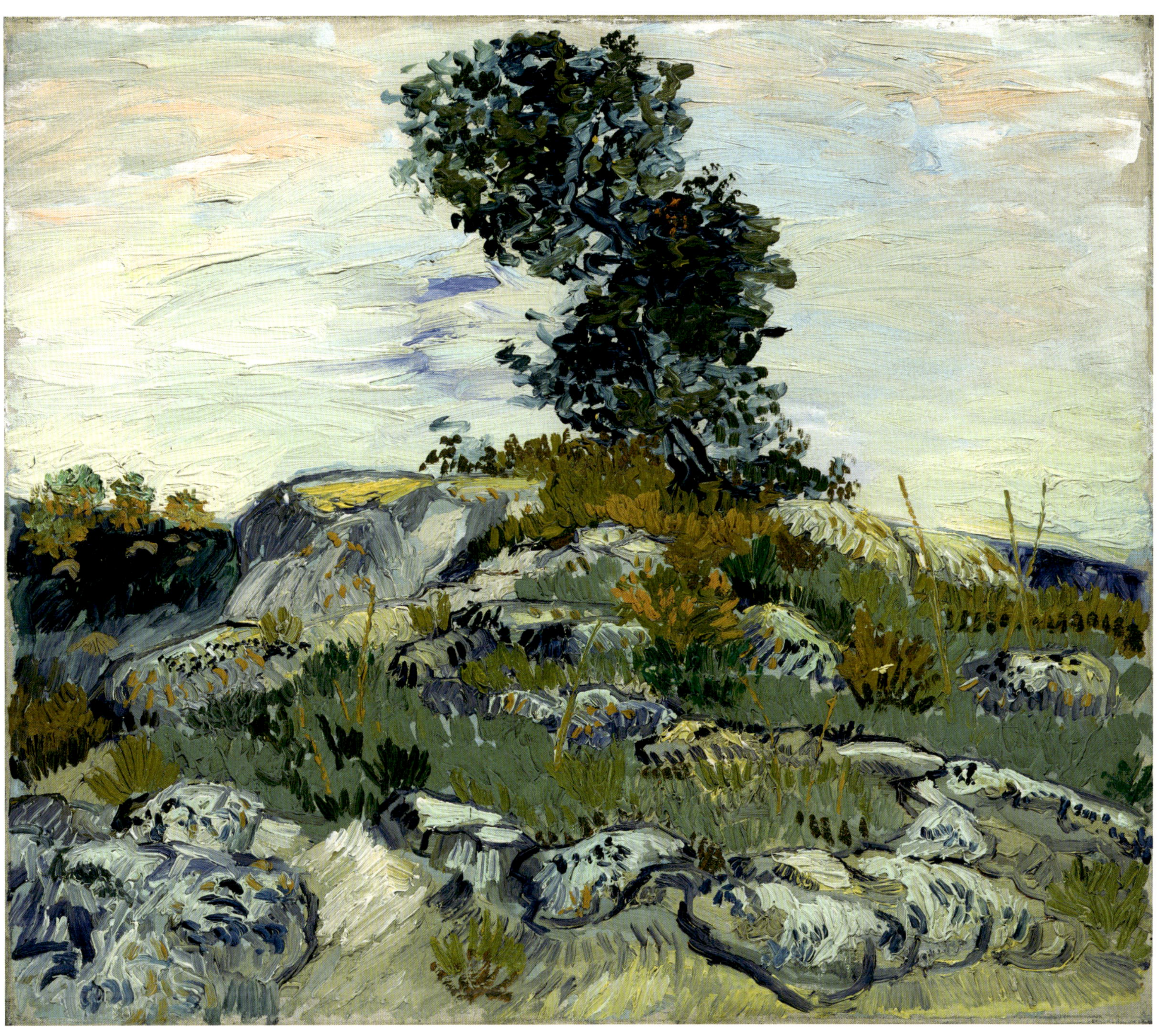

September 1888
Arles

Cat. 33
Café Terrace on the Place du Forum
Reed pen and ink with graphite
on laid paper,
24 ⅛ × 18 ½ inches, (62 x 47 cm)
Dallas Museum of Art,
The Wendy and Emery Reves
Collection
1985.R.79
F1519

Provenance
Sent by the artist to Theo van Gogh,
1888–89; by inheritance to his son,
Vincent Willem van Gogh, Amsterdam,
as part of his collection, administered
by his widow, Johanna van Gogh-Bonger,
Amsterdam, 1891; purchased by Paul
Cassirer, Berlin, December, 1906; purchased by Hugo von Tschudi (died 1911),
Berlin, December 1906; inherited by
his widow, Angela von Tschudi, Munich
(placed on loan at the museum in
Breslau); purchased by the Fritz Nathan
Art Gallery, Zürich, from the Tschudi
family, until 1960; purchased by Emery
Reves, Cabbe-Roquebrune, France,
1960; given to the Dallas Museum of Art,
as part of the Wendy and Emery Reves
collection, 1985.

Notes
1 Letter 159, Vincent van Gogh to Theo van Gogh, Brussels, October 15,
1880. See also Sjraar van Heugten, Maja Hoffmann, and Bice Curiger, *Van
Gogh Drawings: Influences & Innovations* (Amsterdam: Fondation Vincent
van Gogh; Arles: Actes Sud, 2014), 69–71.

2 Letter 620, Vincent van Gogh to Theo van Gogh, Arles, on or about June
5, 1888.

3 Van Heugten, Hoffmann, and Curiger, *Van Gogh Drawings: Influences &
Innovations*, 104.

4 Johannes van der Wolk and Ronald Pickvance and E. B. F. Pey, *Vincent
van Gogh: Drawings*, exh. cat. (New York: Rizzoli, 1990), 237.

5 Letter 678, Vincent van Gogh to Willemien van Gogh, Arles, September
9 and about 14, 1888.

6 Vincent van Gogh, *Café Terrace at Night,* 1889, oil on canvas, Kröller-
Müller Museum, Otterlo, F467, https://krollermuller.nl/en/vincent-van-
gogh-terrace-of-a-cafe-at-night-place-du-forum-1; letter 678; Colta Ives et
al., *Vincent van Gogh: The Drawings* (New York: Metropolitan Museum of
Art, 2005), 284–85, cat. 96.

7 Letter 678.

The pen was one of Van Gogh's most favored drawing
tools, and one he used throughout his career. By the time
he began working in the South of France, his self-assured
reed pen drawings showcased his mastery and expansive
graphic vocabulary. He often combed through book and
print shops for source imagery, and also copied from prints
by artists whom he admired. Once he stated, "Drawing
with the pen is a good preparation if later you might wish
to learn etching."[1] Like the seventeenth-century Dutch
printmaker Rembrandt van Rijn, Van Gogh connected the
skill and quickness of making lines with a reed pen to
the directness and ease of sketching lines on a prepared etching plate.

In the South of France, Van Gogh assimilated artistic influences from his stay in Paris. He collected *ukiyo-e* woodblock
prints, which he admired. "The Japanese draws quickly,
very quickly, like a flash of lightning," he once commented.[2]
Although he soon abandoned his painting experiments
using the Pointillist technique, he modified the style for his
drawings, embracing the use of dots and short lines.[3]

While in Arles, Van Gogh depicted an aspect of the town in
a painting and a drawing of the terrace of a popular coffee-
house on the Place du Forum. He used a large sheet of paper to
delineate the scene with a nimble handling of the pen. His
marks — blunt, heavy, and fine; fluid and twisting; short and
long — highlight his calligraphic expression. He added
graphite for shading and particular details, such as the walls
and wooden floor. The drawing was likely made in the day-
time due to clear signage and the sky's treatment.[4] He later
returned to the café after dark to paint it, commenting that
"the night is even more richly colored than the day."[5] The
painted version, which varies from the drawing somewhat,
was inspired by Guy de Maupassant's book *Bel Ami* (1885),
which describes brightly lit Parisian cafés at night.[6] Van
Gogh excitedly wrote to his sister about the huge yellow gas
lantern and the blue sky studded with stars.[7] DMW

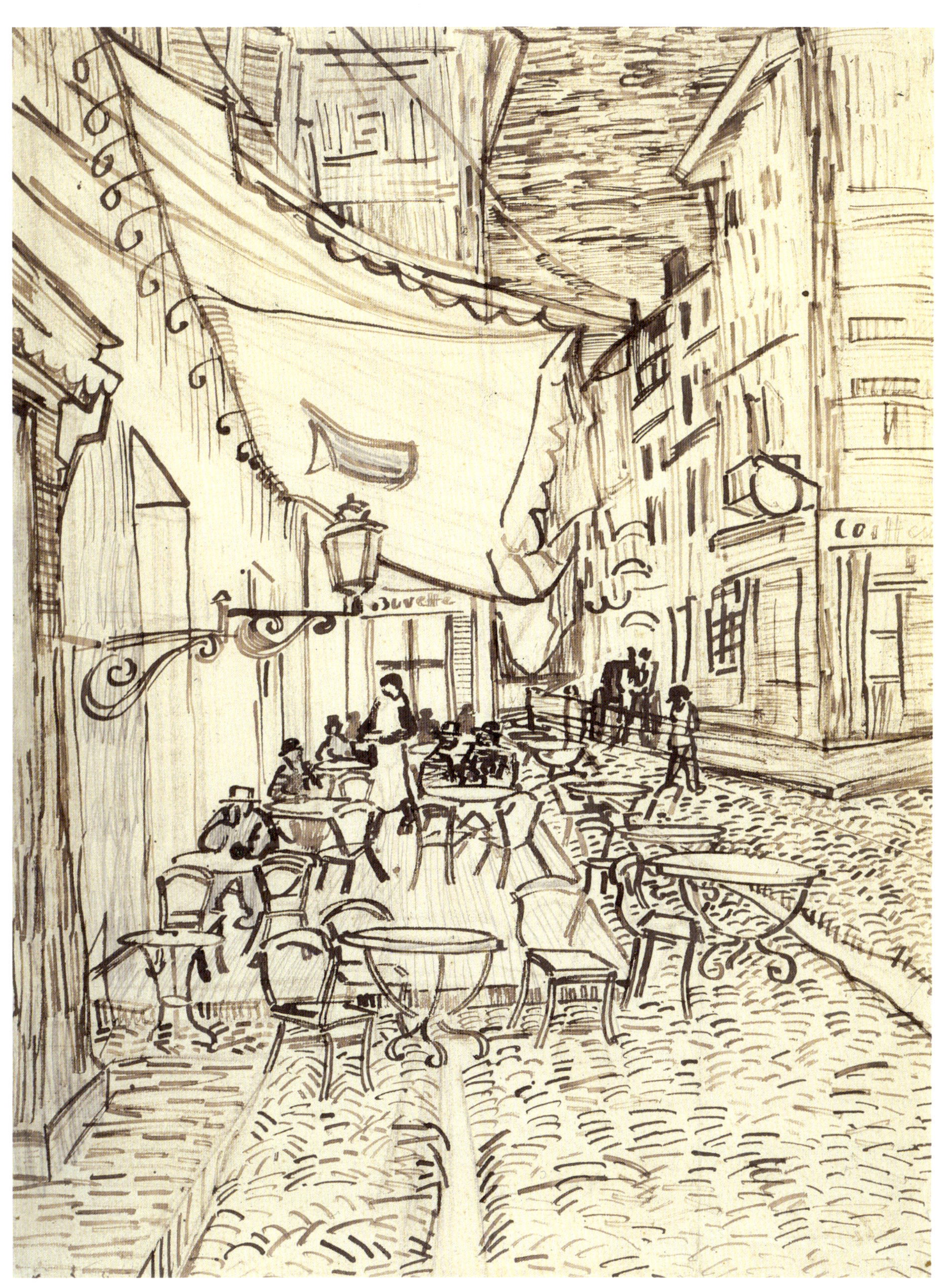

Cat. 34
Ploughed Fields (The Furrows)
Oil on canvas,
28 ½ × 36 ⅜ inches
(72.5 × 92.5 cm)
Van Gogh Museum,
Amsterdam
(Vincent van Gogh Foundation)
s40V1962
F574

Provenance
Sent by the artist to Theo van Gogh, Paris, late April 1889; Jo van Gogh-Bonger and Vincent Willem van Gogh, Paris, January 25, 1891; administered by Jo van Gogh-Bonger, Bussum/Amsterdam/Laren, until September 2, 1925; on loan from Vincent Willem van Gogh to the Stedelijk Museum, October 22, 1931; donated by Vincent Willem van Gogh to the (first) Vincent van Gogh Foundation, Laren, March 11, 1952; transferred to the Theo van Gogh Foundation, Laren, December 28, 1960; agreement July 21, 1962, entrusts collection to the State of the Netherlands until realization of the Rijksmuseum Vincent van Gogh, Amsterdam; donated by the Theo van Gogh Foundation to the (second) Vincent van Gogh Foundation; on loan to Stedelijk Museum, Amsterdam, until opening of Rijksmuseum Vincent van Gogh; Rijksmuseum Vincent van Gogh, Amsterdam, June 2, 1973; Van Gogh Museum, Amsterdam, July 1, 1994.

Following his *Field with Poppies* (cat. 30), painted in May 1888, Van Gogh repeatedly treated the subject of fields throughout the summer of that year. His *View of Arles with Irises in the Foreground*, also painted in May, was followed by *Wheatfield*, dated June 1888. The latter is a pure landscape, featuring the yellow ripened crop, while *The Harvest* from the same month is more anecdotal.[1] A number of farmers are shown performing tasks associated with the cutting and stacking of the crop or driving horse-drawn wagons from the fields to the farms. The intense summer heat is palpable on this canvas dominated by the bright yellow fields of ripe wheat.

The present work, on the other hand, depicts a landscape very similar to *Field with Poppies*, but its stark horizon is interrupted by a few trees and low houses. Instead of a verdant field of unripe corn, the harvested fields have been reduced to bare "furrows in the color of old wooden shoes under a forget-me-not blue sky with white flakes,"[2] stretching in different directions across the foreground. The application of paint is so thick that the clods of earth overturned by the plow appear three-dimensional. Van Gogh described his work of the time in a letter to Theo: "The present studies actually consist of a single flow of impasto. The brushstroke isn't greatly divided, and the tones are often broken. And in the end, without intending to, I'm forced to lay the paint on thickly, à la [Adolphe] Monticelli."[3]

He installed this piece in his Yellow House. He had a teal frame made for it that harmonized with the colors of the fields as well as with some of the teal furniture that he had assembled for his new home.[4] The letters to his brother from these months are filled with his ideas for furnishing his house — simply but comfortably — in anticipation of a visit from Paul Gauguin, who joined him there in October. Unfortunately, their time together ended in the disastrous confrontation in which Van Gogh cut off his ear, followed by Gauguin's immediate departure. HKA

Notes

1 *View of Arles with Irises in the Foreground* (May 1888), *Wheatfield* (June 1888), and *The Harvest* (June 1888) are all in the collection of the Van Gogh Museum, Amsterdam (Vincent van Gogh Foundation).

2 Ronald de Leeuw, *Van Gogh Museum* (Zwolle: Waanders, 1997), 178.

3 Letter 689, Vincent van Gogh to Theo van Gogh, Arles, September 26, 1888.

4 De Leeuw, *Van Gogh Museum*, 178.

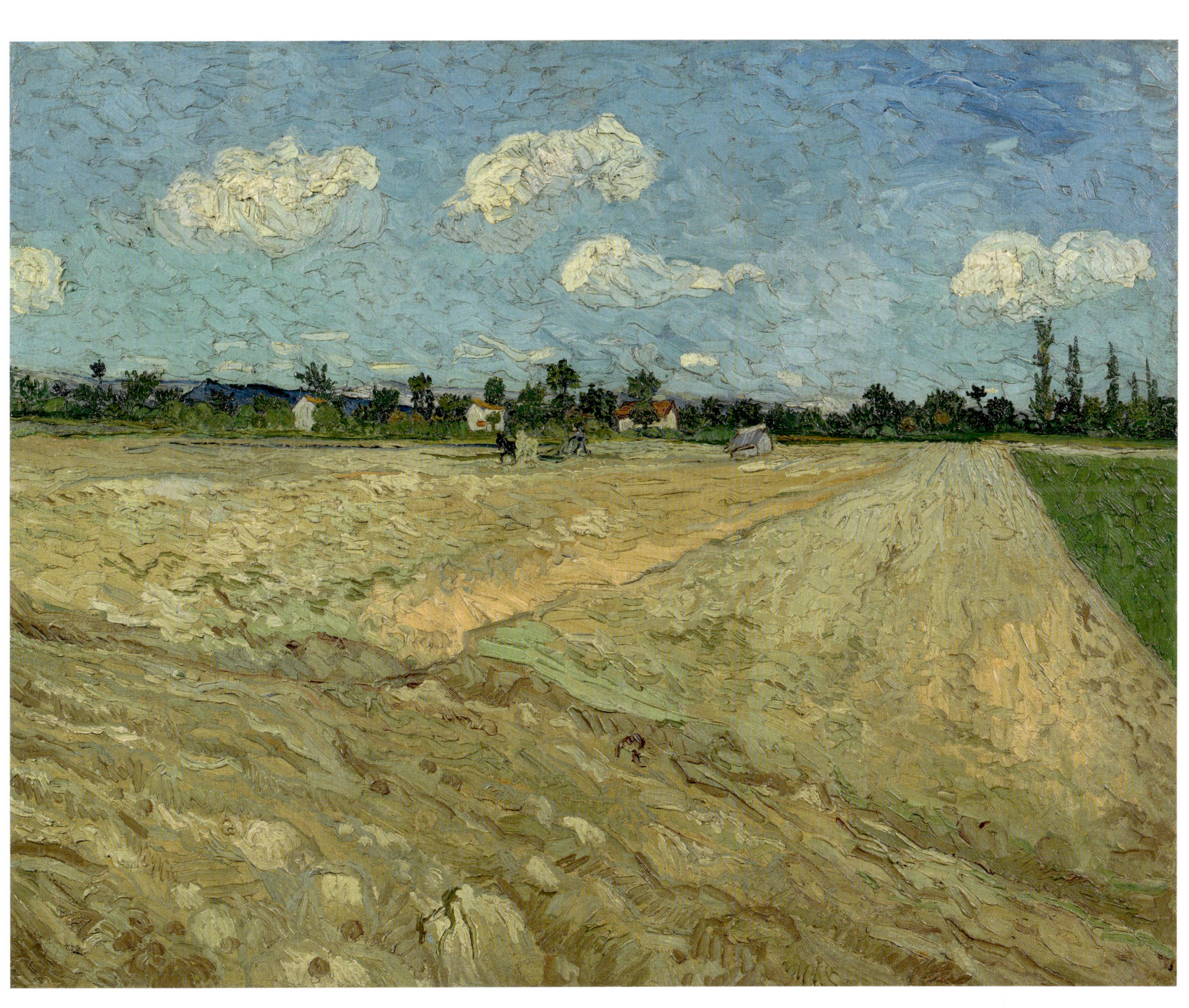

October 1888
Arles

Cat. 35
The Green Vineyard
Oil on canvas,
28 ⅞ × 36 ⅜ inches
(73.5 × 92.5 cm)
Kröller-Müller Museum,
Otterlo
KM 104.607
F475

Provenance
Jo van Gogh-Bonger, Amsterdam;
purchased by M. M. van Valkenburg,
Laren, 1905; probably returned by
Van Valkenburg to Jo van Gogh-Bonger
and traded for F384, Amsterdam;
purchase by L. C. Enthoven, Voorburg,
1905; purchased by H. Kröller-Müller
at Enthoven sale, Amsterdam (Frederik
Muller) May 18, 1920, lot 245: *Champs
de vignes.*

Some three weeks before Paul Gauguin joined him in the Yellow House in Arles, Van Gogh wrote, "I am feverishly active these days. Right now, I'm struggling with a blue sky above an immense green, purple, and yellow vineyard with black and orange vines. Little figures of ladies carrying red parasols and grape pickers in their small cart make it even gayer. There is gray sand in the foreground. It's another size 30 canvas for decorating the house."[1] Along with *The Harvest* and *Wheat Stacks in Provence*,[2] this painting was intended to be one of a series of large works that would greet Gauguin when he arrived at the Yellow House on October 23, 1888.

The site of the vineyard was across the flat plain from Arles, near the hill of Montmajour where Van Gogh often walked. The painting is highly complex, receding in planes from close-up views of leaves, twigs, and tendrils, through the middle ground where grape pickers work and figures leisurely stroll, to the distant fields and houses, and finally to the far horizon, glimpsed under the trees at the left, and the turbulent sky. The paint is piled up, almost interwoven in the foreground, with subtle complementary blues and oranges among the vines. The two red parasols glow against the green background. The sky is a swirling mass of wet-into-wet brushstrokes, the strong blue setting off the two orange roofs at the right.

Vincent wrote to Theo on October 3, "Ah, my study of the vineyard — I sweat blood and tears over it, but it's finally finished."[3] The result is an intricate, powerful work that consciously exploits high impasto for effect, perhaps in imitation of the extreme texture of the paintings of Adolphe Monticelli, whom Van Gogh admired. Van Gogh painted a second vineyard scene one month later, in which the dominant color was red, with a huge setting sun. The two paintings, of equal dimensions, were intended as complementary contrasts to each other.[4] DB

Notes

1 Letter 695, Vincent van Gogh to Paul Gauguin, Arles, October 3, 1888.

2 *The Harvest* (June 1888) is in the collection of the Van Gogh Museum, Amsterdam (Vincent van Gogh Foundation); *Wheat Stacks in Provence* (June 1888) is in the collection of the Kröller-Müller Museum, Otterlo.

3 Letter 694, Vincent van Gogh to Theo van Gogh, Arles, October 3, 1888.

4 See Hildelies Balk, Jos ten Berge, et al., *The Paintings of Vincent van Gogh in the Collection of the Kröller-Müller Museum* (Otterlo: Kröller-Müller Museum, 2003), 249–52.

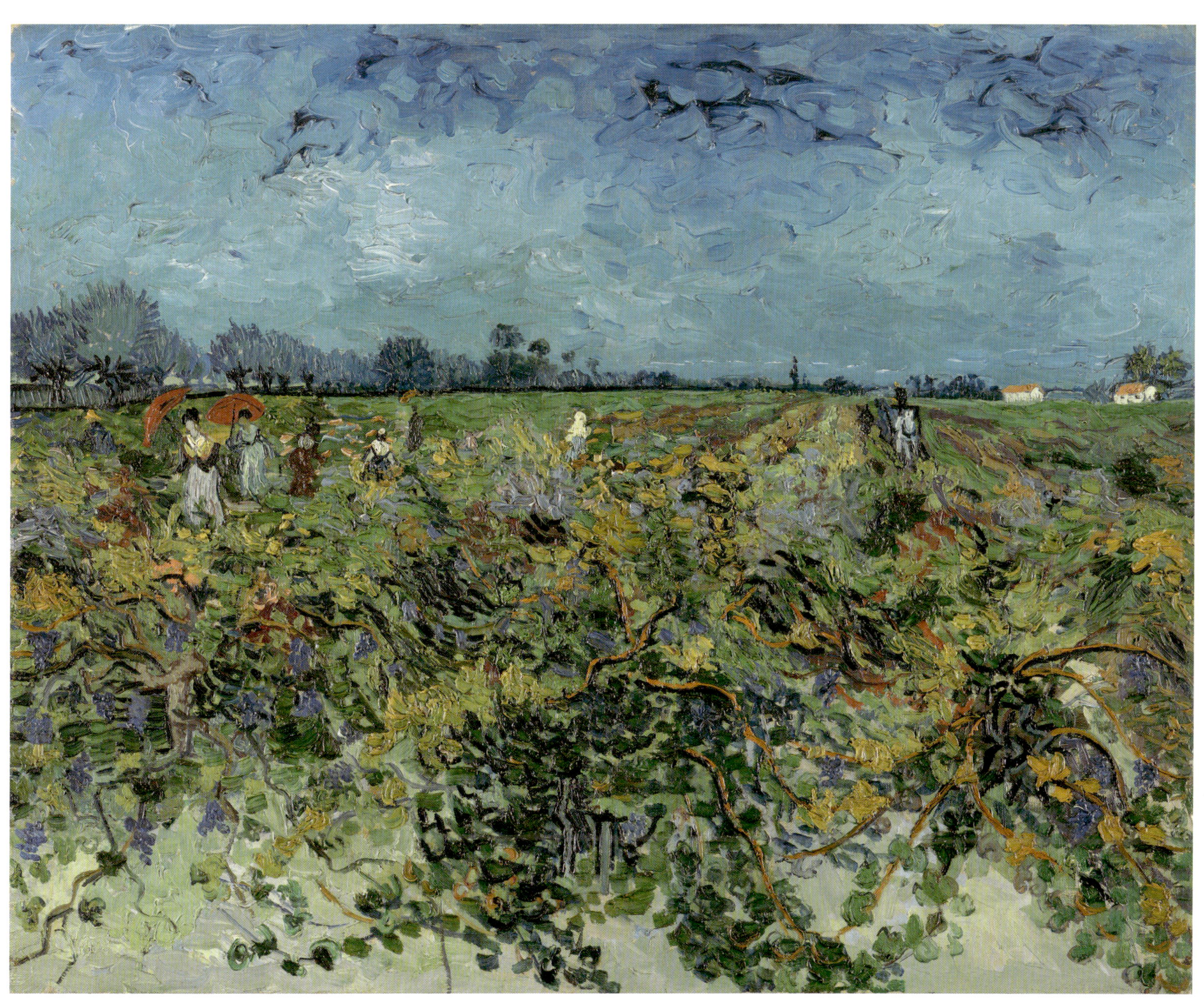

Cat. 36
Portrait of a Man
(Joseph-Michel Ginoux?)
Oil on canvas,
25 ¾ × 21 ⅜ inches
(65.3 × 54.4 cm)
Kröller-Müller Museum,
Otterlo
KM 103.189
F533

Provenance
J.-M. Ginoux, Arles; Abroise Vollard,
 art dealer (c. 1895–96); Bernheim-Jeune,
art dealer, Paris; Eugène Druet, art dealer,
Paris (R 1908, 1909); purchased by
H. Kröller-Müller at Druet, art dealer,
April 13, 1912.

Joseph-Michel Ginoux was the proprietor, with his wife Marie, of the Café de la Gare at 30 Place Lamartine, Arles, the establishment that is seen in the famous *Night Café*. Van Gogh lived there from May 7, 1888, moving in rather suddenly after a dispute about the bill at the Hôtel-Restaurant Carrel, where he had been living previously. He stayed until September 17, paying one franc a night, after which he moved to the Yellow House to await the arrival of Paul Gauguin. Van Gogh first painted Marie Ginoux in November in the celebrated portrait of *L'Arlésienne* (1888, Musée d'Orsay, Paris). Gauguin also drew her and included her portrait in his own version of *The Night Café*.

When Van Gogh painted this portrait of Joseph-Michel in December, Gauguin was positioned right beside him, painting the same sitter at the same time. The particular pose in Van Gogh's painting — angular head leaning back, eyes half closed, looking down his large nose somewhat arrogantly — is echoed precisely in Gauguin's portrait, observed from an oblique view. The same black coat, fashionable high white collar, and knotted bow appear in both paintings. The greenish light in Van Gogh's portrait falls from the left and may be cast by a gas lamp that was installed in the Yellow House so that the two artists could continue to paint after dark.

Marie and Joseph-Michel Ginoux were loyal friends to Van Gogh. They kept in touch with him when he went to the asylum in Saint-Rémy, looking after some of his possessions, and later when he went north to Auvers-sur-Oise. The identity of the sitter for this portrait became obscured at some point after Van Gogh left Arles, and, for most of its existence in the twentieth century, it was simply known as *Portrait of a Man*.[1] DB

Note
1 See Hildelies Balk, Jos ten Berge, et al. *The Paintings of Vincent van Gogh in the Collection of the Kröller-Müller Museum* (Otterlo: Kröller-Müller Museum, 2003), 258–60.

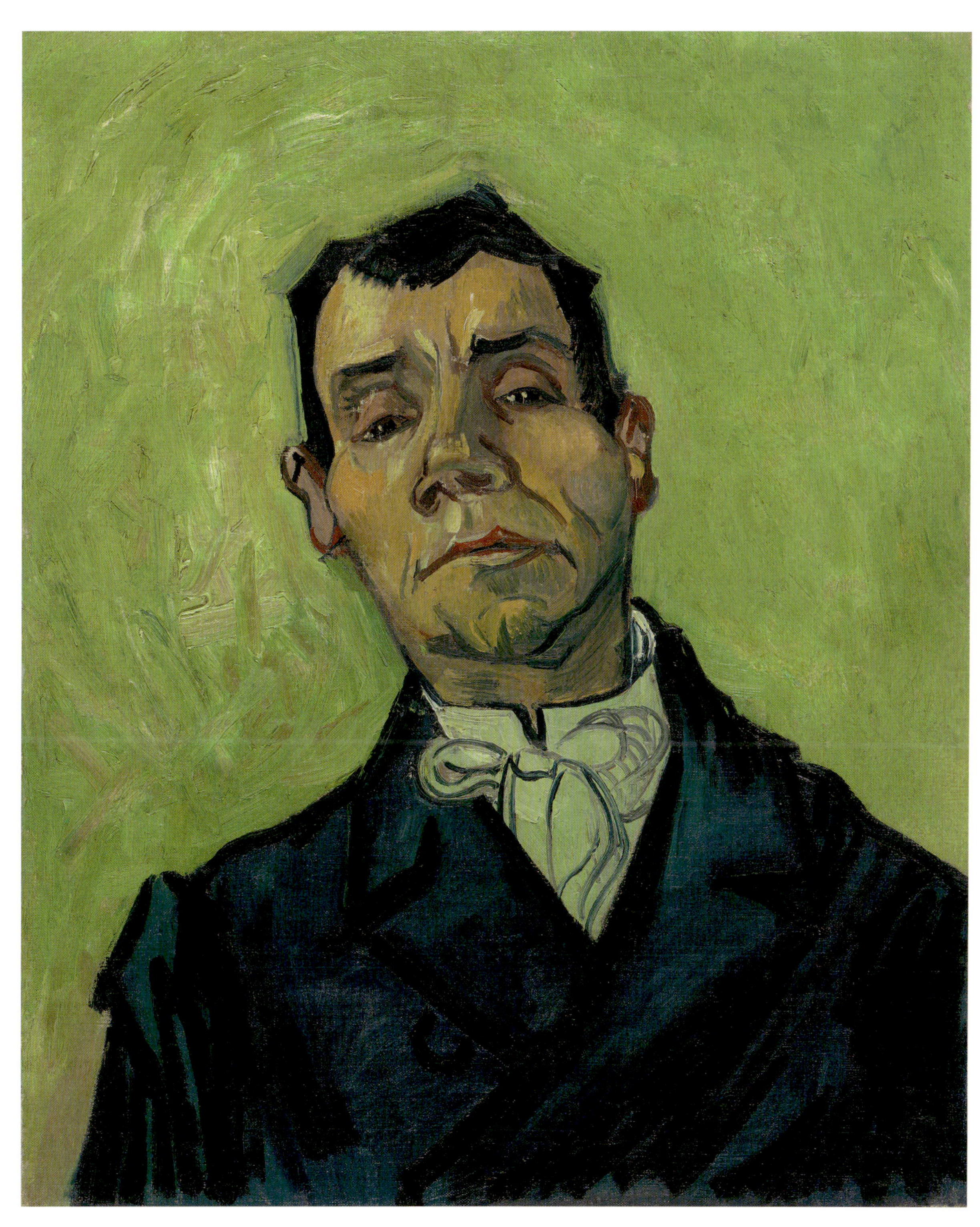

January 1889
Arles

Cat. 37
*Still Life with a Plate
of Onions*
Oil on canvas,
19 ½ × 25 ⅞ inches
(49.6 × 64.4 cm)
Kröller-Müller Museum,
Otterlo
KM 111.075
F604

Provenance
Joseph Hessel, art dealer/coll., Paris
(R 1904, 1909); Bernheim-Jeune, art dealer, Paris, 1910; Paul Cassirer, art dealer,
Berlin, 1910; M. de Nemes coll., Budapest,
1910; purchased for H. Kröller-Müller
by H.P. Bremmer at Nemes sale, Paris
(Manzi-Joyant), June 18, 1913, lot 106:
Nature morte.

Van Gogh imbued this still life of very ordinary objects with so much meaning that it can be understood as a self-portrait. It was painted at a particularly troubled moment in the artist's life, just days after his release from the hospital where he had been treated for the self-inflicted injury to his ear.[1] A confrontation with Paul Gauguin, who had stayed with Van Gogh for a few weeks, took place just before Christmas 1888, culminating in his cutting off his ear and Gauguin's hasty departure. In a sense, this work can be read as Van Gogh's coming-to-terms with the fraught relationship he had with Gauguin — a summing up, but also a first tentative step forward.[2]

Several of the objects displayed on the simple deal table had previously served to characterize Gauguin and Van Gogh in the paintings of their respective chairs (1889, Van Gogh Museum, Amsterdam, and 1889, National Gallery, London). The pipe and tobacco are found on his own simple rush chair, while a box of onions — accented by his signature — is tucked behind it in a corner of the room. Gauguin's more elaborate chair has two books and a candle in the same blue ceramic holder on its seat. Besides these objects arranged around a plate of onions, Van Gogh includes a stick of red sealing wax and matches as well as a letter — from his brother — and a book. It is the *Manuel annuaire de la santé* by François-Vincent Raspail, a handbook for homeopathic medicines and their domestic use, an obvious indication of his struggles with numerous health problems.[3] The large bottle in the foreground most likely held absinthe, the wormwood-based, highly alcoholic drink whose hallucinogenic properties may have been exaggerated, but which nonetheless was anything but salubrious. The large green coffeepot opposite the bottle refers to Van Gogh's love of the more harmless beverage. Despite the light tonality and the delicate yet assured brushwork, this still life offers a peek into Van Gogh's troubled state, his struggles with loneliness, his deteriorating mental and physical health, and his desire to find salvation through his art. HKA

Notes
1 Hildelies Balk, Jos ten Berge, et al., *The Paintings of Vincent van Gogh in the Collection of the Kröller-Müller Museum* (Otterlo: Kröller-Müller Museum, 2003), 261.

2 See letter 737, Paul Gauguin to Vincent van Gogh, Paris, January 17, 1889.

3 Balk, Ten Berge, et al., *The Paintings of Vincent van Gogh*, 262.

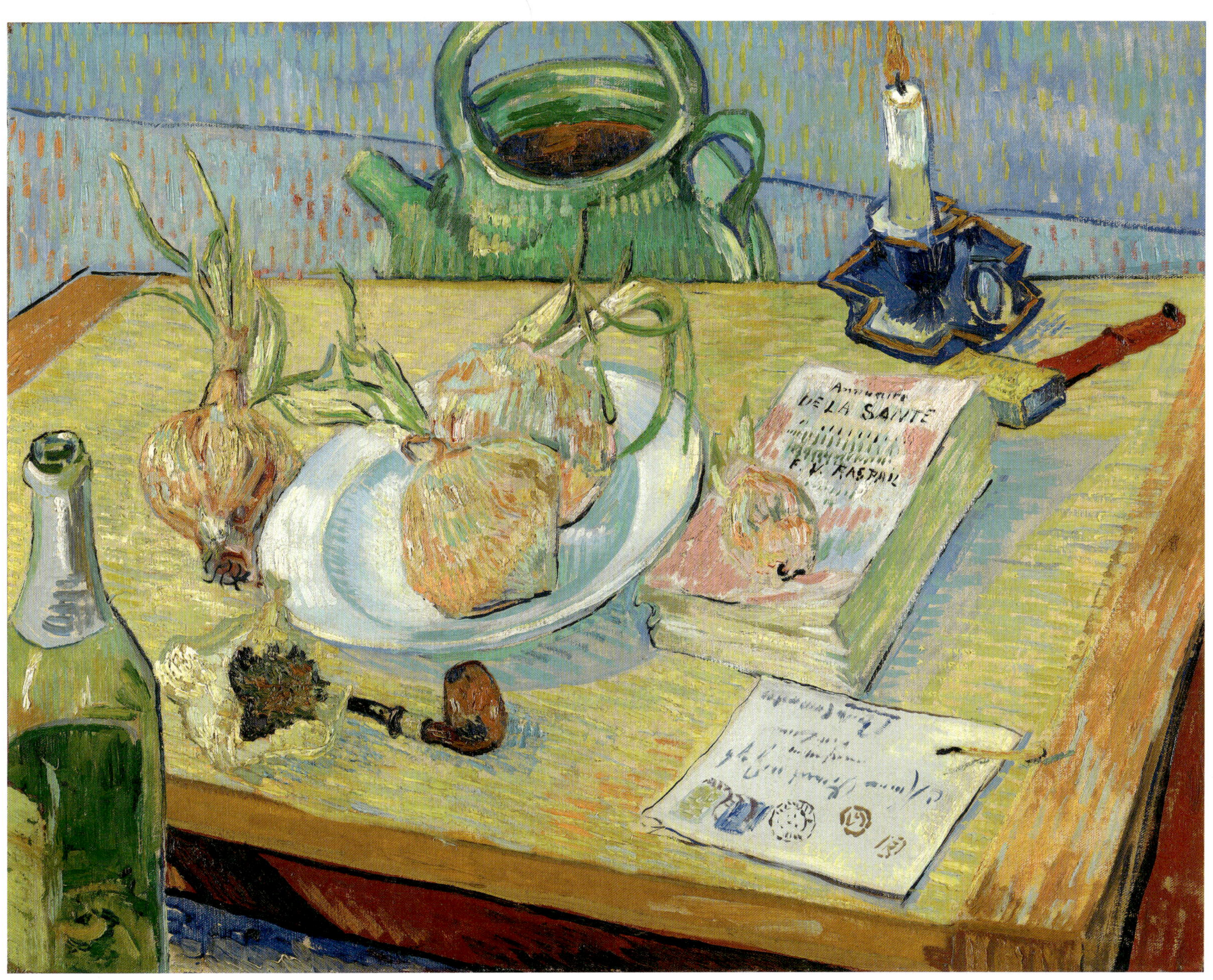

DE LA SANTÉ
F. V. RASPAIL

May 1889
Arles

Cat. 38
Weeping Tree
Reed pen and black-brown
ink, with black chalk on
off-white paper,
19 ⅝ × 24 ⅛ inches
(49.8 × 61.3 cm)
Art Institute of Chicago, gift
of Tiffany and Margaret Blake
1945.31
F1468

Provenance
Sent by the artist to Theo van Gogh, June
19, 1889; by descent to the artist's
sister-in-law, Johanna Cohen van Gogh-
Bonger and by inheritance of his son,
Vincent Willem van Gogh, Amsterdam;
given by the Van Gogh family to Dr. Jan
Pieter Veth, Amsterdam; given by descent
to his daughter-in-law, Christine Veth,
San Francisco, by 1935; [consigned to
Wildenstein and Company, New York,
1945]; purchased by the Art Institute of
Chicago, 1945.

Notes
1 Letter 638, Vincent van Gogh to Theo van Gogh, Arles, July 9 or 10, 1888.

2 Letter 600, Vincent van Gogh to Theo van Gogh, Arles, April 20, 1888.

3 See Louis van Tilborgh, Nienke Bakker, Cornelia Homburg, Tsukasa
Kōdera, and Chris Uhlenbeck, *Van Gogh & Japan*, exh. cat. (Amsterdam:
Van Gogh Museum; Sapporo, Hokkaido Shimbun Press; Brussels:
Mercatorfonds, 2018), 65.

4 See his drawings from Montmajour in Colta Ives, Susan Alyson Stein,
Sjraar van Heuten, and Marije Vellekoop, *Vincent van Gogh: The Drawings*,
exh. cat. (New York: The Metropolitan Museum of Art; Amsterdam: Van
Gogh Museum; New Haven and London: Yale University Press, 2005),
236–47. Beginning in February 1888, the artist produced paintings and
drawings of public gardens that contained the weeping tree, such as *The
Poet's Garden*, 1888, oil on canvas, Mr. and Mrs. Lewis Larned Coburn
Memorial Collection, Art Institute of Chicago (F468) and *Garden with
Weeping Tree, Arles*, August 1888, reed pen, quill and ink over graphite on
wove paper, The Menil Collection, Houston, 1978-172 E (F1451).

5 Letter 768, Vincent van Gogh to Theo van Gogh, Arles, May 3, 1889.

6 See Marije Vellekoop and Roelie Zwikker, *Vincent van Gogh Drawings*,
vol. 4, *Arles, Saint Rémy and Auvers-sur-Oise, 1888–1890*, *Van Gogh
Museum* (Amsterdam: Van Gogh Museum, 1996), 178–79, and *Vincent van
Gogh: The Drawings*, 278–81, 290.

7 Letter 782, Vincent van Gogh to Theo van Gogh, Saint-Rémy-de-
Provence, on or about June 18, 1889.

In Arles, drawing once again became a significant part of
Van Gogh's artistic output. He used drawings in preparation
for paintings, made them after paintings, and used them to
jot down a thought, to explore an element more thoroughly,
and to inform his brother or friends of his artistic pursuits.
Drawing or sketching with pen and paper was more affordable than working with paint and canvas. "I'm doing the
right thing by working chiefly on drawings," he wrote to his
brother, "with paper — if it's not a letter I'm writing but a
drawing I'm doing — it hardly ever goes wrong."[1] The reed
pen was a useful companion to Van Gogh as he explored
the French landscape with rapidity and directness: "These
drawings are done with a reed cut the same way as you'd
cut a goose quill. . . . It's a process I already tried in Holland
in the past, but I didn't have as good reeds there as here."[2]
He also thought his pen manner reflected "the style of
Japanese prints" in its use of concise and varied mark-making.[3]

This reed-pen drawing of a solemn tree with soft, drooping
branches is one of his last made in Arles. The bold outlines
and quick, staccato marks are part of his animated graphic
vocabulary and rival strokes of color in his paintings. He had
been fully engaged in pen drawings of the landscapes and
public gardens around Arles through September 1888, but
abandoned the medium, only to return to it in May, shortly
before leaving the city.[4] He wrote of this drawing: "Today I've
made one of those drawings [with a reed pen] which became very dark and quite melancholic for springtime."[5] He
decorated his hospital room with Japanese prints and mentioned hanging "two large reed-pen drawings" — his latest,
Weeping Tree and *Garden of the Hospital* — on the wall.[6] He
carried these drawings with him to Saint-Rémy and subsequently sent them to his brother Theo.[7] DMW

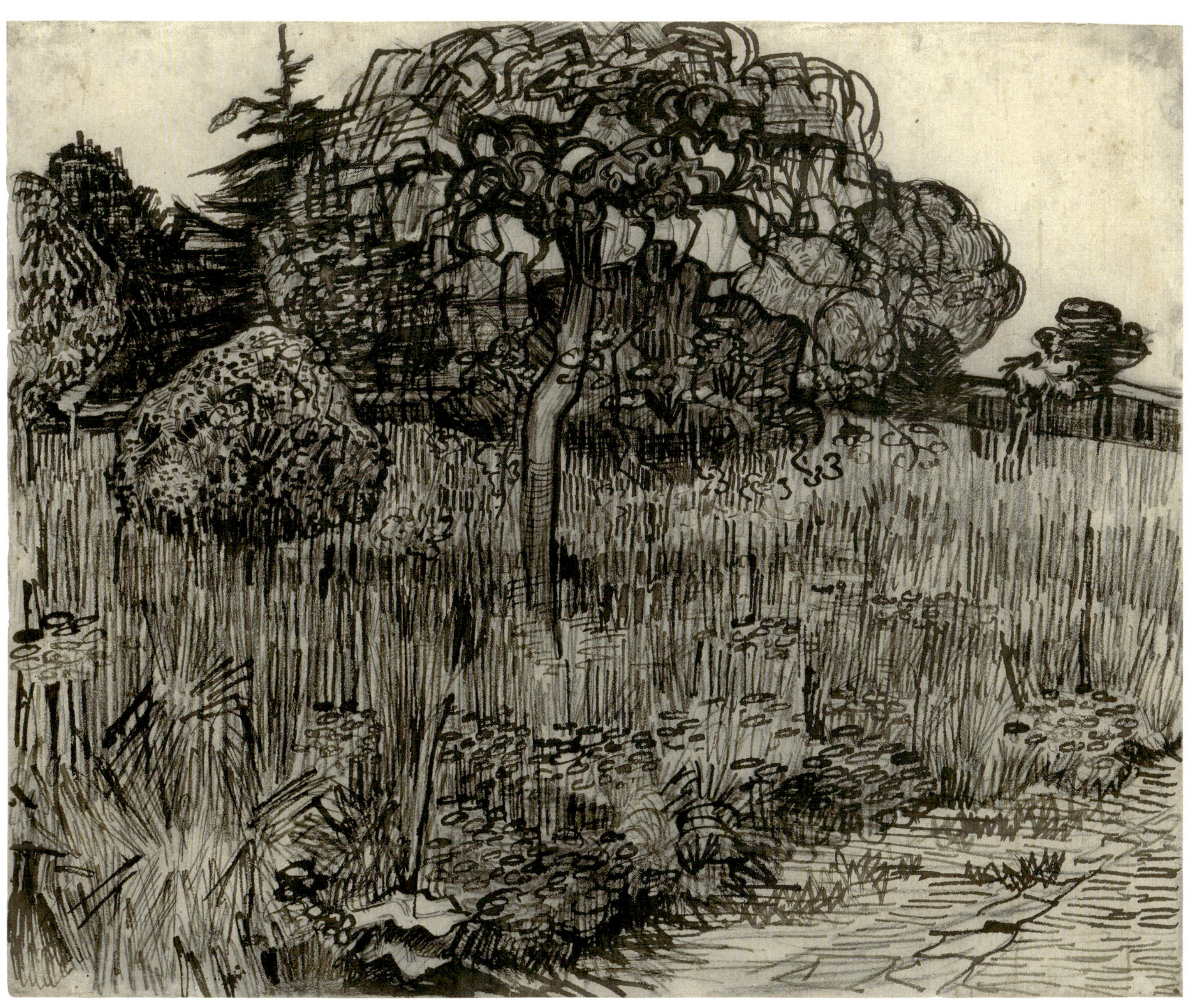

May 1889
Saint-Rémy

Cat. 39
*The Garden of the Asylum at
Saint-Rémy*
Oil on canvas,
36 × 28 ⅜ inches (91.5 × 72 cm)
Kröller-Müller Museum,
Otterlo
KM 101.508
F734

Provenance
L. C. Enthoven coll., Voorburg (R 1904);
purchase by H. Kröller-Müller at
Enthoven sale, Amsterdam (Frederik
Muller), May 18, 1920, lot 247: *Jardin
de l'hôpital à Arles.*

Notes
1 Letter 776, Vincent van Gogh to Theo van Gogh, Saint-Rémy-de-
Provence, on or about May 23, 1889.

2 See Hildelies Balk, Jos ten Berge, et al., *The Paintings of Vincent van
Gogh in the Collection of the Kröller-Müller Museum* (Otterlo: Kröller-
Müller Museum, 2003), 283–86.

3 Letter 772, Vincent van Gogh to Jo van Gogh-Bonger, Saint-Rémy-de-
Provence, May 9, 1889.

4 Letter 776.

After his breakdown, Van Gogh voluntarily entered the
Saint-Paul-de-Mausole asylum at Saint-Rémy in May 1889.
For the first few weeks, he was confined to the building
and grounds and immediately looked for subjects to paint
behind the walls of the institution: "Since I've been here,
the neglected garden planted with tall pines and badly tended
grass intermingled with various weeds has provided me
with enough work and I haven't yet gone outside."[1] He made
a number of paintings of the garden on the west side of
the asylum, both in general views and in close-up studies of
plants and bushes. It was here that the famous *Irises* (cat. 48)
and *Lilacs* were painted.

The present painting, on a large size 30 canvas, offers a
view along the wall of the north wing of the men's block,
with its characteristic drain pipes projecting outward
halfway up the facade. The steep perspective is something
he had mastered earlier in his career, and it is sketched out
in an underdrawing of pencil or black chalk, visible in places
under the paint layers.

In swathes of brilliant brushstrokes, Van Gogh captures
the luxuriant growth of trees and flowers and weeds that
pressed close to and overshadowed the buildings. At ground
level, the grasses are shown as swirls, clumps, and long
ranks of short verticals in green, blue-green, and gold, with
flat green patches for the grass between the trees to the
right. Moving up the canvas, individual flowers and bushes
give way to a tree canopy of dazzling color and wildness —
like an exploding firework display — set against a deep blue
Provençal sky. The painting is signed, which is significant
in that Van Gogh consciously distinguished between finished,
signed paintings (*tableaux*) and studies (*études*) in his letters to Theo: this work was mentioned as more of an *étude*,
but he signed it anyway.[2]

Van Gogh's painting activities were of great interest to his
fellow patients. He wrote to his sister-in-law Jo: "They all come
to see when I'm working in the garden, and I can assure
you are more discreet and more polite to leave me in peace
than, for example, the good citizens of Arles."[3] He was
determined not to fall into the "extreme lethargy suffered by
those who have been here for some years already. Now
my work will protect me from this to a certain extent."[4] DB

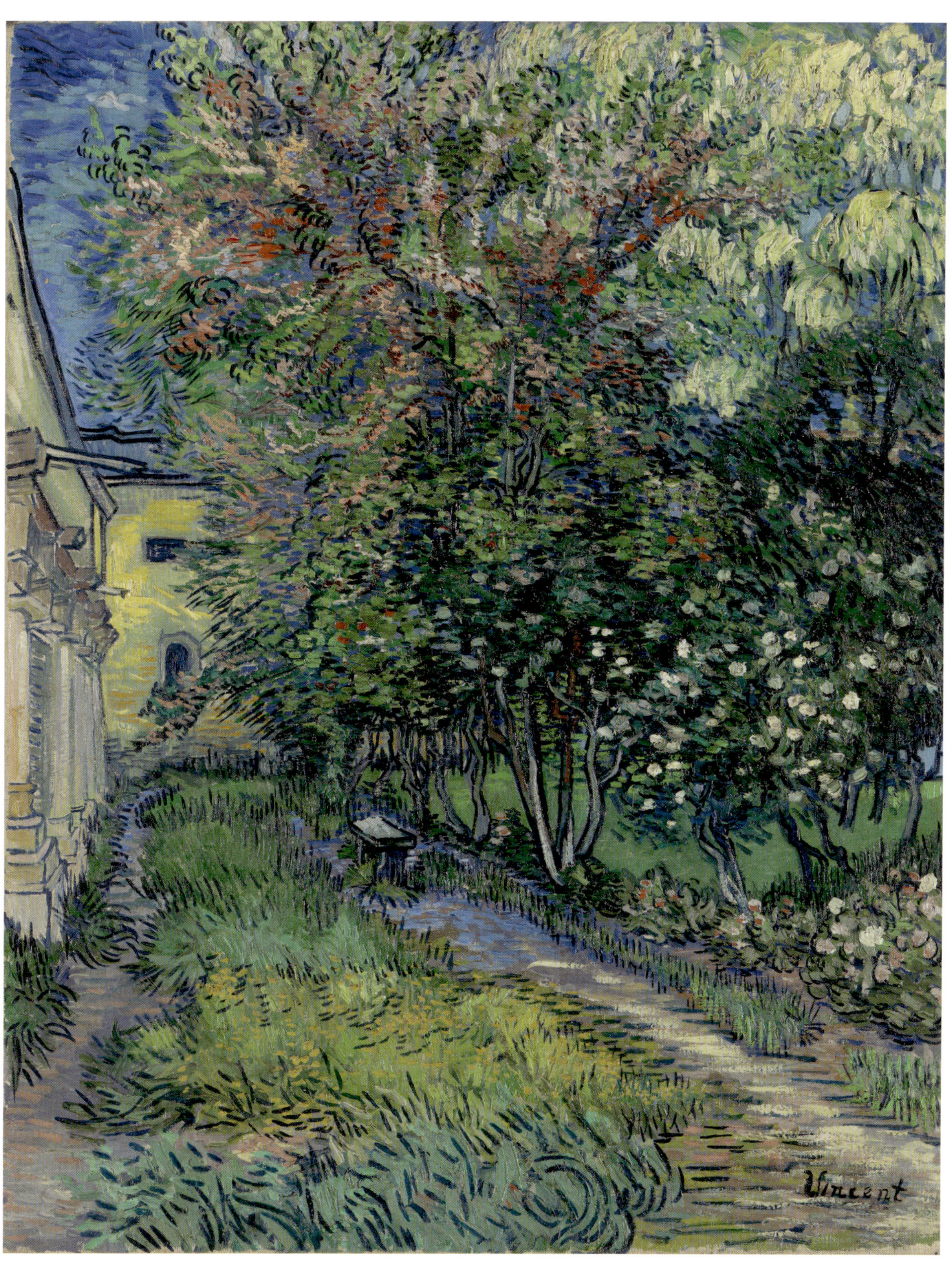

Cat. 40
Entrance to a Quarry
Oil on canvas,
23 ⅝ × 29 ⅜ inches (60 × 74.5 cm)
Van Gogh Museum,
Amsterdam
(Vincent van Gogh Foundation)
s41V1962
F744

Provenance
Sent by the artist to Theo van Gogh, Paris, late September 1889; Jo van Gogh-Bonger and Vincent Willem van Gogh, Paris, January 25, 1891; administered by Jo van Gogh-Bonger, Bussum/Amsterdam/Laren, until September 2, 1925; on loan from Vincent Willem van Gogh, Laren, to the Stedelijk Museum, Amsterdam, October 22, 1931; transferred to Vincent van Gogh Foundation, Amsterdam, July 10, 1962; agreement July 21, 1962, entrusts collection to the State of the Netherlands until realization of the Rijksmuseum Vincent van Gogh, Amsterdam; on loan to Stedelijk Museum, Amsterdam, until opening of Rijksmuseum Vincent van Gogh; Rijksmuseum Vincent van Gogh, Amsterdam, June 2, 1973; Van Gogh Museum, Amsterdam, July 1, 1994.

The asylum at Saint-Rémy was near the low mountain range of the Alpilles, the other side of which Van Gogh had seen daily from Arles. He described them to his sister-in-law as "little grey or blue mountains with very, very green wheatfields at their foot, and pines."[1] It was here that he drew and painted his celebrated studies titled *Wheat Fields with Cypresses*, inspired by the view from his window.

After a few weeks, he was permitted to leave the confines of the asylum and paint outside, but always accompanied by an orderly. He painted the Alpilles from far away and close up, showing wide views of the receding line of hills and also the rugged rock formations of the individual peaks. He was particularly fascinated by a quarry not far from the asylum: he painted it twice, in mid-July (the present work) and again in October. This painting was done at a moment of renewed crisis. On the windy day he was working on it, he experienced the panic of immense loneliness: he finished the painting, but quickly retreated to the asylum, where he was confined to his room for a month and not allowed to paint. He had his painting materials taken away because he would attempt to swallow them. He wrote to Theo: "For many days I have been absolutely distraught as in Arles, just as much if not worse, and it's to be presumed that these crises will recur in the future. It is abominable."[2] After a month, he was cautiously allowed out to begin painting again.[3]

Entrance to a Quarry is remarkable for its swirling angular forms and rich but subdued palette of colors. It consists almost entirely of vegetation and tawny rocks, but the mountain ridge and a glimpse of deep blue sky are just visible at the top. Van Gogh wrote to Theo that it was "precisely a more sober attempt, matte in color without looking impressive, broken greens, reds and rusty ochre yellows, as I told you that from time to time I felt a desire to begin again with a palette like the one in the north."[4] DB

Notes
1 Letter 772, Vincent van Gogh to Jo van Gogh-Bonger, Saint-Rémy-de-Provence, May 9, 1889.

2 Letter 797, Vincent van Gogh to Theo van Gogh, Saint-Rémy-de-Provence, August 22, 1889.

3 See Ronald Pickvance, *Van Gogh in Saint-Rémy and Auvers* (New York: The Metropolitan Museum of Art, 1986), 119–20, cat. 21.

4 Letter 797.

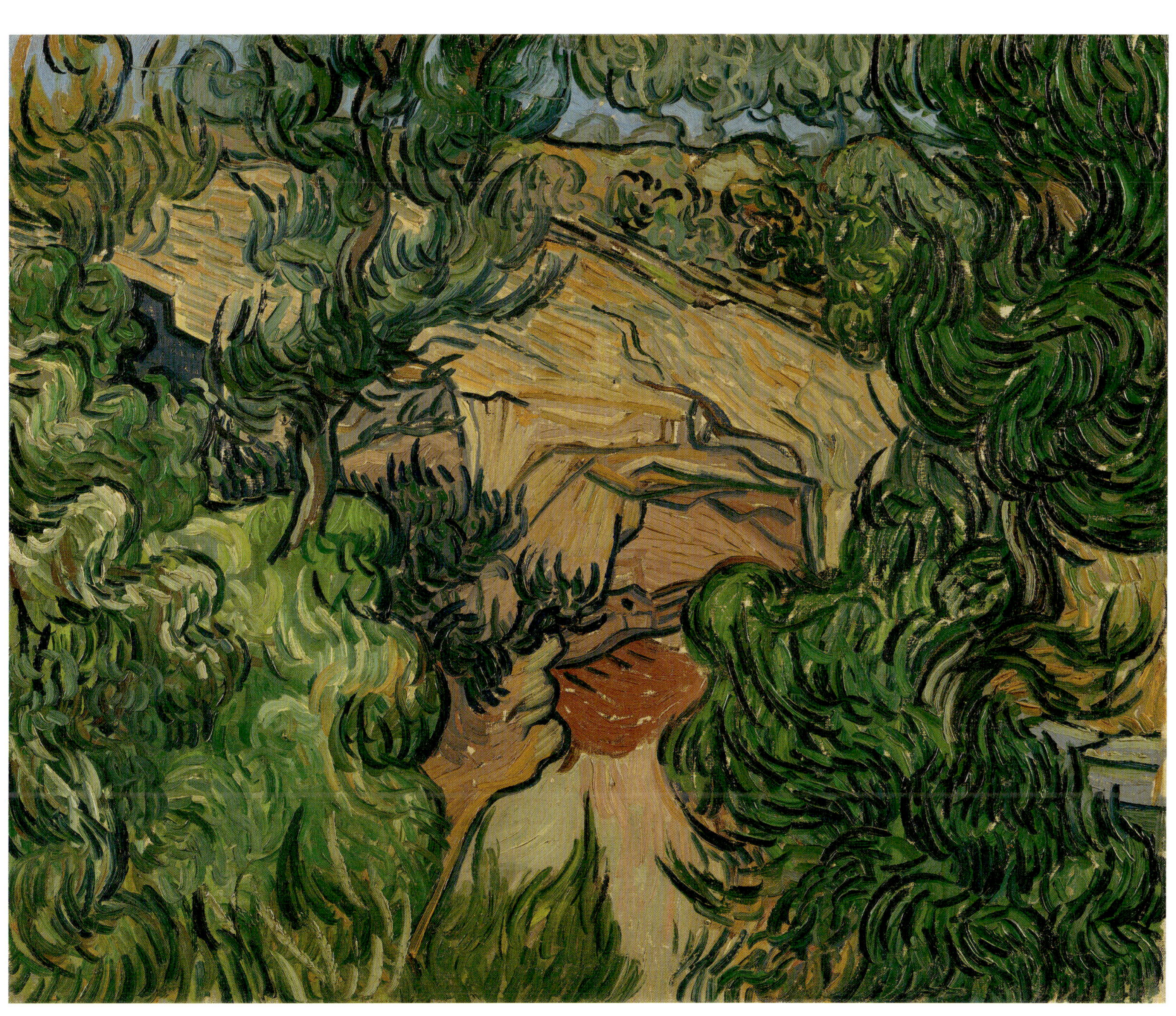

Cat. 41
Tree Trunks with Ivy
Oil on canvas,
19 ¼ × 25 ½ inches (49 × 64.7 cm)
Kröller-Müller Museum,
Otterlo
KM 100.398
F747

Provenance
Jo van Gogh-Bonger, Amsterdam; C. M.
van Gogh, art dealer, Amsterdam, 1910;
purchased by H. Kröller-Müller at C. M.
van Gogh, art dealer, June 24, 1910.

At the beginning of May 1889, Van Gogh checked himself into the Saint-Paul-de-Mausole mental hospital at Saint-Rémy because he no longer felt strong enough to live on his own.[1] His doctor thought that a form of epilepsy was triggering his attacks and that a complete recovery was unlikely. Van Gogh was allowed to paint out-of-doors, but he was confined to the garden of the hospital, where he painted several versions of this *sous-bois* of tree trunks and undergrowth.

The relationship of this canvas to a larger painting of the same subject in the Van Gogh Museum, titled *Tree Trunks in the Garden of the Asylum*, also dated to July 1889, is unclear. It may be a preliminary study or an autograph copy on a smaller scale.[2] Besides the notable difference in size, the two works differ significantly in their tonality. Although the tree trunks are captured in a virtually identical disposition, the smaller painting almost entirely lacks the sunlight playing among them and in the background. The overall effect of this composition in dark shades of greens and browns, without any hint of sky, is rather gloomy. The impasto is heavy, laid on in directional brushstrokes that emphasize the vegetative growth of the dense underwood. At this moment, during the early months of his confinement to the asylum, Van Gogh was experimenting with a style uniquely his own. This highly emotive manner informs his paintings of cypress trees and wheat fields, dated June and early July, and includes the celebrated *Starry Night* (June 1889, Museum of Modern Art, New York).

It is possible that this is a preliminary study for the larger version, but Van Gogh also made copies on a reduced scale of his most important works to send to his mother and sisters in Holland. "I've taken the best of 12 subjects, so in any case they will get things that are well thought out and well chosen,"[3] Van Gogh wrote to his brother Theo in September 1889, but, unfortunately, he did not mention *Tree Trunks with Ivy* specifically. HKA

Notes

1 Ronald de Leeuw, *Van Gogh Museum* (Zwolle: Waanders, 1997), 183.

2 Hildelies Balk, Jos ten Berge, et al., *The Paintings of Vincent van Gogh in the Collection of the Kröller-Müller Museum* (Otterlo: Kröller-Müller Museum, 2003), 311. The work is slightly cut down.

3 Letter 806, Vincent van Gogh to Theo van Gogh, Saint-Rémy-de-Provence, September 28, 1889.

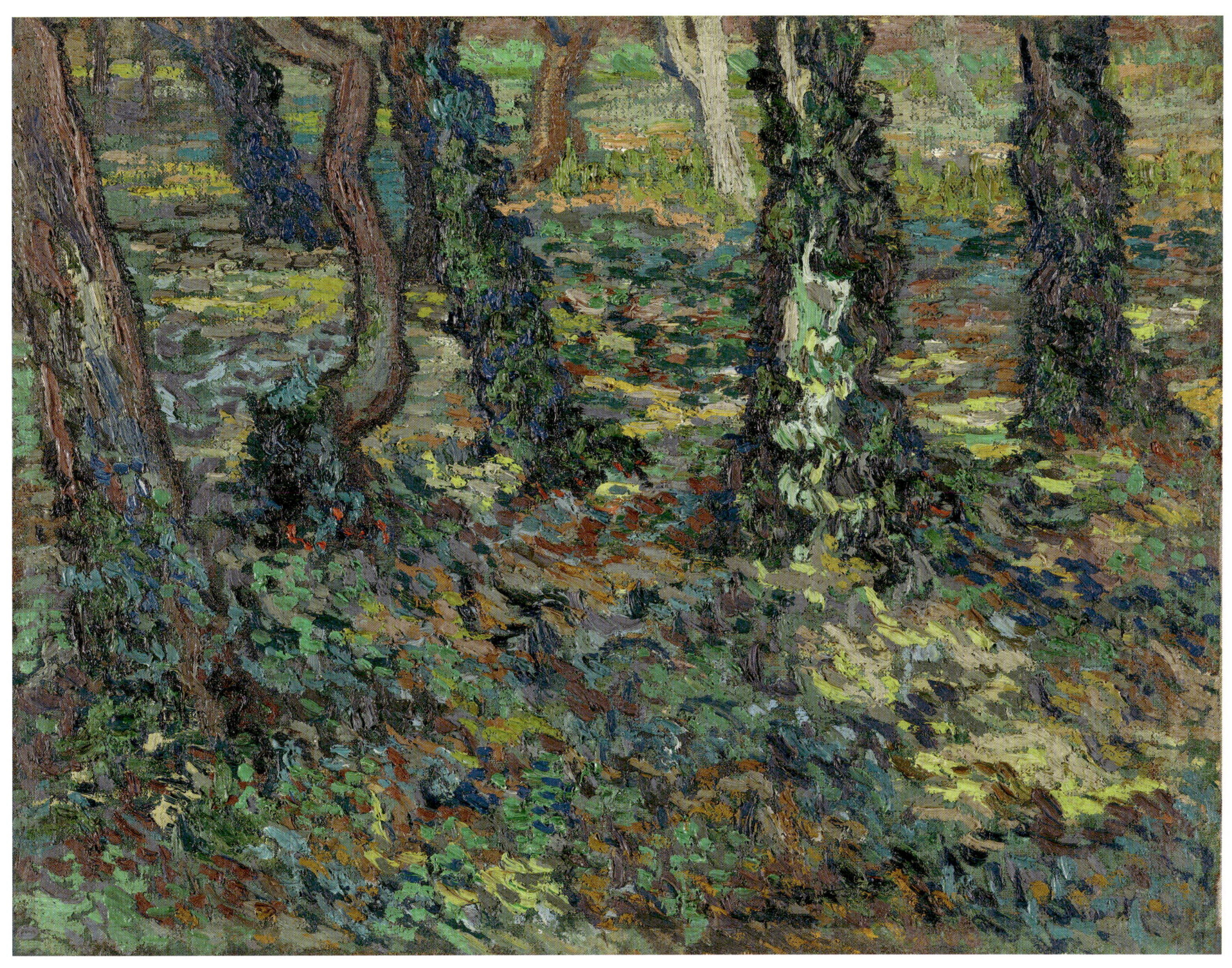

Cat. 42
Peasant Woman Binding Sheaves
(after Millet)
Oil on canvas on cardboard,
17 × 13⅛ inches (43.2 × 33.2 cm)
Van Gogh Museum,
Amsterdam
(Vincent van Gogh Foundation)
s172V1962
F700

Provenance
Sent by the artist to Theo van Gogh,
Paris, late April 1890; Jo van Gogh-
Bonger and Vincent Willem van
Gogh, Paris, January 25, 1891; sold to
Henri Bonger, Amsterdam, August
1905; Betsy Bonger, Amsterdam,
May 17, 1929; Vincent Willem van
Gogh, Laren, January 17, 1944; donated
by Vincent Willem van Gogh to the
(first) Vincent van Gogh Foundation,
Laren, March 11, 1952; transferred
to the Theo van Gogh Foundation,
Laren, December 28, 1960; agreement
July 21, 1962, entrusts collection to the
State of the Netherlands until realiza-
tion of the Rijksmuseum Vincent
van Gogh, Amsterdam; donated by the
Theo van Gogh Foundation to the
(second) Vincent van Gogh Foundation,
July 21, 1962; on loan to Stedelijk
Museum, Amsterdam, until opening
of Rijksmuseum Vincent van Gogh;
Rijksmuseum Vincent van Gogh,
Amsterdam, June 2, 1973; Van Gogh
Museum, Amsterdam, July 1, 1994.

From September 1889, Van Gogh made twenty paintings, copying images in prints by or after Jean-François Millet. It was another moment of crisis for Van Gogh in the Saint-Rémy asylum, and, for consolation and rebuilding his self-confidence, he returned to the painter who had inspired him in his early years. These two paintings are from Millet's *Travaux des champs* (Work in the Fields) series. In a letter to Theo, Van Gogh wrote, "At present I have 7 copies out of ten of Millet's *Travaux des champs*. I can assure you that it interests me enormously to make copies, and that not having any models for the moment it will ensure that I don't lose sight of the figure."[1]

He acknowledged his current difficulties and described his working method and intentions: "Since I'm above all ill at present, I'm trying to do something to console myself, for my own pleasure. I put the black-and-white by Delacroix or Millet in front of me as a subject. And then I improvise color on it but, being me, not completely of course, but seeking memories of *their* paintings—but the memory, the vague consonance of colors that are in the same sentiment, if not right—that's my interpretation."[2]

The paintings are strikingly composed in tones of blue and yellow. For the more subdued *Peasant Woman Binding Sheaves*, Van Gogh has invented a landscape background with receding fields and a village on the horizon. *The Sheaf-Binder* (cat. 43) is an extraordinary essay in color: linked forms of bright blue limbs define the crouching figure against a swirling golden yellow sea of wheat sheaves, under a brilliant pale blue sky. Although the composition is Millet's, the exuberance of colored patterns and the sheer energy of the brushwork is all Van Gogh's.[3] DB

Notes
1 Letter 805, Vincent van Gogh to Theo van Gogh, Saint-Rémy-de-Provence, on or about September 20, 1889.

2 Ibid.

3 Ronald de Leeuw, *Van Gogh Museum* (Zwolle: Waanders, 1997), 190–91.

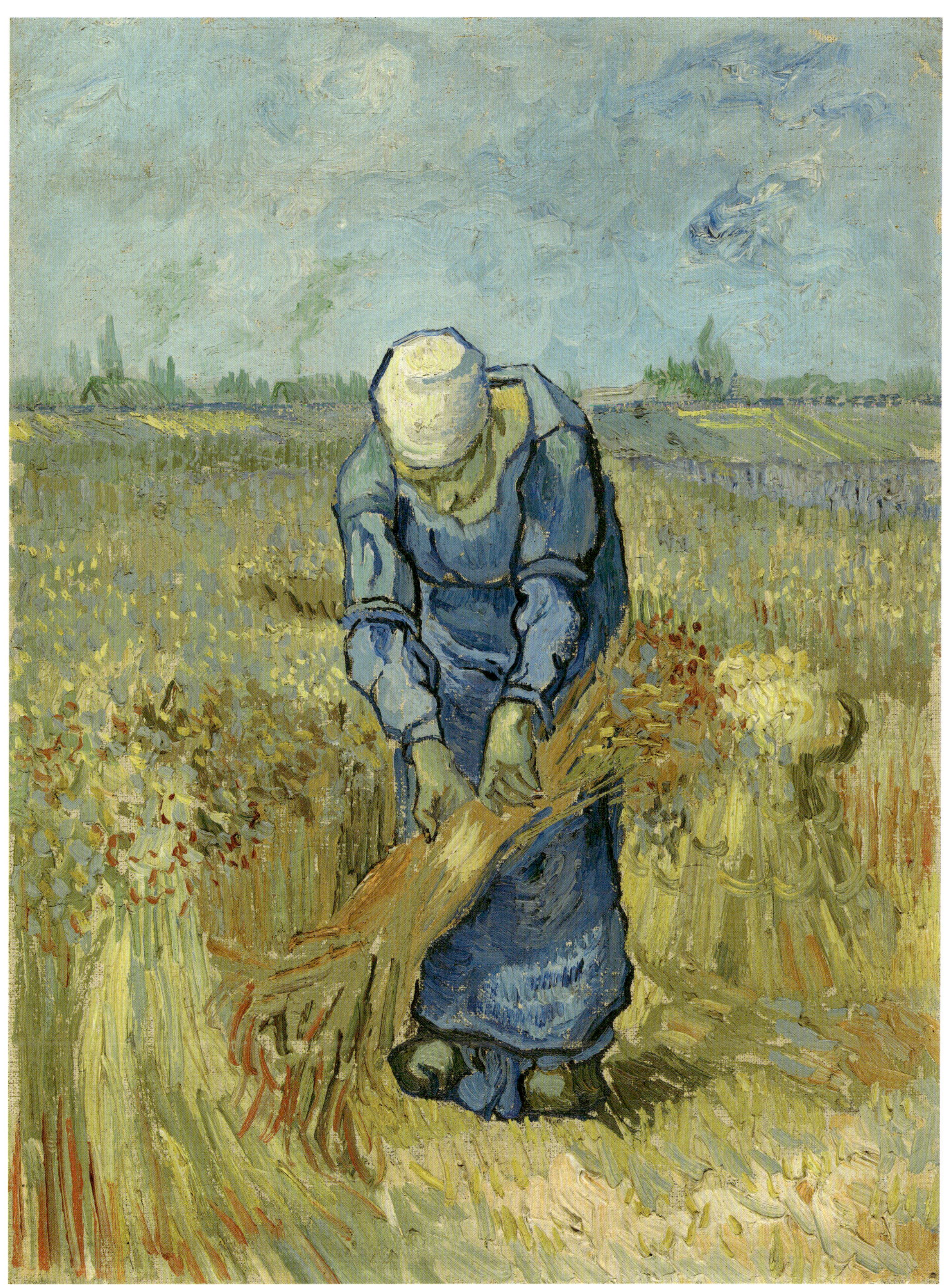

Cat. 43
The Sheaf-Binder (after Millet)
Oil on canvas,
17 ½ × 13 inches (44.5 × 33.1 cm)
Van Gogh Museum,
Amsterdam
(Vincent van Gogh Foundation)
s173V1962
F693

Provenance
Sent by the artist to Theo van Gogh,
Paris, late April 1890; Jo van Gogh-
Bonger and Vincent Willem van Gogh,
Paris, January 25, 1891; administered
by Jo van Gogh-Bonger, Bussum/
Amsterdam/Laren, until September 2,
1925; donated by Vincent Willem van
Gogh to the (first) Vincent van Gogh
Foundation, Laren, March 11, 1952; trans-
ferred to the Theo van Gogh Foundation,
Laren, December 28, 1960; agreement
July 21, 1962, entrusts collection to the
State of the Netherlands until realization
of the Rijksmuseum Vincent van Gogh,
Amsterdam; donated by the Theo van
Gogh Foundation to the (second) Vincent
van Gogh Foundation, July 21, 1962; on
loan to Stedelijk Museum, Amsterdam,
until opening of Rijksmuseum Vincent
van Gogh; Rijksmuseum Vincent van
Gogh, Amsterdam, June 2, 1973; Van
Gogh Museum, Amsterdam, July 1, 1994.

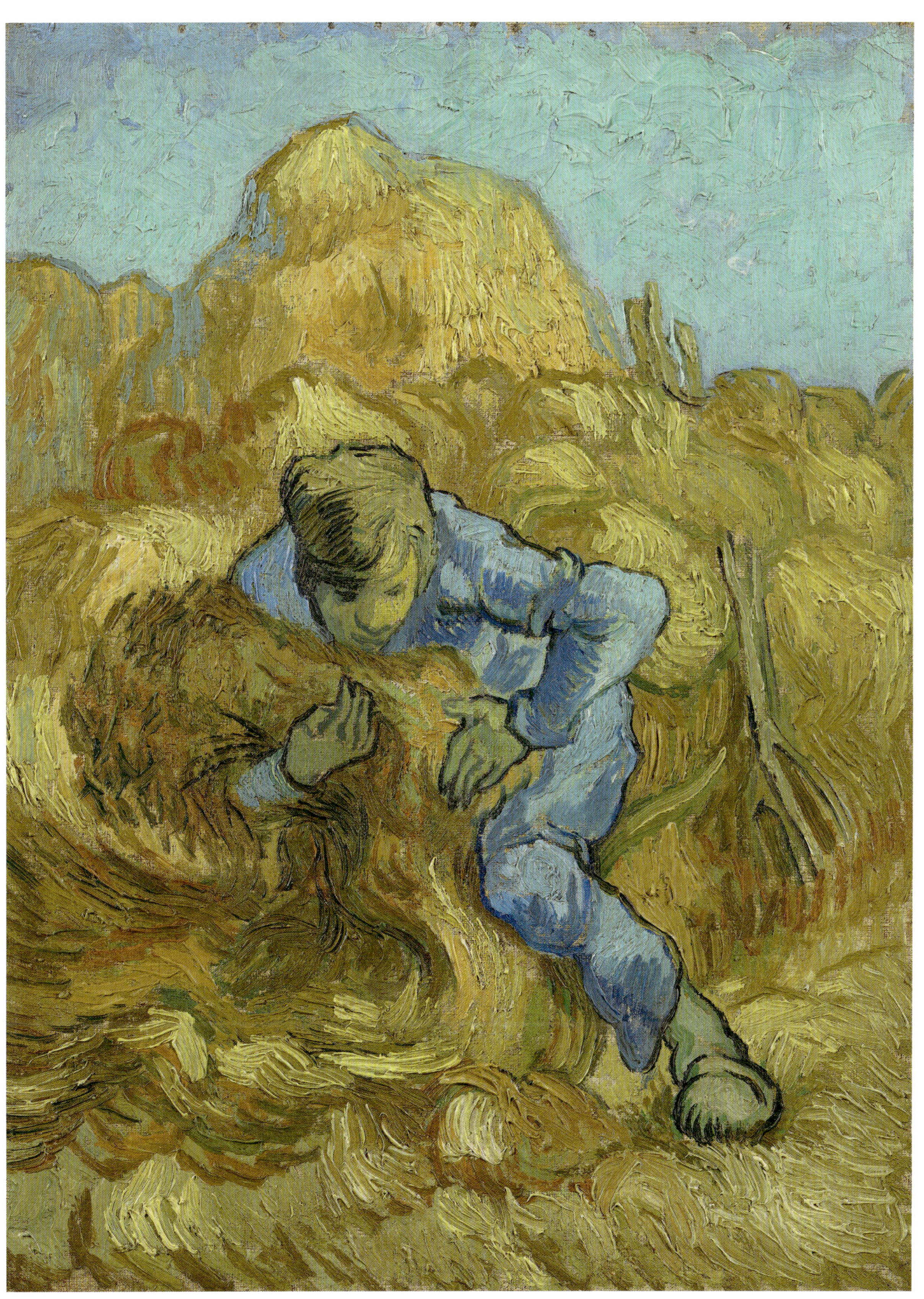

Autumn 1889
Saint-Rémy

Cat. 44
A *Pair of Leather Clogs*
Oil on canvas,
12 ⅝ × 16 inches (32.2 × 40.5 cm)
Van Gogh Museum,
Amsterdam
(Vincent van Gogh Foundation)
s120V1962
F607

Provenance
Theo van Gogh, Paris, after autumn 1889; Jo van Gogh-Bonger and Vincent Willem van Gogh, Paris, January 25, 1891; administered by Jo van Gogh-Bonger, Bussum/Amsterdam/Laren, until September 2, 1925; on loan from Vincent Willem van Gogh, Laren, to the Stedelijk Museum, Amsterdam, December 16, 1930; transferred to Vincent van Gogh Foundation, Amsterdam, July 10, 1962; agreement July 21, 1962, entrusts collection to the State of the Netherlands until realization of the Rijksmuseum Vincent van Gogh, Amsterdam; on loan to Stedelijk Museum, Amsterdam, until opening of Rijksmuseum Vincent van Gogh; Rijksmuseum Vincent van Gogh, Amsterdam, June 2, 1973; Van Gogh Museum, Amsterdam, July 1, 1994.

In this still life of shoes, Van Gogh returns to a subject he had already painted repeatedly between 1886 and 1888. Living in Paris at the time, he produced four canvases of single pairs of boots and one larger composition featuring three pairs. They were not his own boots, but ones that Van Gogh had picked up at flea markets.[1] He returned to the motif of footwear again during his years in the South of France, when he painted a pair of peasant shoes (1888, The Metropolitan Museum of Art, New York) and these leather clogs, dated 1889.

The bright tonality and emotive brushwork of this still life reflects the artistic development Van Gogh achieved during his final years. He captured these rustic, wooden-soled leather clogs up close and seen from an odd angle. Both the insides and outsides are meticulously depicted with wide, parallel brushstrokes that follow the different parts of the shoes. The intensity of his gaze makes a powerful statement of these simple, everyday objects. It is assumed that Van Gogh painted this work while confined to the mental hospital at Saint-Rémy in the autumn of 1889. Given his limited access to the outside world, it is assumed that these were his own shoes.

Much has been written about the meaning of these still lifes, starting with an intriguing discussion of reality and how we perceive it by the philosopher Martin Heidegger.[2] Whether these clogs can actually be read as a self-portrait also persists as a question that interests scholars. Petra ten-Doesschate Chu has suggested the possibility that they can be seen as referring to specific walks taken by the artist, as symbols of his spiritual wanderings, or even his entire concept of a walk, a path, or of his journey through life.[3] Interestingly, the directional brushwork is used to greatest effect by Van Gogh in his self-portraits of 1886–87 (cat. 24), and its use here may seem to further support the argument that these shoes are symbolic self-portraits. HKA

Notes
1 Louis van Tilborgh and Ella Hendriks, *Vincent van Gogh Paintings*, vol. 2, *Antwerp and Paris, 1885–1888, Van Gogh Museum* (Amsterdam and Zwolle: Van Gogh Museum / Waanders, 2011), 257.

2 Ibid., 260.

3 "Browse the Collection: Shoes" (entry for Vincent Van Gogh, *Shoes*, 1888, accession number 1992.374), The Metropolitan Museum of Art, https://www.metmuseum.org/art/collection/search/436533.

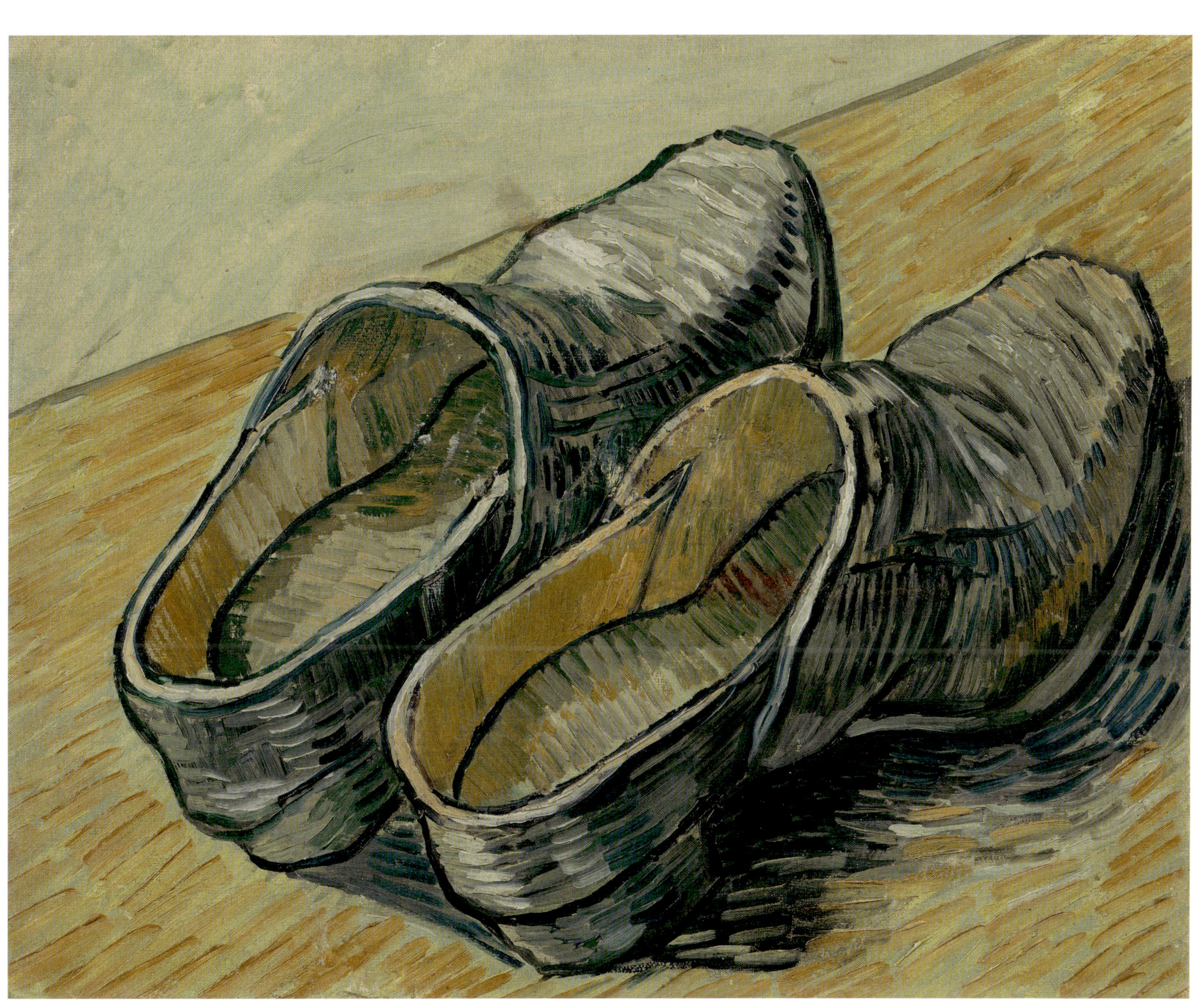

Cat. 45
*Olive Grove with Two
Olive Pickers*
Oil on canvas,
28 ⅞ × 36 ¼ inches
(73.3 × 92.2 cm)
Kröller-Müller Museum,
Otterlo
KM 104.796
F587

Provenance
Jo van Gogh-Bonger, Amsterdam; purchased by Bernheim-Jeune, art dealer,
Paris, March 1907; A. Schuffenecker
coll., Meudon; purchased by H. Kröller-
Müller from A. Schuffenecker, April
1912.

"The thing is, the olive tree and the cypress have rarely been painted," Vincent van Gogh wrote to his brother Theo in late November 1889. But, as he explained, he was addressing the problem: "I've been messing about in the groves morning and evening on these bright and cold days, but in very beautiful, clear sunshine. . . . The olive tree is variable like our willow or pollard in the north. You know that willows are very picturesque, despite the fact that it appears monotonous, it's the tree typical of the country. Now what the willow is in our native country, the olive tree and the cypress have exactly the same importance here."[1] The olive trees' old, twisted trunks and the silvery tonality of their leaves are indeed typical for the ancient countryside of Provence.

Van Gogh included this painting of two olive pickers in an olive grove in a shipment of twelve canvases — among them six of olive groves — to his brother in Paris.[2] This painting, which features a woman in the foreground and a man at the center of the canvas, both raising their arms to the lower branches of an olive tree, is closely related to *Olive Grove* (November–December 1889, Gothenburg Museum of Art). The view of the olive grove is virtually identical, yet in the work without the figures the trees play an even more expressive role. This is due in part to its more intense colors; the Kröller-Müller Museum's painting has suffered from discoloration and overpainting.[3] For instance, the woman's dress retains only a part of its allover pink color, now forming much less of a contrast with her surroundings. The addition of the people extends this work beyond the realm of pure landscape and invokes the eternal rhythm of country life, moving at the same languid pace each year, punctuated by planting and harvesting. Van Gogh had earlier attempted but twice failed to use an olive grove as the setting of Christ in the Garden of Gethsemane. His renewed interest in the motif of the olive trees was a reaction to paintings of this subject by Paul Gauguin and Émile Bernard.[4] HKA

Notes
1 Letter 823, Vincent van Gogh to Theo van Gogh, Saint-Rémy-de-Provence, November 26, 1889.

2 Ibid.

3 Hildelies Balk, Jos ten Berge, et al., *The Paintings of Vincent van Gogh in the Collection of the Kröller-Müller Museum* (Otterlo: Kröller-Müller Museum, 2003), 330–31.

4 Ibid., 329.

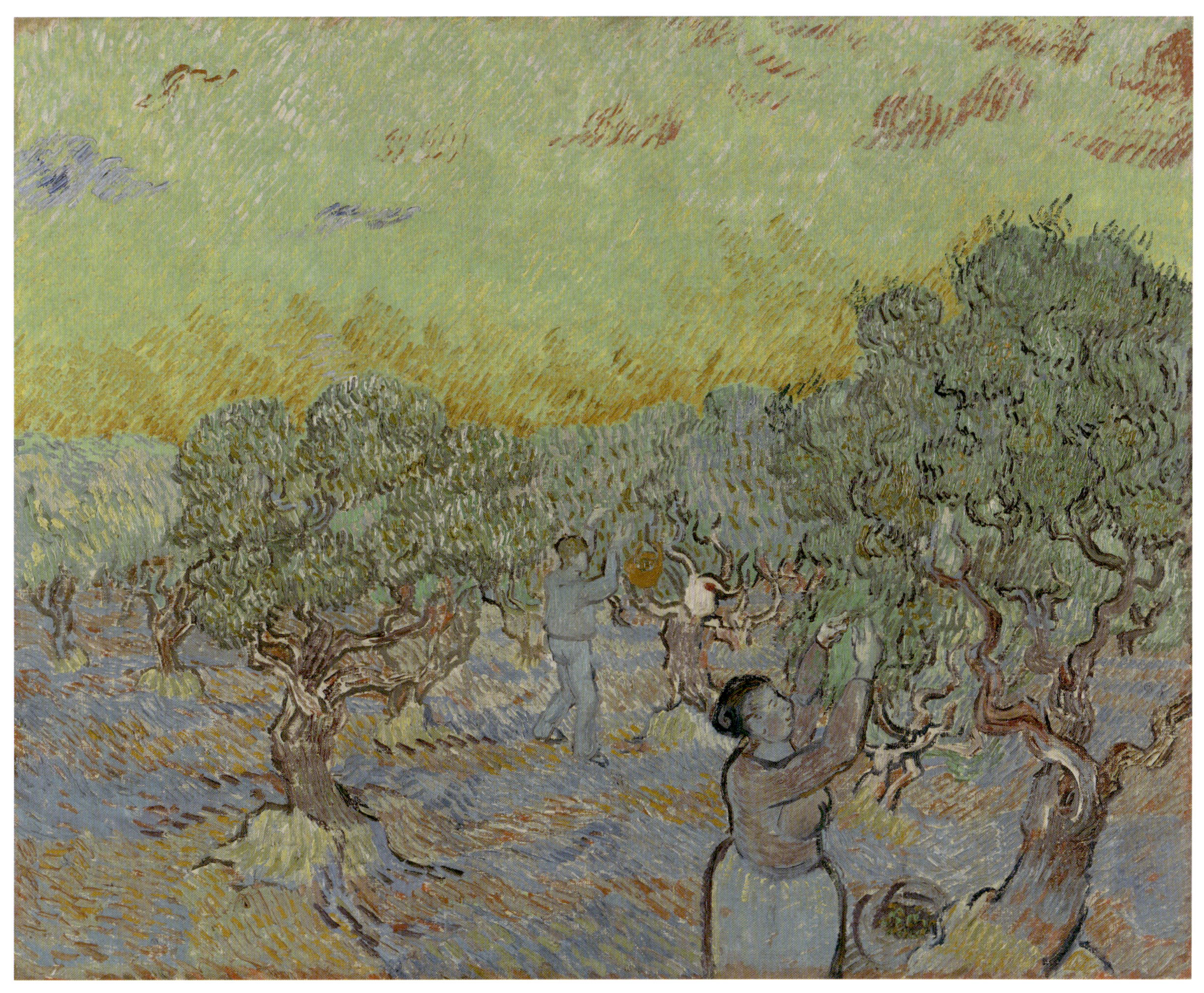

Cat. 46
Field with Sower
Graphite on wove paper,
9 ⅜ × 12 ½ inches
(23.8 × 31.9 cm)
Van Gogh Museum,
Amsterdam
(Vincent van Gogh Foundation)
d186V1962v
F1592v

Provenance
Theo van Gogh, Paris, after April 1890;
Jo van Gogh-Bonger and Vincent Willem
van Gogh, Paris, January 25, 1891; administered by Jo van Gogh-Bonger, Bussum/
Amsterdam/Laren, until September 2,
1925; on loan from Vincent Willem van
Gogh, Laren, to the Stedelijk Museum,
Amsterdam, October 22, 1931; transferred to Vincent van Gogh Foundation,
Amsterdam, July 10, 1962; agreement
July 21, 1962, entrusts collection to the
State of the Netherlands until realization of the Rijksmuseum Vincent van
Gogh, Amsterdam; on loan to Stedelijk
Museum, Amsterdam, until opening
of Rijksmuseum Vincent van Gogh;
Rijksmuseum Vincent van Gogh,
Amsterdam, June 2, 1973; Van Gogh
Museum, Amsterdam, July 1, 1994.

Van Gogh moved to Arles in the South of France in 1888 and, by 1889–90, relocated to the psychiatric asylum in Saint-Rémy. He returned to familiar rural subjects from his earlier Dutch period, while reflecting on the dramatic wheat fields and skies of Provence. During this period, the work of Jean-François Millet also continued to be an important influence. Theo wrote to Vincent in 1889, "The Millet copies are perhaps the finest things you've done yet."[1] Van Gogh had previously read the pivotal biography of Millet by Alfred Sensier, who portrayed the Realist artist as a man of virtue, simplicity, and perseverance.[2] The French painter's closeness with nature and with peasants who worked the land conveyed a spirituality that connected with Van Gogh's own search for life's purpose.

As one of the most persistent figures in Van Gogh's oeuvre, the sower had a quasi-religious, emblematic connotation for him. He wrote to his brother, "I feel so strongly that the story of people is like the story of wheat, if one isn't sown in the earth to germinate there, what does it matter, one is milled in order to become bread."[3] While in Arles, he had embraced the reed pen and ink, but he returned to his faithful pencil in Saint-Rémy, as seen in this drawing. The field where the peasant stands gives way to farmhouses and mountains in the background. Van Gogh produced subjects from memory at this time, as he was too ill to work outside. His agitated, staccato lines were made either with a carpenter's pencil with which he could manipulate the thickness of the strokes or with three pencils of varied widths.[4] DMW

Notes
1 Letter 867, Theo van Gogh to Vincent van Gogh, Saint-Rémy-de-Provence, May 3, 1890.

2 Alfred Sensier, *La vie et l'oeuvre de J.-F. Millet* (Paris: A. Quantin, 1881). In a letter to his brother Theo, Vincent wrote, "When you read Sensier's book about Millet you take courage from it." It is worth noting that Sensier had idolized Millet and embellished his biography of the artist with partial truths, since Millet was generally an agnostic and enjoyed his friendships with writers and artists more than with peasants. Letter 258, Vincent van Gogh to Theo van Gogh, The Hague, August 20, 1882.

3 Letter 805, Vincent van Gogh to Theo van Gogh, Saint-Rémy-de-Provence, on or about September 20, 1889.

4 See Marije Vellekoop and Roelie Zwikker, *Vincent van Gogh: Drawings*, vol. 4, *Arles, Saint-Rémy and Auvers-sur-Oise, 1888–1890, Van Gogh Museum* (Amsterdam: Van Gogh Museum; London: Lund Humphries, 1996), 299–303, cat. 400.

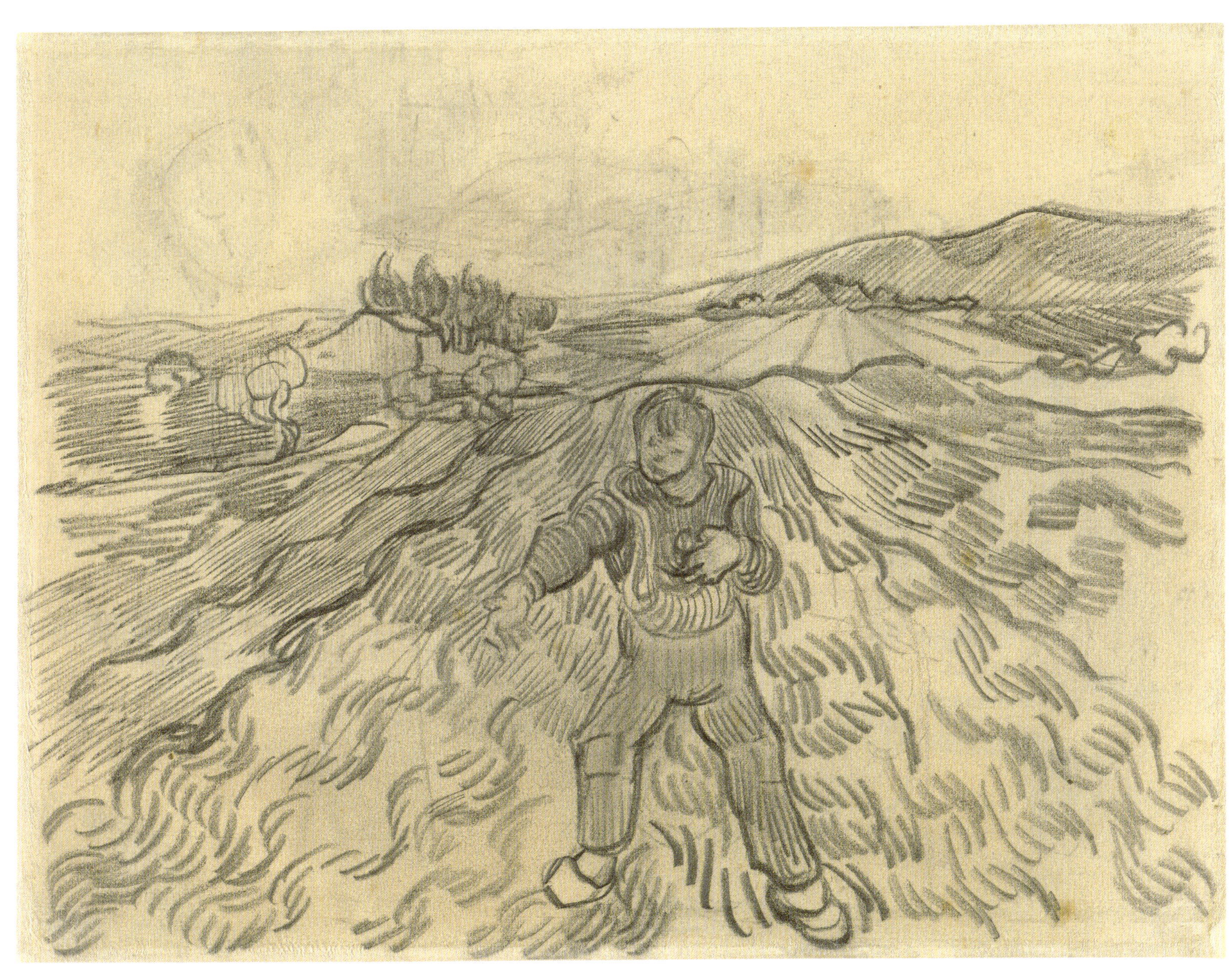

Cat. 47
The Good Samaritan
(after Delacroix)
Oil on canvas,
28 ¾ × 23 ⅜ inches (73 × 59.5 cm)
Kröller-Müller Museum,
Otterlo
KM 104.010
F633

Provenance
Jo van Gogh-Bonger in storage with Tanguy, Paris; Willy Grétor (W. R. J. Petersen), Paris, 1891; P. Goldmann coll., Paris; Ambroise Vollard, art dealer, Paris, December 1895; E. Schuffenecker, Paris, December 1895; Prince of Wagram coll., Paris; Barbazanges, art dealer, Paris; purchased for H. Kröller-Müller by Leonard in Paris, May–July 1912.

In the same September 1889 letter in which Van Gogh described to Theo his paintings of subjects after Jean-François Millet, he announced, "I'm going to copy Delacroix's *Good Samaritan* too."[1] But it was not until some eight months later, in May 1890, that he actually painted the subject. In that earlier campaign of copying, beginning in September 1889, he had completed his version of another Delacroix, the *Pietà*, but he did not get around to fulfilling his intention to copy the *Good Samaritan* until early May the following year, when he briefly stated in a letter to Theo, "I've also attempted a copy of Delacroix's *Good Samaritan*."[2] There is no more mention of it in the correspondence, so that is all the information that we have.

The source for the painting had long been in Van Gogh's possession. He owned a lithograph of the Delacroix composition by Jules-Joseph-Augustin Laurens, and it had been among the works decorating his hospital room in Arles in May 1889. As with his copies of Millet, Van Gogh's versions of Delacroix were very much his own interpretation, since all he had in front of him was a black-and-white image. In fact, Van Gogh's colors are markedly different from those in Delacroix's painting, which he had probably never seen. In contrast to the rich reds and browns of Delacroix's original, the colors here consist of cool blues and violets and dull oranges, with just one red accent in the turban of the Samaritan. Van Gogh concentrates on expressive brushwork, varying from staccato diagonals in the foreground to great swathes of undulating forms in the landscape background, highly reminiscent of his paintings of the nearby Alpilles mountains.[3] DB

Notes
1 Letter 805, Vincent van Gogh to Theo van Gogh, Saint-Rémy-de-Provence, on or about September 20, 1889.

2 Letter 866, Vincent van Gogh to Theo van Gogh, Saint-Rémy-de-Provence, on or about Friday, May 2, 1890.

3 See Hildelies Balk, Jos ten Berge, et al., *The Paintings of Vincent van Gogh in the Collection of the Kröller-Müller Museum* (Otterlo: Kröller-Müller Museum, 2003), 347–50.

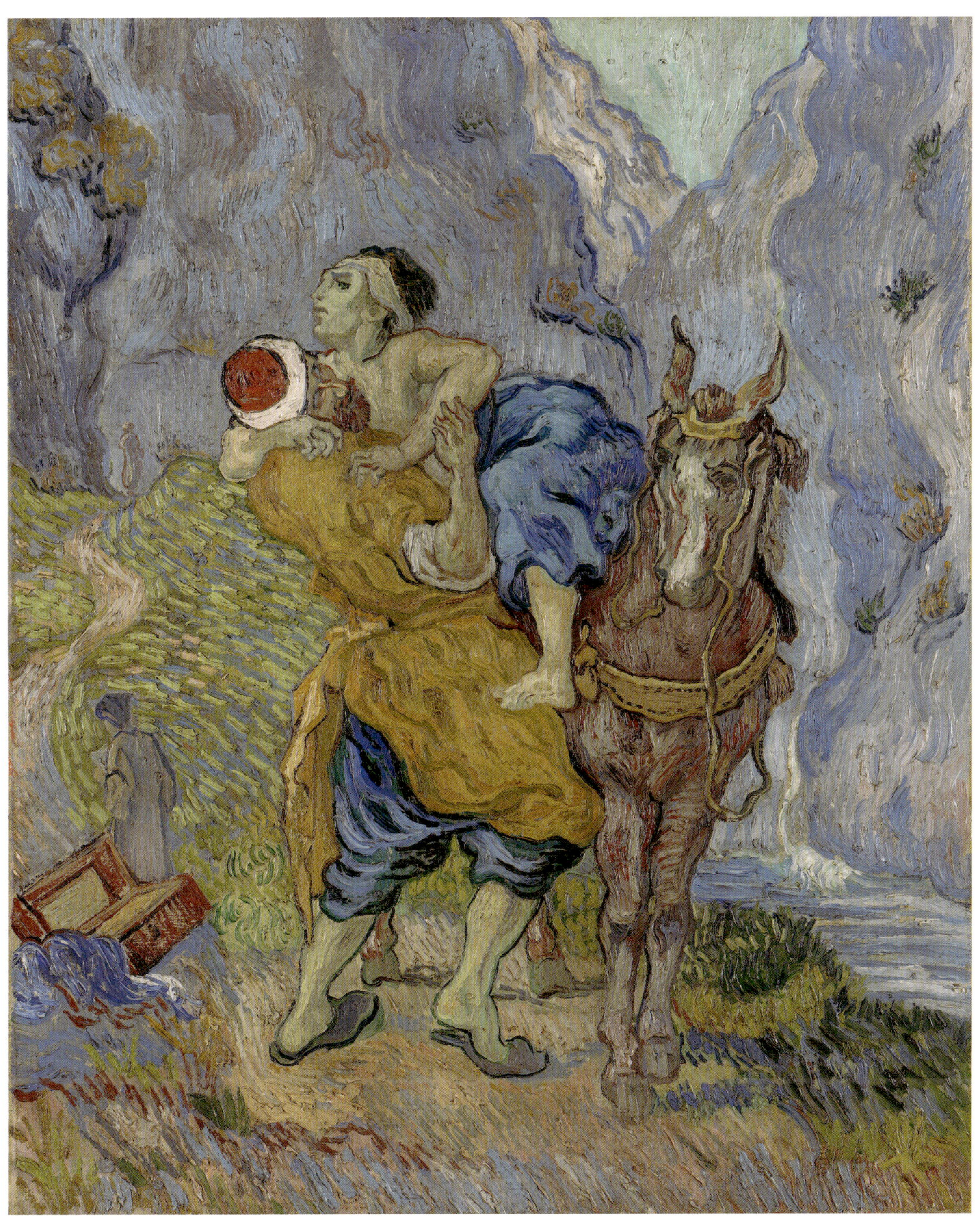

May 1890
Saint-Rémy

Cat. 48
Irises
Oil on canvas,
36 ½ × 29 ⅛ inches
(92.7 × 73.9 cm)
Van Gogh Museum,
Amsterdam
(Vincent van Gogh Foundation)
s50V1962
F678

Provenance
Theo van Gogh, Paris, after late June
1890; Jo van Gogh-Bonger and Vincent
Willem van Gogh, Paris, January 25,
1891; administered by Jo van Gogh-
Bonger, Bussum/Amsterdam/Laren,
until September 2, 1925; on loan from
Vincent Willem van Gogh, Laren, to
the Stedelijk Museum, Amsterdam,
October 22, 1931; transferred to Vincent
van Gogh Foundation, Amsterdam,
July 10, 1962; agreement July 21, 1962,
entrusts collection to the State of the
Netherlands until realization of the
Rijksmuseum Vincent van Gogh,
Amsterdam; on loan to Stedelijk
Museum, Amsterdam, until opening
of Rijksmuseum Vincent van Gogh;
Rijksmuseum Vincent van Gogh,
Amsterdam, June 2, 1973; Van Gogh
Museum, Amsterdam, July 1, 1994.

This glorious bouquet of irises is without a doubt one of Van Gogh's greatest still lifes, not only a painting of beautifully rendered flowers, but a work that allows a multiplicity of interpretations. It was part of a group, an ensemble of still lifes of roses and irises, that he painted in 1890, just before his departure from the mental hospital at Saint-Rémy.[1] Its pendant, a horizontal still life of irises, is one of the masterpieces of the Metropolitan Museum of Art, New York.[2]

In this vertical version, the deep blue irises are arranged in a simple yellow earthenware vase, set just off-center on a yellow table in front of a lighter yellow background. The densely grouped blue flowers are punctuated by swordlike leaves, whose upward thrust is countered by several drooping stems at the right. Van Gogh created a complex composition by emphasizing the sharp angles of the leaves in contrast to the amorphous mass of blossoms and the rounded form of the vase. However, most important to Van Gogh, who had been fascinated by the theory of complementary colors for years, were the effects of the yellow against the purple (now faded to blue) and green.

Van Gogh loved irises, and these elegant, lily-like spring flowers, which grow in luscious profusion in Provence, appear in one of his earliest works from Arles, *View of Arles with Irises in the Foreground* (1888, Van Gogh Museum, Amsterdam). The following year, he reached a new height of painterly expression in his wonderful *Irises* (May 1889, J. Paul Getty Museum, Los Angeles), but the culmination of his efforts are the present bouquet and its pendant at the Metropolitan Museum of Art. Van Gogh was surely aware of the flowers' Christian symbolism, but for him they simply may have been the harbingers of spring, warmth, and hope.[3] Since the bouquet's abundance is countered by the falling stems, this painting may be interpreted as a sign of his troubled state, even as a premonition of his tragic suicide just two months later. HKA

Notes
1 Jennifer Helvey, *Irises: Vincent Van Gogh in the Garden* (Los Angeles: J. Paul Getty Museum, 2009), 18.

2 "Browse the Collection: Irises" (entry for Vincent Van Gogh, *Irises*, 1890, accession number 58.187), The Metropolitan Museum of Art, New York, https://www.metmuseum.org/art/collection/search/436528.

3 Helvey, *Irises*, 96.

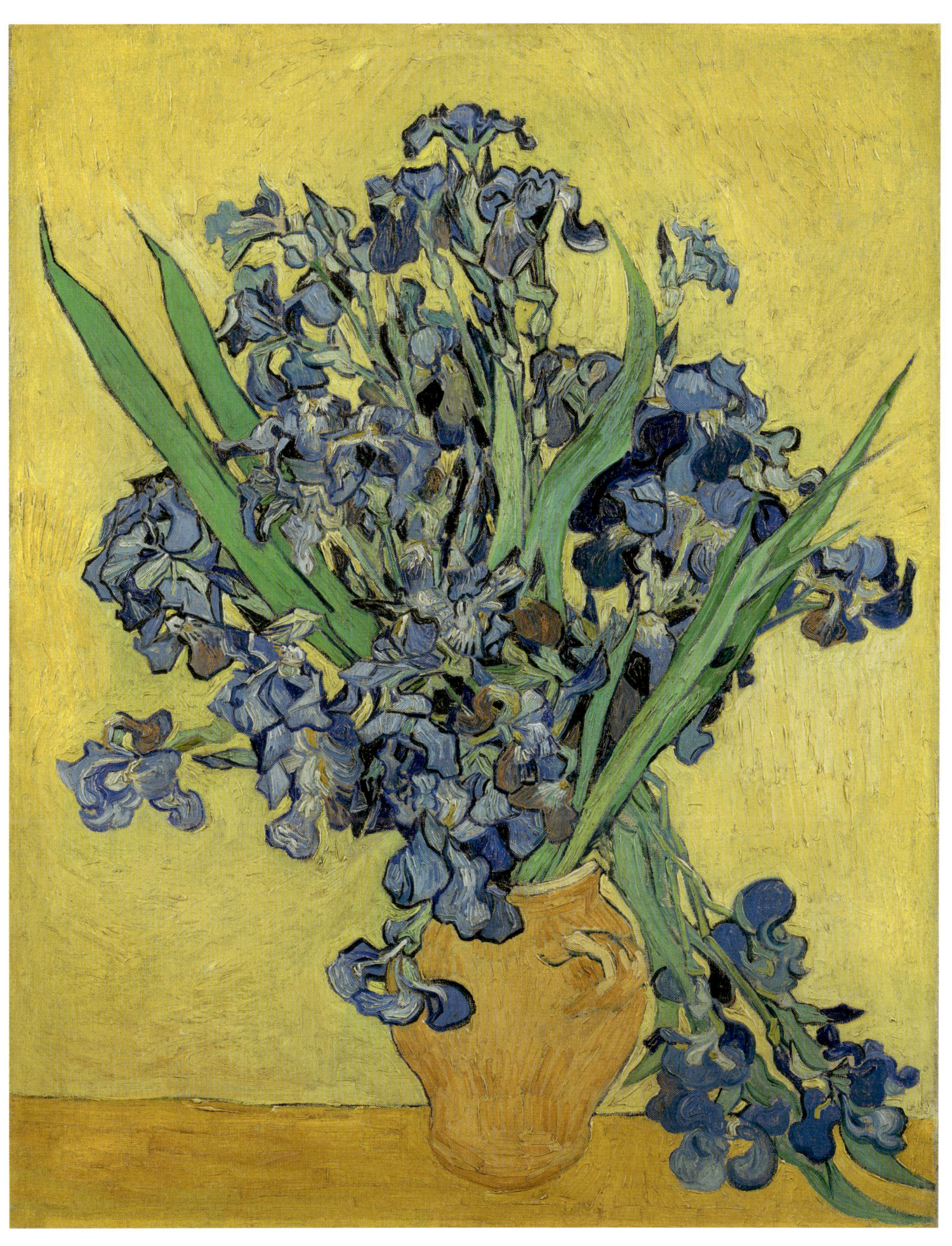

May 1890
Auvers-sur-Oise

Cat. 49
Blossoming Chestnut Trees
Oil on canvas,
24 ⅞ × 19 ⅝ inches
(63.3 × 49.8 cm)
Kröller-Müller Museum,
Otterlo
KM 105.479
F752

Provenance
Jo van Gogh-Bonger, Amsterdam; C. M. van Gogh (J. H. de Bois), art dealer, Amsterdam, 1909; C. Sternheim, Munich, 1909; returned in October 1909 to C. M. van Gogh, art dealer, Amsterdam; purchased by H. Kröller-Müller at C. M. van Gogh, art dealer, June 24, 1910.

This small work is a study executed during Van Gogh's early days in Auvers-sur-Oise. After a two-year stay in southern France, he had returned to the North in May 1890, but his time in Auvers would be just a brief two months before it tragically ended in suicide. At the moment of his arrival, however, he seemed in good health to both his family and Dr. Gachet, the homeopathic physician living at Auvers into whose care his brother Theo had committed him. Yet, despite outward appearances, Van Gogh was unsettled, writing, "I can do nothing about my illness — I am suffering a little these days. . . . But as work is proceeding a little, serenity will come."[1]

Nonetheless, Van Gogh explored the little town with enthusiasm. Above all, he saw his stay as a chance to become reacquainted with the light of northern France, so much softer and gentler than that of the South.[2] Within days after arriving in Auvers, he completed four painted studies and two drawings, including this work and another larger and more finished version.[3] Although it is less obvious here than it is in the preparatory drawing, there are actually two tree trunks visible, but the crowns have grown together. Most of the canvas is taken up by the massive foliage of the trees with their distinctive candle-like flowers. Whereas the brushwork here consists of short, spiky dabs, the bushes at right are made up of circular strokes, which he presaged in the drawing. The cool tonality, characteristic of the northern light, is reduced to green, blue, and white, with a bit of bare canvas visible at the lower right, suggesting the work's purpose as a sketch.

This work is closely linked with *Chestnut Trees in Bloom*, also painted in May 1890 and today in a private collection, yet it is not the preliminary sketch for it. The related example offers a much more expansive view of the town, depicting a major street that is enlivened by a group of passersby and a large building in the background. Nevertheless, the main focus, the magnificent chestnut trees, is definitely based on the same sketch. HKA

Notes
1 Letter 874, Vincent van Gogh to Theo van Gogh and Jo van Gogh-Bonger, Auvers-sur-Oise, on or about May 21, 1890.

2 Ibid., 20.

3 Hildelies Balk, Jos ten Berge, et al., *The Paintings of Vincent van Gogh in the Collection of the Kröller-Müller Museum* (Otterlo: Kröller-Müller Museum, 2003), 371.

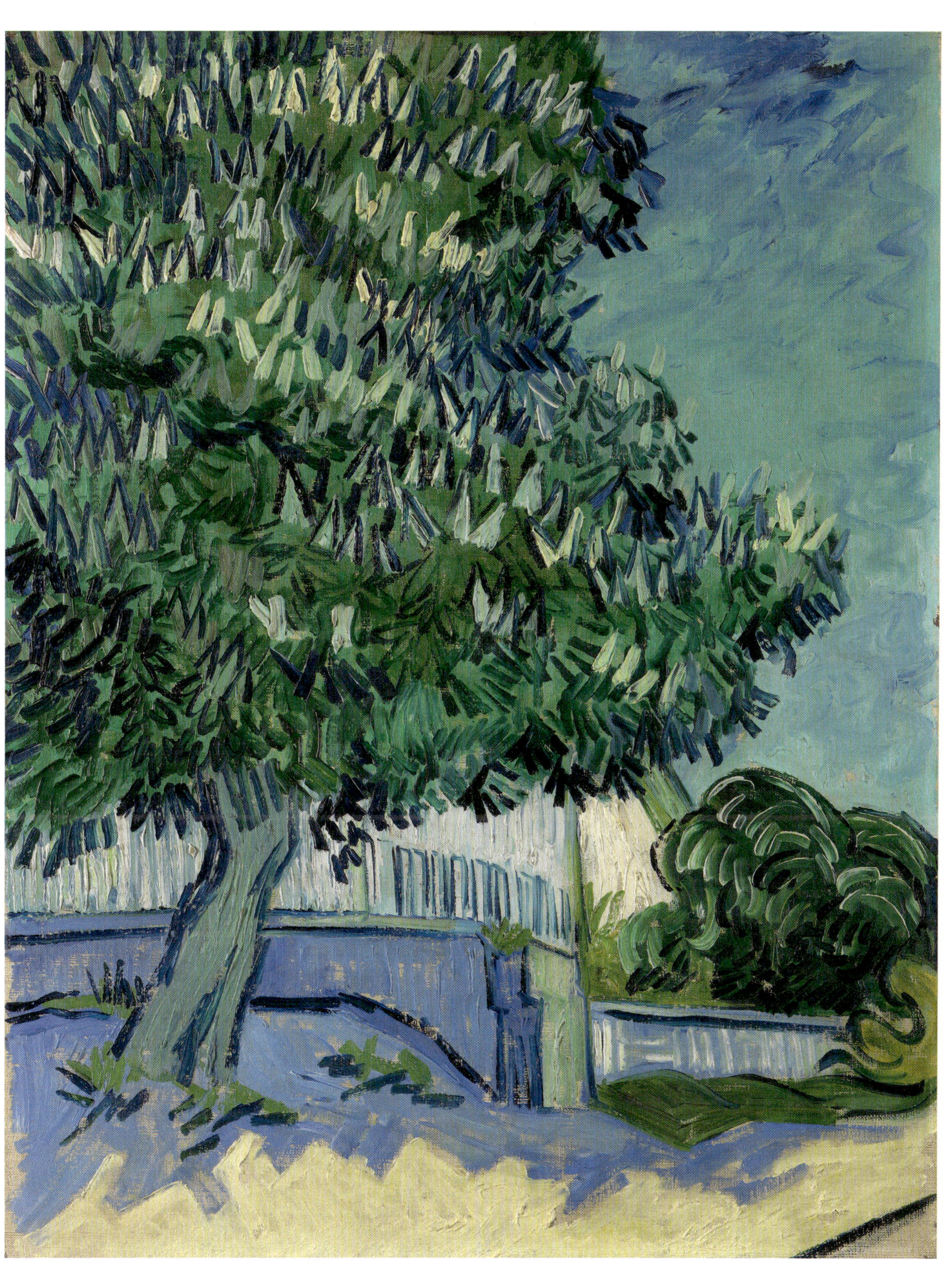

Cat. 50
Portrait of Dr. Gachet
(*L'Homme à la Pipe*)
Etching, with black chalk
on laid paper,
7 × 6 inches (18 × 15 cm)
Private collection
F1664

Provenance
P. F. and P. L. L. Gachet (Lugt 1195b and
Lugt 2807c); Mrs. Romano, New York,
until September 1982; [David Tunick,
New York], September 1982 to May 1983;
bought by the family of the present
owner, May 1983.

Notes
1 The artist Camille Pissarro suggested to Theo that Vincent should go
to Dr. Gachet in Auvers. See Janine Bailly-Herzberg, *Correspondance
de Camille Pissarro* (Paris and Pontoise: Presses Universitaires de France,
1980–91), 2:297–99, and Jan Hulsker, *Vincent and Theo van Gogh: A Dual
Biography* (Ann Arbor: Fuller Publications, 1990), 418.

2 Van Gogh also produced painted portraits of Dr. Gachet. See
Ronald Pickvance, *Van Gogh in Saint-Rémy and Auvers* (New York: The
Metropolitan Museum of Art and Harry N. Abrams, 2013), 195.

3 "I really think that I'll stay friends with him and that I'll do his portrait."
Letter 873, Vincent van Gogh to Theo van Gogh and Jo van Gogh-Bonger,
Auvers-sur-Oise, May 20, 1890.

4 Letter 889, Vincent van Gogh to Theo van Gogh, Auvers-sur-Oise, June
17, 1890. Vincent also wrote to Paul Gauguin about making etchings.
See letter RM23, Vincent van Gogh to Paul Gauguin, Auvers-sur-Oise, on
or about June 17, 1890.

5 See Sjraar van Heugten and Fieke Pabst, *The Graphic Work of Vincent
van Gogh* (Zwolle: Waanders, 1995), 30.

6 See William H. Robinson and Galina K. Olmsted, "Dr. Gachet (Man
with a Pipe): Van Gogh's Final Print," in *Van Gogh: New Research
and Perspectives* (Cleveland: Cleveland Museum of Art, 2014), http://www.
clevelandart.org/events/exhibitions/van-gogh-repetitions/supplement/
dr-gachet-etching.

7 Letter 890, Theo van Gogh to Vincent van Gogh, Paris, June 23, 1890.

8 Sixty-one known impressions of this etching exist. The printing
plate is now housed at the Musée d'Orsay in Paris, having been given to
the Musée du Louvre by Gachet's son, Paul, in 1951.

Shortly after his arrival in Auvers, and based on his brother's recommendation, Van Gogh met Dr. Paul-Ferdinand Gachet, a homeopathic doctor who specialized in "nervous disorders."[1] The doctor was well known for his patient care; he was also an amateur artist, and the owner of a printmaking press and a notable art collection.[2] Van Gogh considered the doctor "rather eccentric, but his doctor's experience must keep him balanced himself while combating the nervous ailment from which it seems to me he's certainly suffering at least as seriously as I am."[3]

Vincent was eager to experiment with Dr. Gachet's etching press. He wrote to his brother about wanting to make six etchings of Southern subjects, because Dr. Gachet could print them free of charge.[4] He had made nine lithographs in the 1880s, and at the time was enthusiastic about the possibilities afforded by printmaking — as a means of supporting himself, dispersing imagery to a wider audience, and later having his work better known in avant-garde art circles.[5] The print project was never realized due to his death in July, but he did produce this portrait of Dr. Gachet holding a pipe, which was his last print and only etching. Van Gogh, with Dr. Gachet's aid, is believed to have printed fourteen of these etchings, experimenting with the colors of the ink, varying the wiping of the plate, and reinforcing areas with drawn materials, such as in this impression with black chalk on and above the right shoulder. According to Gachet's son and as the inscription, probably in Dr. Gachet's hand, suggests, it was made on May 25. However, Van Gogh probably made his etching on June 15, based on his letters.[6] Theo praised this print in a letter to his brother six days later, stating, "it's a real painter's etching. No refinement in the procedure, but a drawing done in metal."[7] After Van Gogh's death, Dr. Gachet and his son continued to print posthumous impressions from the copper plate they possessed, often giving them to friends with handwritten notes.[8] DMW

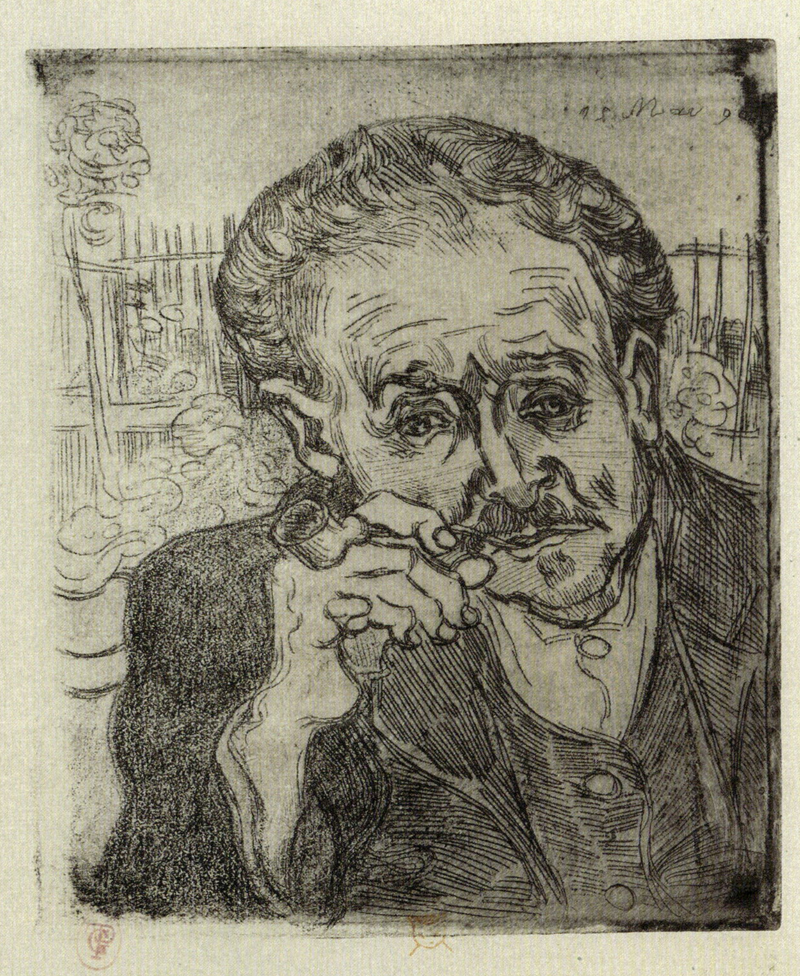

Portrait du Dr Gachet
(Eau forte de Vangogh)

Cat. 51
Farmhouse
Oil on canvas,
15 ¼ × 18 ¼ inches
(38.9 × 46.4 cm)
Van Gogh Museum,
Amsterdam
(Vincent van Gogh Foundation)
s108V1962
F806

Provenance
Theo van Gogh, Paris, after June 1890;
Jo van Gogh-Bonger and Vincent Willem
van Gogh, Paris, January 25, 1891;
administered by Jo van Gogh-Bonger,
Bussum/Amsterdam/Laren, until
September 2, 1925; on loan from Vincent
Willem van Gogh, Laren, to the
Stedelijk Museum, Amsterdam, October
22, 1931; transferred to Vincent van
Gogh Foundation, Amsterdam, July 10,
1962; agreement July 21, 1962, entrusts
collection to the State of the Netherlands
until realization of the Rijksmuseum
Vincent van Gogh, Amsterdam; on loan
to Stedelijk Museum, Amsterdam,
until opening of Rijksmuseum Vincent
van Gogh; Rijksmuseum Vincent van
Gogh, Amsterdam, June 2, 1973; Van
Gogh Museum, Amsterdam, July 1, 1994.

Van Gogh arrived in Auvers-sur-Oise from Paris on May 20, 1890, and his first impressions were very positive. He loved the houses, which he was immediately determined to paint. In his first letter from the town to his brother and sister-in-law, he wrote, "Auvers is really beautiful — among other things many old thatched roofs, which are becoming rare. I'd hope, then, that in doing a few canvases of that really seriously, there would be a chance of recouping some of the costs of my stay — for really it's gravely beautiful, it's the heart of the countryside, distinctive and picturesque."[1]

In a fragmentary note to his sister, written the following day but never sent, Van Gogh described "roofs of mossy thatch which are superb, and of which I'll certainly do something."[2] He must have worked fast, because the same day he wrote to Theo and Jo, "Now I have a study of old thatched roofs with a field of peas in flower and some wheat in the foreground, hilly background. A study which I think you'll like. And I perceive already that it did me good to go into the south the better to see the north."[3]

He went on to paint an extensive view of thatched cottages in the Auvers landscape (*Farms near Auvers*, 1890, Tate, London), and also the present smaller study, which is repeated in the right-hand part of the larger composition. This rough, presumably unfinished and certainly unsigned work is rapidly painted in tones of green and gray-blue, with one complementary accent in the red chimney — a color not repeated in the composition. This may be one of the first studies that Van Gogh made shortly after his arrival.[4] DB

Notes
1 Letter 873, Vincent van Gogh to Theo van Gogh and Jo van Gogh-Bonger, Auvers-sur-Oise, May 20, 1890.

2 Letter RM19 (unsent), Vincent van Gogh to Willemien van Gogh, Auvers-sur-Oise, on or about May 21, 1890.

3 Letter 874, Vincent van Gogh to Theo van Gogh and Jo van Gogh-Bonger, Auvers-sur-Oise, on or about May 21, 1890.

4 See Ronald Pickvance, *Van Gogh in Saint-Rémy and Auvers* (New York: The Metropolitan Museum of Art, 1986), 269.

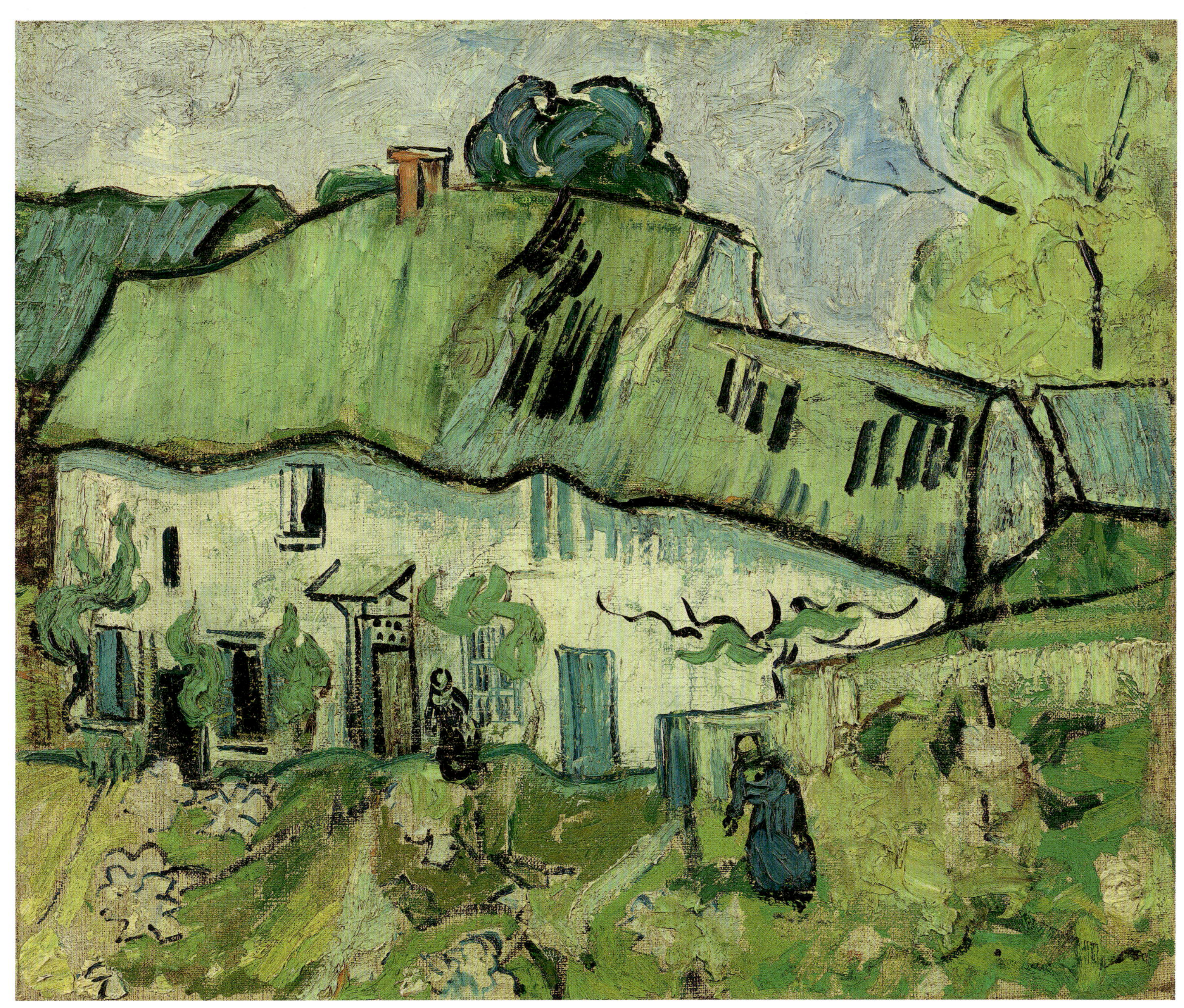

Cat. 52
Ears of Wheat
Oil on canvas,
25 ¼ × 18 ⅝ inches (64 × 48 cm)
Van Gogh Museum,
Amsterdam
(Vincent van Gogh Foundation)
s88V1962
F767

Provenance
Theo van Gogh, Paris, after June 1890;
Jo van Gogh-Bonger and Vincent Willem
van Gogh, Paris, January 25, 1891;
administered by Jo van Gogh-Bonger,
Bussum/Amsterdam/Laren, until
September 2, 1925; on loan from Vincent
Willem van Gogh, Laren, to the
Stedelijk Museum, Amsterdam, October
22, 1931; transferred to Vincent van
Gogh Foundation, Amsterdam, July 10,
1962; agreement July 21, 1962, entrusts
collection to the State of the Netherlands
until realization of the Rijksmuseum
Vincent van Gogh, Amsterdam; on loan
to Stedelijk Museum, Amsterdam,
until opening of Rijksmuseum Vincent
van Gogh; Rijksmuseum Vincent
van Gogh, Amsterdam, June 2, 1973;
Van Gogh Museum, Amsterdam,
July 1, 1994.

In an unsent, unfinished letter to Paul Gauguin composed in Auvers-sur-Oise about June 17, 1890, Van Gogh wrote:

Look, an idea which will perhaps suit you. I'm trying to do studies of wheat like this … nothing but ears, blue-green stems, long leaves like ribbons, green and pink by reflection, yellowing ears lightly bordered with pale pink due to the dusty flowering. A pink bindweed at the bottom, wound around a stem. On it, a very alive and tranquil background, I would like to paint portraits. It is greens of a different quality, of the same value, in such a way as to form a green whole which would by its vibration make one think of a soft sound of the ears swaying in the breeze. It's not at all easy as a color scheme.[1]

In the letter, Van Gogh made two little sketches of ears of wheat, and the painting is just as he describes, with pink bindweed flowers at the lower right and a blue cornflower at the top left. He did indeed follow his plan of using the motif as a background for portraits, and two are known, including *Girl in White* in the National Gallery of Art, Washington, D.C.

Van Gogh also describes painting arrangements of wild flowers to Theo in a letter written around the same time: "At the moment, I have two studies on the go — one a bouquet of wild plants, thistles, ears of wheat, leaves of different kinds of greenery. One almost red, the other very green, the other yellowing."[2]

Wheat was a constant theme in Van Gogh's work, from vast wheat fields, which he painted over and over again, to close-up studies of individual stalks and ears laden with grain. For him, wheat was a symbol of life, from sowing, through germination and growing, to reaping and harvesting. It represented the eternal struggle of man with the earth he cultivated.[3] DB

Notes
1 Letter RM23 (unsent), Vincent van Gogh to Paul Gauguin, Auvers-sur-Oise, on or about June 17, 1890.

2 Letter 889, Vincent van Gogh to Theo van Gogh, Auvers-sur-Oise, June 17, 1890.

3 See Ronald Pickvance, *Van Gogh in Saint-Rémy and Auvers* (New York: The Metropolitan Museum of Art, 1986), 243.

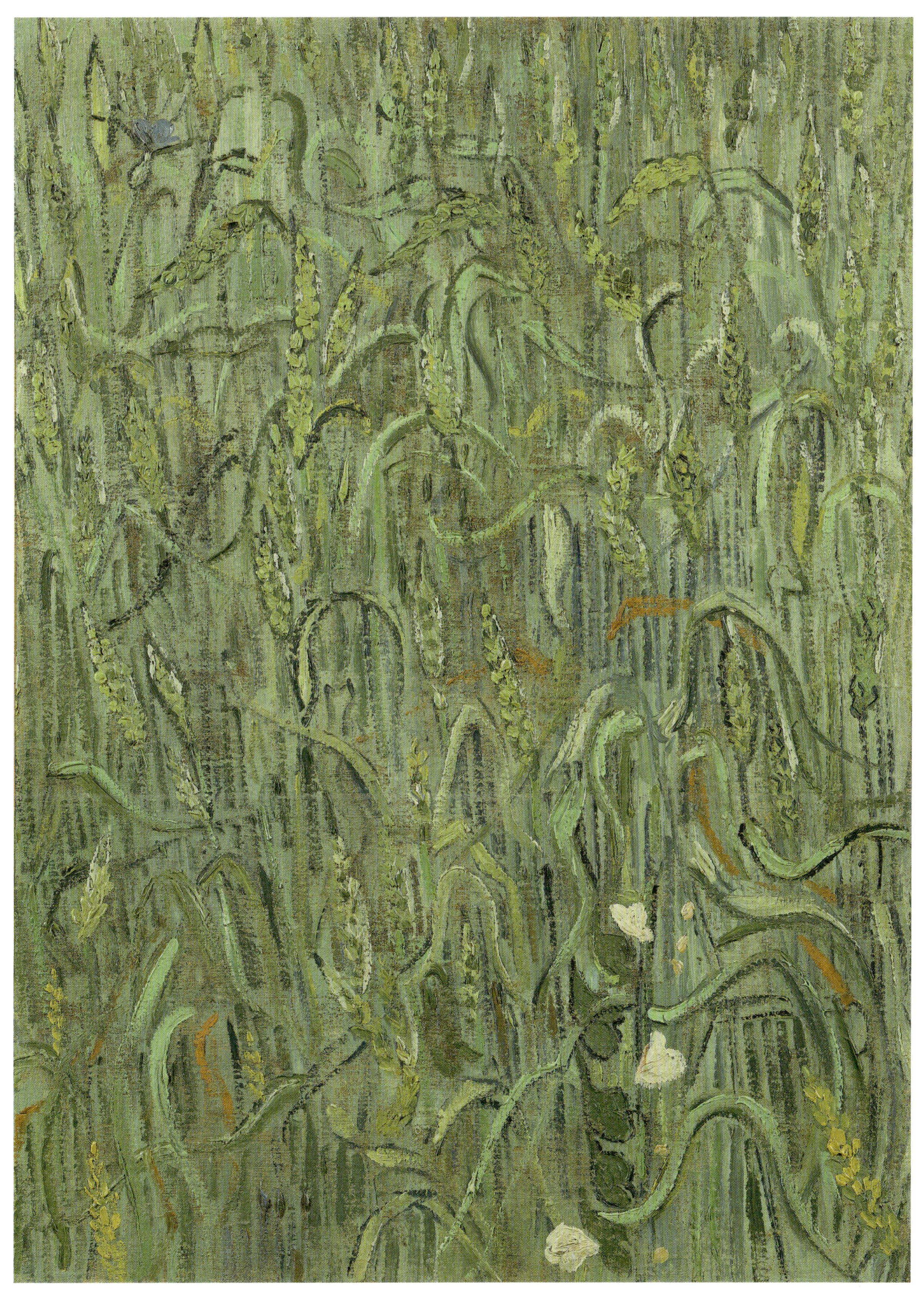

July 1890
Auvers-sur-Oise

Cat. 53
Women Crossing the Fields
Oil on paper,
11 ⅞ × 23 ½ inches
(30.3 × 59.7 cm)
McNay Art Museum,
San Antonio, bequest of
Marion Koogler McNay
150.49
F819

Provenance
Jo van Gogh-Bonger, Amsterdam; sold
by Leicester Galleries, London, 1927;
Chester H. Johnson Galleries, Chicago,
by 1933; Marion Koogler McNay
purchased from Chester H. Johnson,
October 13, 1934; bequeathed by McNay
upon the founding of the McNay Art
Museum, San Antonio, 1950.

In a letter dated just a month before he died, Vincent wrote to Theo, "And then this has been gained, that in women's clothes one sees very pretty arrangements of bright colors. If only one could have the individuals one sees pass by to do their portraits, it would be as pretty as any past era, and I even think that often in nature there is currently all the grace of Puvis's painting, *Between Art and Nature*. Thus yesterday I saw two figures, the mother in dark carmine dress, the daughter in pale pink with a yellow hat without any ornamentation, very healthy figures, rustic, well tanned by the open air."[1] Although the colors of the clothing do not exactly correspond to Van Gogh's description, there can be little doubt that this rapidly sketched painting on a sheet of now darkened paper was inspired not only by such encounters in the fields around Auvers but also by the frieze-like compositions of Puvis de Chavannes that he so admired.

Women Crossing the Fields shows straight rows of flowering potato plants and fields of green wheat set against the characteristic scenery of the Vexin plateau near the town, giving way to turbulent contours behind the figures. The two women, yellow-hatted, one clad in white and the other in an orange-dotted blue dress, walk across the fields, with a house and blue hills visible in the background. The modeling of the figures is simplified, with the nearer woman defined by a single outline that calls to mind the work of Paul Gauguin or Émile Bernard. The long, narrow horizontal shape of the composition was a format that Van Gogh favored in these final weeks of his life. It was in one of the Auvers wheat fields that he shot himself with a revolver on July 27, 1890.[2] DB

Notes
1 Letter 893, Vincent van Gogh to Theo van Gogh, Auvers-sur-Oise, June 28, 1890.

2 See Ronald Pickvance, *Van Gogh in Saint-Rémy and Auvers* (New York: The Metropolitan Museum of Art, 1986), 253–55.

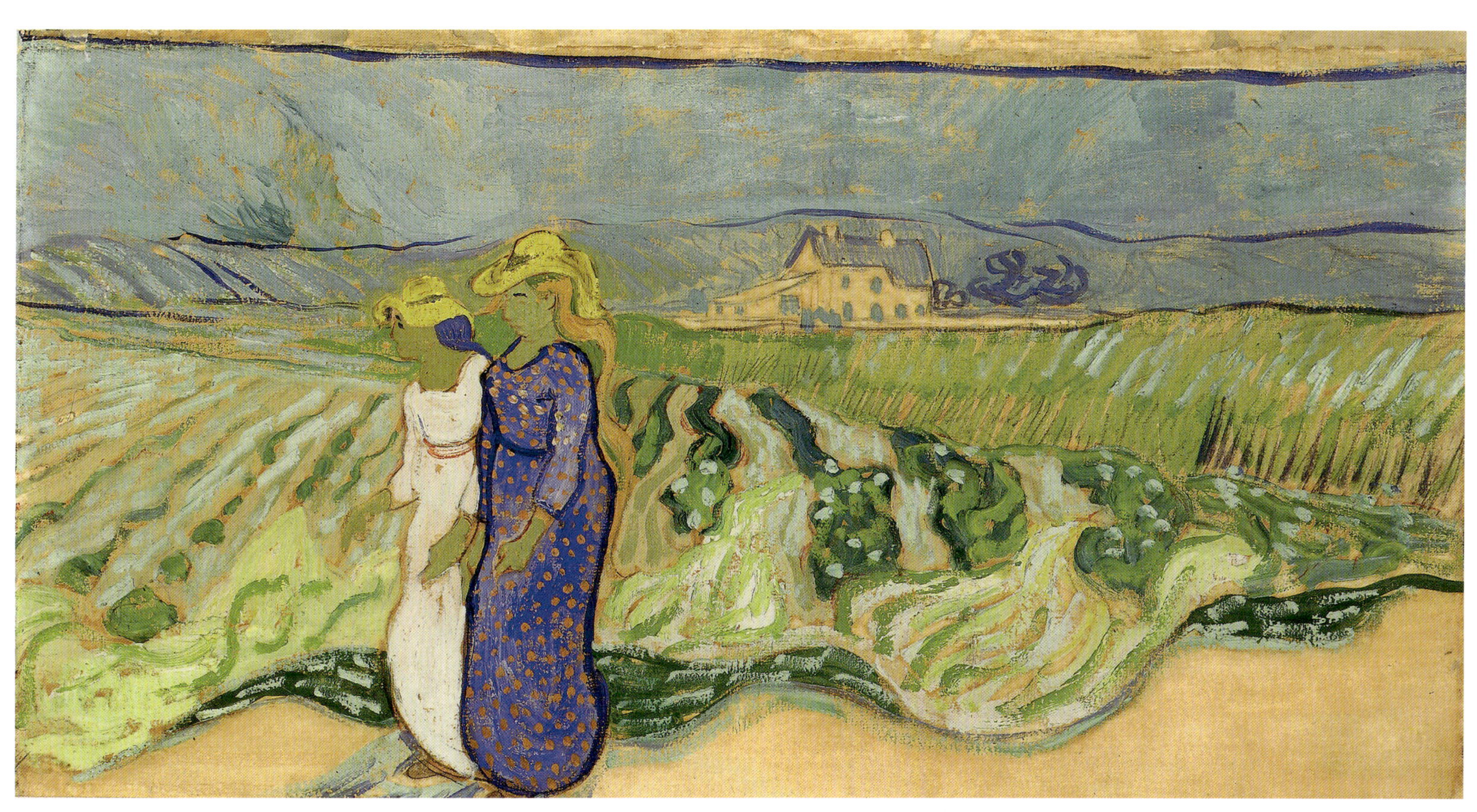

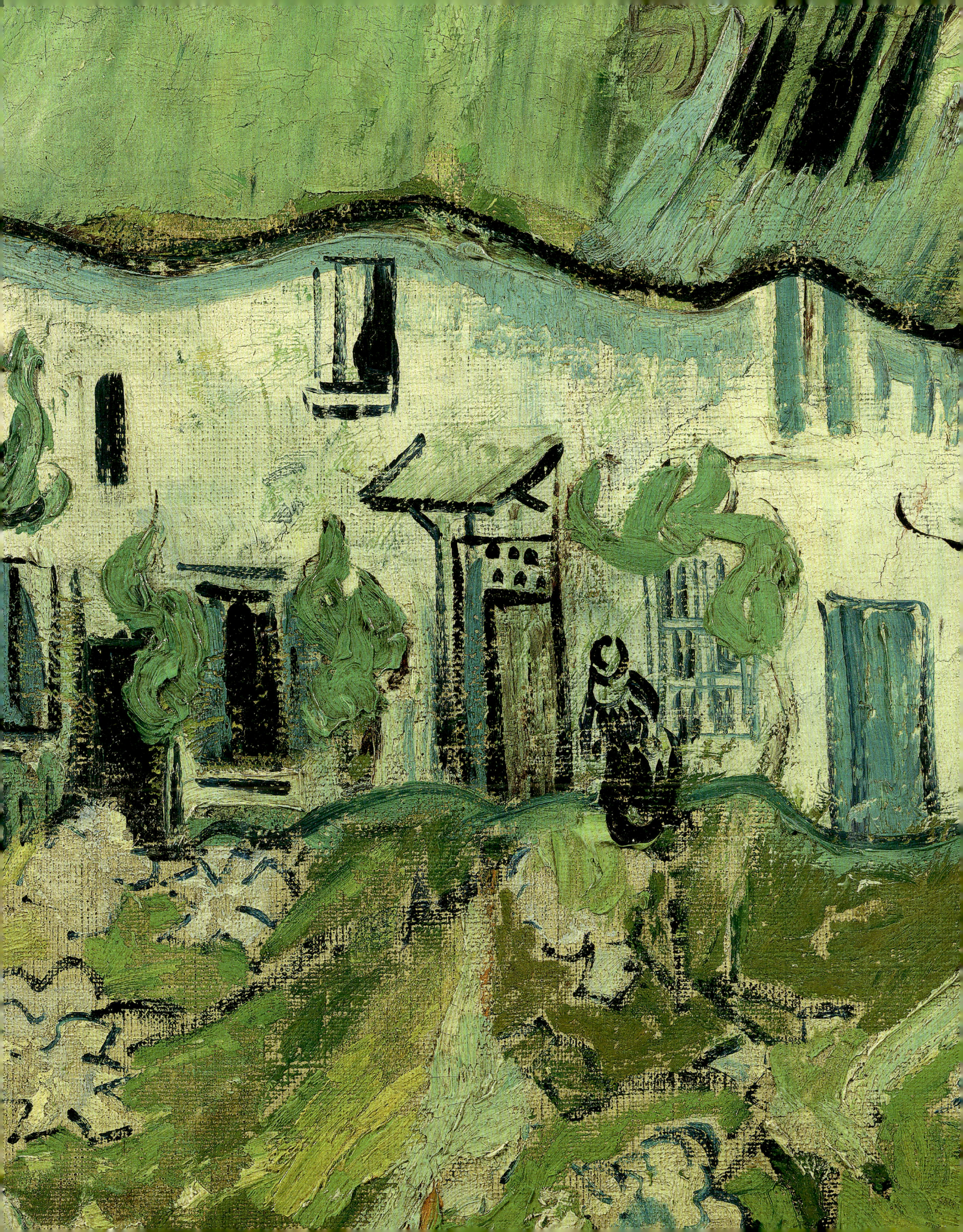

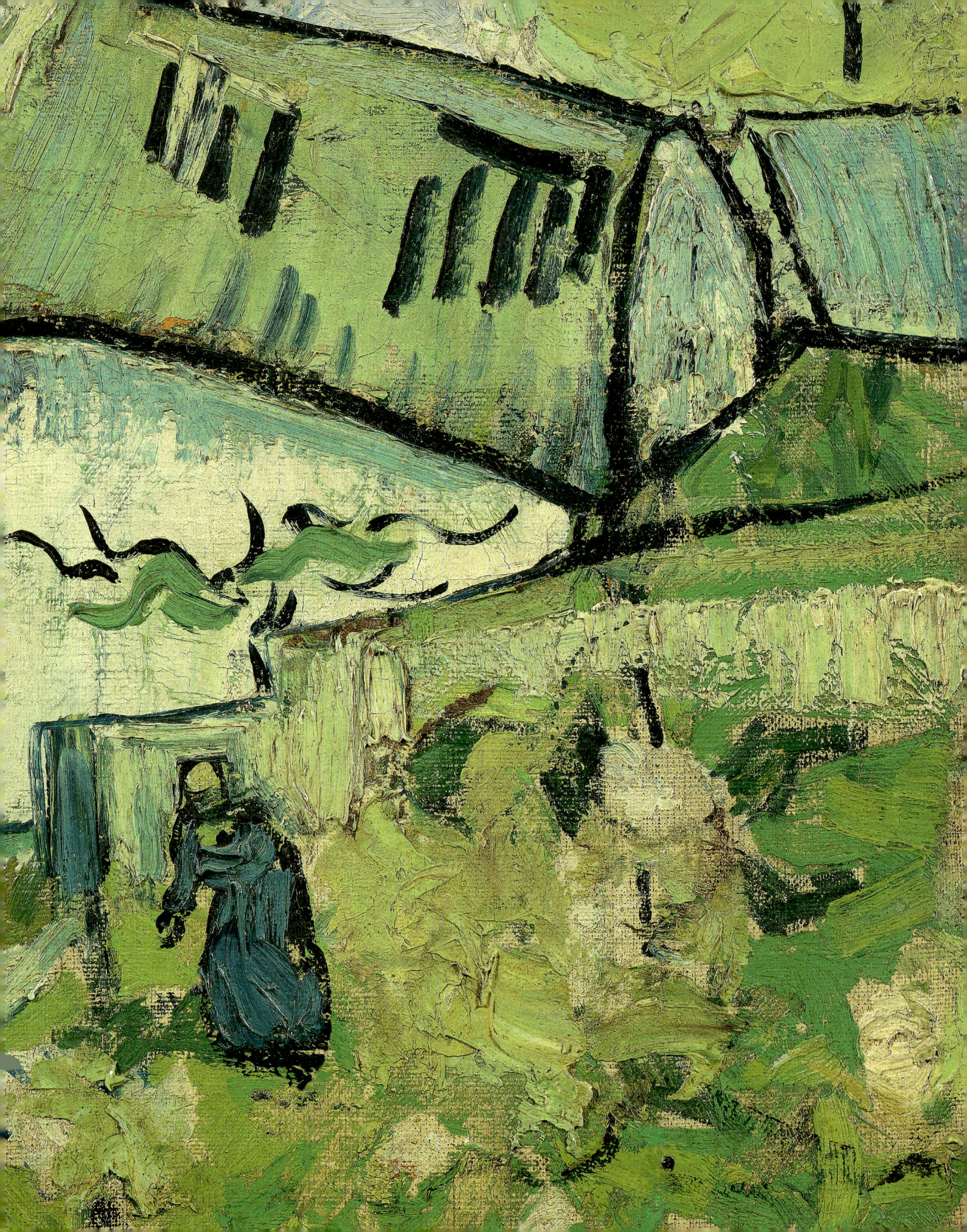

Chronology

by Laura Minton

by Laura Minton

1850s

1853 Vincent Willem van Gogh is born on March 30 in Groot-Zundert, the Netherlands, to Theodorus van Gogh and Anna Carbentus, a Protestant minister and a bookseller's daughter.

1857 His brother Theodorus "Theo" van Gogh is born on May 1.

1860s

1864 Van Gogh leaves the local village school for Jan Provily's boarding school for boys in Zevenbergen, where he completes his elementary schooling.

1866–68 Van Gogh attends King William II Secondary School in Tilburg, leaving partway through his second year. He does not return to his formal education.

1869 After leaving school at age sixteen, Van Gogh becomes the youngest clerk at Goupil & Cie, an international art dealer where his uncle, also named Vincent and known to his family as "Uncle Cent," was a partner. He works at the branch in The Hague.

1872 In September, Van Gogh and his younger brother Theo begin their lifelong correspondence.

1873 Theo begins working at Goupil in Brussels. Van Gogh is transferred to the company's London branch. He is moved by the life of the poor in large cities. While in London, he visits the British Museum and the National Gallery.

1874–75 Van Gogh is briefly transferred in October to Goupil's Paris office, returning to London in January 1875.

1875 In May, Van Gogh is transferred back to Paris. He becomes increasingly religious at this time.

1876 Van Gogh is fired from Goupil & Cie; his religious fervor conflicts with the commercial nature of his employer. He returns to his family's new home in Etten, the Netherlands.

In April, Van Gogh goes back to England, working as an assistant teacher at a boarding school for boys in Ramsgate. He then finds employment at a private school run by a vicar in Isleworth, near London. He is able to preach at the school and in the surrounding villages of Turnham Green and Petersham.

Van Gogh spends Christmas with his family in Etten and decides not to return to England.

1877 In early 1877, Van Gogh's Uncle Cent finds him a job at a bookseller, Blussé & Van Braam, in Dordrecht, near Rotterdam. Several months later, his family agrees to support his decision to study theology and become a minister.

Van Gogh then moves to Amsterdam to prepare for his theology entrance exam, living with his uncle Johannes van Gogh, a rear admiral in the navy. His uncle Johannes Paulus Stricker, who was a preacher, assists Van Gogh in his studies. However, Van Gogh is not diligent in his preparations, and after a year he abandons his plan to enter theology school.

1878–80 Although he no longer intends to study theology formally, Van Gogh is still eager to work in a religious vocation and trains for three months in Laken, Belgium, outside of Brussels, to be an evangelist.

In early December, Van Gogh moves to the Borinage, a depressed coal-mining region located in southwest Belgium. He works as a lay preacher until October 1880, sharing in the poverty of the miners and their families. He makes a number of drawings of the landscape and the rural workers. Although Van Gogh would destroy much of the work he made during this time, the motifs he explored would remain interests throughout his artistic career.

1880 Van Gogh travels on foot from Cuesmes, Belgium, to the village of Courrières in northern France, where the Realist painter Jules Breton lives and works. Van Gogh greatly admires Breton's work but writes in a letter to Theo that he did not dare introduce himself to the painter, instead standing outside his studio.

During the summer, Van Gogh decides to become an artist.

In October, Van Gogh travels to Brussels to study at the Royal Academy of Fine Arts.

1881 In April, Van Gogh moves to Etten to live at the home of his parents; he spends a great deal of time drawing figures and working outdoors. Drawings made during his stay in Etten demonstrate his development as an artist as he practiced and learned from books and prints. Theo is appointed manager of Goupil & Cie in Paris and begins to financially support Vincent. Their parents are disappointed with Vincent's failed career choices and his decision to become an artist.

For three weeks in November and December, Van Gogh begins studying under his cousin, the Dutch landscape painter Anton Mauve. He continues to practice drawing, and Mauve teaches him techniques in watercolor and oil painting.

Van Gogh falls in love with his widowed cousin, Kee Vos, but his affections are not reciprocated. Van Gogh persists and has an argument with his father, walking out on his family on Christmas Day.

Van Gogh moves to The Hague following the row with his family and continues his studies with Mauve.

1882 Van Gogh meets Sien Hoornik in early 1882. Hoornik, a former prostitute, is pregnant, unmarried, and has a five-year-old daughter. She becomes Van Gogh's model and lover. Van Gogh rents a studio on Schenkweg and moves in with Hoornik, her newborn baby, and her daughter. He plans to marry her, but his family, including Theo and Mauve, do not approve of the union.

His uncle, the art dealer Cornelis Marinus van Gogh, commissions Van Gogh to produce twelve drawings of city views in The Hague. Van Gogh finishes the drawings in two weeks, and his uncle places another order for six additional drawings of the city. Van Gogh completes the order in May, sending seven instead of six drawings to his uncle. The drawings are not sold until an auction in the early 1900s.

In November, he produces a series of six lithographs: five of working-class figures and one of a female personification of sorrow.

1883 Van Gogh makes two additional lithographs in July, depicting an old gardener by an apple tree and a man and woman burning weeds.

Van Gogh ends his relationship with Hoornik and moves in September to Hoogeveen, a small town located in the province of Drenthe. In October, he moves to Nieuw-Amsterdam/Veenoord, Drenthe. He plans to draw and paint the landscape of the moors, but in December, after less than three months, the cold, rainy weather and his unbearable loneliness drive him to Nuenen, his parents' new home in the Brabant region. He continues to clash with his father over their differing opinions and views about life.

1884 Early in the year, Vincent proposes to give Theo artworks in exchange for financial support. Theo could then sell the paintings in Paris. However, the plan does not yield any results; Van Gogh's works fail to satisfy French tastes.

Van Gogh rents a larger studio in Nuenen after working in a small studio at the back of his parents' parsonage.

1885 Van Gogh finds that Nuenen, home to many rural laborers, farmers, and weavers, facilitates his interest in being a painter of peasants and peasant life, which he sketches and paints often.

His parents find it difficult to live with Van Gogh, and he moves into his studio just before his father's death.

In March, Van Gogh's father, Theodorus, dies.

In April, Van Gogh paints *Still Life with Bible* in his father's memory. The painting depicts his father's open Bible in juxtaposition with Van Gogh's copy of Émile Zola's *La joie de vivre*, symbolizing the differences in their worldviews.

From April to May, he produces one of his most ambitious paintings, *The Potato Eaters*. The painting depicts the harshness of country life and labor. Van Gogh also makes a lithograph after the first version of the scene.

In November, Van Gogh heads to Antwerp, Belgium, and takes lessons at the Royal Academy of Fine Arts in figure painting and drawing from plaster casts, but he finds these classes to be too traditional.

1886 By mid-March, Van Gogh moves to Paris to live with Theo and study in the atelier of the painter Fernand Cormon. Theo introduces him to the work of Claude Monet. Van Gogh meets and gets to know artists Henri de Toulouse-Lautrec, Louis Anquetin, Paul Signac, Lucien Pissarro, and Émile Bernard. Under the influence of the Impressionists and Neo-Impressionists, his work becomes much brighter, and he starts to develop his characteristic brushstrokes.

From March to April, Van Gogh organizes an exhibition of Japanese woodcuts in the café Le Tambourin; both he and Theo collect these prints. His work is influenced by the colors, bold outlines, and innovative cropping of the woodcuts.

Van Gogh paints his earliest known self-portrait in a series of twenty-seven between fall 1886 and 1888. While in Paris, the subjects of his paintings change from rural laborers to cafés, the countryside along the Seine, and floral still lifes.

1887 From November to December, Van Gogh organizes an exhibition at the Grand Bouillon-Restaurant du Chalet and meets the artists Georges Seurat and Paul Gauguin.

1888 In February, Van Gogh begins to tire of city life in Paris and departs. He rents a room in Arles and uses the covered terrace on the roof as his studio. Van Gogh is inspired by the sun and bright colors of southern France.

In March and April, Van Gogh paints a series of orchards with flowering fruit trees. He also makes a number of landscape drawings using a reed pen, which he cuts and fashions himself.

On May 1, Van Gogh signs the lease for four rooms in a house at 2 Place Lamartine, known as the "Yellow House," and moves in on September 17. He plans to set up a "Studio of the South" in Arles for artists whose work Theo could then sell in Paris.

From the end of May to the beginning of June, Van Gogh visits the Mediterranean fishing village Saintes-Maries-de-la-Mer in southern France. He draws and paints boats on the beach, fishermen's cottages, and views of the village. He then returns to Arles.

In September, Van Gogh paints *The Night Café* and *Terrace of a Café at Night (Place du Forum)*.

On October 16 and 17, Van Gogh paints *The Bedroom*, a depiction of his own room in the Yellow House.

On October 23, the artist Paul Gauguin moves into the Yellow House with Van Gogh. Several months earlier, Van Gogh made paintings of vases of sunflowers to hang in Gauguin's bedroom. Gauguin and Van Gogh make collaborative progress for a time but frequently argue about their radically different views on art. Their personalities clash, and tensions rise steadily. In December, Van Gogh menaces Gauguin with a razor when he threatens to leave Arles. The same night, Van Gogh cuts off his ear and presents it to a prostitute with whom he is acquainted.

Van Gogh is admitted to the hospital on December 24, the morning after he cuts off his ear. Theo rushes to Arles and returns to Paris with Gauguin the next day.

1889 Van Gogh comes back to the Yellow House from the hospital in January but is soon hospitalized again in February after another attack. His doctor thinks he may have a form of epilepsy. He is confined to the hospital at the end of February on police orders as a result of a citizen's petition against him.

Theo marries Johanna "Jo" Bonger in April in Amsterdam.

In May, Van Gogh voluntarily admits himself to the clinic of Saint-Paul-de-Mausole in Saint-Rémy-de-Provence. Once he has recovered, he begins to paint in the walled garden and is later allowed to work outside of the clinic. Although his mental health continues to fluctuate, his time at Saint-Rémy is artistically productive; he completes more than 150 paintings. It is at Saint-Rémy that he paints olive trees and cypresses.

Van Gogh paints *The Starry Night* in June at Saint-Rémy.

Van Gogh visits Arles and then returns to the clinic in Saint-Rémy in July.

In mid-July, he has his first mental breakdown in Saint-Rémy.

He paints second and third versions of *The Bedroom* in September. He makes a series of works after prints of paintings by such artists as Rembrandt and Millet.

1890 Van Gogh experiences additional mental breakdowns in December 1889 and January 1890.

Van Gogh receives a birth announcement from Theo and Jo in January; his nephew has been named after him: Vincent Willem van Gogh. Van Gogh sends the painting *Almond Blossom* to Theo and Jo in honor of the new baby.

His reputation continues to grow, and he is invited to exhibit six paintings with the Belgian artist group Les Vingt. One of the paintings, *The Red Vineyard*, sells during the exhibition. The critic Albert Aurier writes a lengthy and positive review on Van Gogh's work, published in January.

In February, Van Gogh visits Arles and then returns to the clinic in Saint-Rémy.

Van Gogh experiences another mental breakdown from February to April and afterward returns to motifs that he explored in Nuenen. His last works made at the clinic in Saint-Rémy are still lifes of roses and irises.

In March, ten paintings are selected for inclusion in the annual *Salon des Indépendants* in Paris. The works are positively received but fail to sell.

Van Gogh is discharged from the clinic of Saint-Paul-de-Mausole in Saint-Rémy in May; he goes to Paris to stay with Theo, finally meeting his sister-in-law, Jo.

In mid-May, Van Gogh travels to Auvers-sur-Oise, near Paris, in order to be close to Theo but still in the countryside. In Auvers, the physician and amateur painter Dr. Paul Gachet keeps an eye on Van Gogh. Van Gogh paints members of the Gachet family and produces an etching of Paul Gachet, the only etching he ever makes. He also paints the small houses of the village and the surrounding landscape, particularly the wheat fields.

Vincent van Gogh dies on July 29, 1890, at the age of thirty-seven in Auvers-sur-Oise, France, from a self-inflicted gunshot wound occurring on July 27. His brother Theo dies in January of the following year.

Selected References

Bailey, Martin. *Studio of the South: Van Gogh in Provence*. London: Frances Lincoln, 2016.

Bailey, Martin. *The Sunflowers Are Mine: The Story of Van Gogh's Masterpiece*. London: Frances Lincoln, 2013.

Bailey, Martin. *Young Vincent: The Story of Van Gogh's Years in England*. London: W. H. Allen, 1990.

Bakker, Nienke. *Vincent van Gogh and Paris*. Van Gogh in Focus. Amsterdam: Van Gogh Museum, 2017.

Bakker, Nienke, Leo Jansen, and Hans Luijten, eds. *Vincent van Gogh: The Letters: The Complete Illustrated and Annotated Edition*. 6 vols. New York: Thames & Hudson, 2009.

Bakker, Nienke, Louis van Tilborgh, and Laura Prins. *On the Verge of Insanity: Van Gogh and His Illness*. Exh. cat. Brussels: Mercatorfonds, 2016.

Blotkamp, Carel, Gottfried Boehm, Bernhard Mendes Bürgi, Laura Coyle, Walter Feilchenfeldt, Seraina Werthemann, and Nina Zimmer. *Vincent van Gogh: Between Earth and Heaven, The Landscapes*. Exh. cat. Ostfildern, Germany: Hatje Cantz Verlag, 2009.

Cahn, Isabelle, Natacha Allet, Nienke Bakker, and Paul Denis. *Van Gogh/Artaud: Le Suicidé de La Société*. Exh. cat. Paris: Musée d'Orsay, 2014.

Callow, Phillip. *Vincent van Gogh: A Life*. London: W. H. Allen, 1990.

Collins, Bradley. *Van Gogh and Gauguin: Electric Arguments and Utopian Dreams*. Cambridge, MA: Westview Press, 2001.

Cooper, Douglas. *Drawings and Watercolours by Vincent van Gogh*. New York: Macmillan, 1955.

Denekamp, Nienke. *Vincent van Gogh Atlas*. New Haven, CT: Yale University Press, 2016.

Dumas, Ann, Nienke Bakker, Leo Jansen, and Hans Luijten. *The Real Van Gogh: The Artist and His Letters*. Exh. cat. London: Royal Academy of Arts, London, 2010.

Esner, Rachel, and Margriet Schavemaker, eds. *Vincent Everywhere: Van Gogh's (Inter) National Identities*. Amsterdam: Amsterdam University Press, 2010.

Fondation Vincent van Gogh-Arles. *Van Gogh à Arles: Dessins 1888–1889*. Arles: Actes Sud, 2003.

Gayford, Martin. *The Yellow House: Van Gogh, Gauguin, and Nine Turbulent Weeks in Arles*. New York: Little, Brown, 2008.

Gogh-Bonger, Johanna van. *A Memoir of Vincent van Gogh*. Los Angeles: J. Paul Getty Museum, 2018.

Grant, Patrick. *Reading Vincent van Gogh: A Thematic Guide to the Letters*. Edmonton, AB: Athabasca University Press, 2016.

Groom, Gloria Lynn, ed. *Van Gogh's Bedrooms*. Exh. cat. Chicago: Art Institute of Chicago, 2016.

Helvey, Jennifer. *Irises: Vincent van Gogh in the Garden*. Los Angeles: The J. Paul Getty Museum, 2009.

Hendriks, Ella, and Louis van Tilborgh. *Vincent van Gogh Paintings*. 2 vols. Amsterdam: Van Gogh Museum, 1999.

Heugten, Sjraar van. *Van Gogh and the Seasons*. Exh. cat. Princeton: Princeton University Press, 2018.

Heugten, Sjraar van. *Van Gogh Drawings: Influences and Innovations*. Exh. cat. Arles: Actes Sud, 2015.

Heugten, Sjraar van. *Vincent van Gogh Drawings*. 4 vols. Amsterdam: Van Gogh Museum, 1996.

Heugten, Sjraar van, ed. *Van Gogh: The Birth of an Artist*. Exh. cat. Brussels: Mercatorfonds, 2015.

Heugten, Sjraar van, and Fieke Pabst. *The Graphic Work of Vincent van Gogh*. Zwolle, the Netherlands: Waanders, 1995.

Heugten, Sjraar van, Joachim Pissarro, and Chris Stolwijk. *Van Gogh and the Colors of the Night*. Exh. cat. New York: The Museum of Modern Art, 2008.

Heugten, Sjraar van, Marije Vellekoop, and Roelie Zwikker. *Van Gogh: Master Draughtsman*. New York: Harry N. Abrams, 2005.

Homburg, Cornelia. *The Copy Turns Original: Vincent van Gogh and a New Approach to Traditional Art Practice*. OCULI: Studies in the Arts of the Low Countries, vol. 6. Amsterdam: John Benjamins, 1996.

Homburg, Cornelia, ed. *Van Gogh: Up Close*. Exh. cat. New Haven, CT: Yale University Press, 2012.

Homburg, Cornelia, ed. *Vincent van Gogh and the Painters of the Petit Boulevard*. Exh. cat. Saint Louis: Saint Louis Art Museum, 2001.

Homburg, Cornelia, ed. *Vincent van Gogh: Timeless Country — Modern City*. Milan: Skira, 2010.

Homburg, Cornelia, Simon Kelly, Laura Prins, and Jenny Reynaerts. *Van Gogh: Into the Undergrowth*. Exh. cat. Cincinnati: Cincinnati Art Museum, 2016.

Hulsker, Jan. *The New Complete Van Gogh: Paintings, Drawings, Sketches, Revised and Enlarged Edition of the Catalogue Raisonné of the Works of Vincent van Gogh*. Amsterdam: J. M. Meilenhoff, 1996.

Ives, Colta, Susan Alyson Stein, Sjraar van Heugten, and Marije Vellekoop. *Vincent van Gogh: The Drawings*. Exh. cat. New York: The Metropolitan Museum of Art, 2005.

Jansen, Leo. *Vincent van Gogh and His Letters*. Van Gogh in Focus. Amsterdam: Van Gogh Museum, 2007.

Jansen, Leo, Hans Luijten, and Nienke Bakker. *Vincent van Gogh: Painted with Words, The Letters to Émile Bernard*. New York: Rizzoli, 2007.

Jansen, Leo, and Jan Robert, eds. *Brief Happiness: The Correspondence of Theo van Gogh and Jo Bonger*. Cahier Vincent 7. Zwolle, the Netherlands: Waanders, 1999.

Keyes, George S., Joseph J. Rishel, and George T. M. Shackelford. *Van Gogh Face to Face: The Portraits*. Exh. cat. Detroit: Detroit Institute of Arts, 2000.

Kōdera, Tsukasa. *Vincent van Gogh: Christianity versus Nature*. Amsterdam: John Benjamins, 1990.

Kōdera, Tsukasa, and Yvette Rosenberg, eds. *The Mythology of Vincent van Gogh*. Tokyo: TV Asahi, 1992.

Kooten, Toos van, and Mieke Rijnders, eds. *The Paintings of Vincent van Gogh in the Collection of the Kröller-Müller Museum*. Otterlo, the Netherlands: Kröller-Müller Museum, 2003.

Kosinski, Dorothy. *Van Gogh's Sheaves of Wheat*. Exh. cat. Dallas: Dallas Museum of Art, 2006.

Lloyd, Jill, and Michael Peppiatt. *Van Gogh and Expressionism*. Exh. cat. Ostfildern, Germany: Hatje Cantz Verlag, 2007.

Leeman, Fred, and John Sillevis. *De Haagse School en de Jonge Van Gogh*. Zwolle, the Netherlands: Waanders, 2005.

Leeuw, Ronald de. *Van Gogh Museum*. Zwolle, the Netherlands: Waanders, 1997.

Leeuw, Robert de, comp. *The Letters of Vincent van Gogh*. London: Penguin, 1997.

Masheck, Joseph D., ed. *Van Gogh 100*. Westport, CT: Greenwood Press, 1996.

Maurer, Naomi Margolis. *The Pursuit of Spiritual Wisdom: The Thought and Art of Vincent van Gogh and Paul Gauguin*. Madison, NJ: Fairleigh Dickinson University Press, 1998.

Meedendorp, Teio. *Drawings and Prints by Vincent van Gogh in the Collection of the Kröller-Müller Museum*. Otterlo, the Netherlands: Kröller-Müller Museum, 2007.

Naifeh, Steven, and Gregory White Smith. *Van Gogh: The Life*. London: Profile Books, 2011.

New York Graphic Society. *The Complete Letters of Vincent van Gogh*. 2nd ed. 3 vols. Greenwich, CT: New York Graphic Society, 1959.

Ozanne, Marie-Angélique, and Frédérique de Jode. *Theo: The Other Van Gogh*. New York: Magowan, 1999.

Pickvance, Ronald. *Van Gogh in Arles*. Exh. cat. New York: The Metropolitan Museum of Art, 1984.

Pickvance, Ronald. *Van Gogh in Saint-Rémy and Auvers*. Exh. cat. New York: The Metropolitan Museum of Art, 1986.

Porter, Lynnette. *Van Gogh in Popular Culture*. Jefferson, NC: McFarland, 2016.

Rappard-Boon, Charlotte van, Willem R. van Gulik, and Keiko van Bremen-Ito. *Catalogue of the Van Gogh Museum's Collection of Japanese Prints*. Amsterdam: Van Gogh Museum, 1991.

Rathbone, Eliza E., William H. Robinson, Elizabeth Steele, and Marcia Steele. *Van Gogh Repetitions*. Exh. cat. New Haven, CT: Yale University Press, 2013.

Restellini, Marc, Sjraar van Heugten, Wooter van der Veen, and Gabriel P. Weisberg. *Van Gogh: Rêves de Japon*. Exh. cat. Paris: Pinacothèque de Paris, 2012.

Rijksmuseum Kröller-Müller. *Vincent van Gogh: A Detailed Catalogue of the Paintings and Drawings by Vincent van Gogh in the Collection of the Kröller-Müller National Museum*. Otterlo, the Netherlands: Kröller-Müller National Museum, 1980.

Robertis, Antonio de, and Matteo Smolizza. *Vincent van Gogh: Le Opere Disperse: Oltre 1000 Disegni e Dipinti Citati Dall'Artista e Introvabili*. Nuoro, Italy: Ilisso, 2005.

Silverman, Debora. *Van Gogh and Gauguin: The Search for Sacred Art*. New York: Farrar, Straus and Giroux, 2000.

Standring, Timothy, and Louis van Tilborgh, eds. *Becoming Van Gogh*. Exh. cat. Denver: Denver Museum of Art, 2012.

Stolwijk, Chris, and Richard Thomson. *Theo van Gogh, 1857–1891: Art Dealer, Collector, and Brother of Vincent*. Exh. cat. Zwolle, the Netherlands: Waanders, 1999.

Sund, Judy. *True to Temperament: Van Gogh and French Naturalist Literature*. Cambridge: Cambridge University Press, 1992.

Tilborgh, Louis van. "Van Gogh in Cormon's Studio: A Chronological Puzzle." In *Current Issues in 19th Century Art*, edited by Chris Stolwijk, 53–72. Van Gogh Studies 1. Zwolle, the Netherlands: Waanders, 2007.

Tilborgh, Louis van, Nienke Bakker, Cornelia Homburg, Tsukasa Kōdera, and Chris Uhlenbeck. *Van Gogh and Japan*. Exh. cat. Amsterdam: Van Gogh Museum, 2018.

Tilborgh, Louis van, and Marie-Pierre Salé. *Millet/Van Gogh*. Exh. cat. Paris: Musée d'Orsay, 1998.

Uitert, Evert van. *Van Gogh in Brabant: Paintings and Drawings from Etten and Nuenen*. Exh. cat. Zwolle, the Netherlands: Waanders, 1987.

Van Heugten, Sjraar, et al. *Van Gogh and the Seasons*. Exh. cat. Melbourne: National Gallery of Victoria, 2017.

Van Gogh Museum. "Vincent van Gogh: The Letters." 2009. www.vangoghletters.org.

Veen, Wouter van der. *Van Gogh in Auvers: His Last Days*. New York: Monacelli Press, 2010.

Vellekoop, Marije. *Van Gogh at Work*. Exh. cat. Brussels: Mercatorfonds, 2013.

Vellekoop, Marije, Muriel Geldof, Ella Hendriks, Leo Jansen, and Alberto de Tagle. *Van Gogh's Studio Practice*. Brussels: Mercatorfonds, 2013.

Walther, Ingo F., and Rainer Metzger. *Vincent van Gogh: The Complete Paintings*. 2 vols. Cologne: Benedikt Taschen, 1990.

Welsh-Ovcharov, Bogomila. *Vincent van Gogh and the Birth of Cloisonism*. Exh. cat. Toronto: Art Gallery of Ontario, 1981.

Wolk, Johannes van der. *The Seven Sketchbooks of Vincent Van Gogh*. New York: Harry N. Abrams, 1987.

Zemel, Carol. *Van Gogh's Progress: Utopia, Modernity, and Late-Nineteenth-Century Art*. Berkeley: University of California Press, 1997.

Copyright and Photography Credits